Mental Health
&
Mental Illness

Mental Health
&
Mental Illness

Arthur James Morgan, M.D.

Associate in Psychiatry, University
of Pennsylvania; Director of Clinical
Services, Hall-Mercer Community Mental
Health and Mental Retardation Center,
Pennsylvania Hospital, Philadelphia

Mabyl K. Johnston,
R.N., B.S., M.S. Ed.

Late Director of Nursing Education
Brainerd State Hospital
Brainerd, Minnesota

J. B. Lippincott Company

Philadelphia • Toronto

ISBN 0-397-54189-9

Library of Congress Catalog Card Number: 76-14855

Printed in the United States of America

10   12   14   16   18   19   17   15   13   11

Library of Congress Cataloging in Publication Data

Morgan, Arthur James
  Mental health & mental illness.

  First ed. (1971) by M. K. Johnston.
  Bibliography: p.
  Includes index.
  1. Psychiatry.   2. Psychology.   3 Psychiatric
nursing.   I.   Johnston, Mabyl K., joint author.
II.   Title.   [DNLM: 1.   Mental health.   2.   Psychiatric
nursing.   WY160 M847m]
RC454.M67   1976   616.8ꞌ9   76-14855
ISBN 0-397-54189-9

Preface

As the second edition of *Mental Health & Mental Illness* was nearing completion, Mabyl K. Johnston, already in semiretirement, died. The first edition of *Mental Health & Mental Illness* reflected Miss Johnston's vast experience in the management and nursing care of mentally ill hospitalized adults, children, and the mentally retarded.

As I began the revision of this most popular text, I made every effort to retain Miss Johnston's style and prose and rich examples of psychodynamic principles. I, like Miss Johnston, have had experience in the state hospital system and was trained with a strong psychoanalytic background; but I have spent the last two decades working to return the chronically institutionalized to the community using an eclectic theoretical approach that can best be described as psychobiological and reality-oriented.

Today, even more than in the beginning of this decade when the first edition of this book was written, practitioners often find themselves thinking about, and understanding the manifestations of mental illness in psychodynamic terms while applying treatment measures that are designed to remove symptoms and modify behavior regardless of the particular psychodynamics we envision. For example, while we may see depression as springing from a real or imagined loss, or schizophrenia as a disease of genetic predisposition with defective parenting, our treatment approach will most likely be a combination of psychopharmacology, milieu therapy, and individual and group psychotherapy. The emphasis today is on the restoration of function rather than "cure" or the elimination of disease.

To bring the text up-to-date, sections on community psychiatry, genetics, and psychopharmacology were either heavily revised or completely rewritten. The order in which specific illnesses are considered was changed to reflect the modern classification system embodied in the July 1974 edition of the American Psychiatric Association's Diagnostic and Statistical Manual II (DSM II). We have yet to meet an experienced practitioner who is comfortable or satisfied with DSM II or any other method of classifying the subtle and varied ways nature manifests herself in humankind, but we are compelled by utilization reviewers and audit teams to give the names and numbers that "best" describe our patients. The reorganization of the mental illness portion of this book in the manner described will make the finding of this information easier, and will help the student to begin to think in the terms we are now required to use. While there is considerable discussion and argument today regarding the role of biogenic amines and neurotransmitters in emotional illness, and efforts are continuing to make the present system of classification of mental disorder more coherent and scientific, there is not yet enough information which compels universal assent to make any *major* changes in our diagnostic labels.

The second edition of *Mental Health & Mental Illness* is an introductory text addressed to students of nursing, psychology and social work, and to psychiatric technicians and mental health workers who are beginning their study of mental health and mental illness. For practitioners, it serves as a useful review of both the normal and disturbed patterns of behavior.

Each chapter is preceded by a list of behavioral objectives to help students, instructors and practitioners in formulating their goals. Discussion and study questions are included. A glossary has been added.

The increasing (and sometimes overwhelming) demands for documentation of clinical observations and treatments have been taken into account. Our focus is, however, as it always has been, on the patient and on the helping relationship.

A. James Morgan, M.D.
Philadelphia 1976

Contents

viii

Contents

x

Contents

The Psychology
of Human
Behavior

Normal Growth and Development

Behavioral Objectives

The student successfully attaining the goals of this chapter will be able to:

- Identify the physical and mental characteristics that constitute a person's heredity and explain the role genes play in heredity.
- List two main factors that make up an infant's environment.
- Name two forces that influence the development of a person's personality.
- Explain the importance of the mother-child relationship in the development of a child's personality by describing both a good and bad relationship and the types of personalities each fosters.
- Describe the process of identification and explain how it influences a child's personality.

Heredity

When a sperm unites with an ovum to form a new life, each germ cell contributes 23 chromosomes on which are arranged a vast number of genes or genetic factors. These genes determine the type of body build the child will have, the texture of his skin and hair, the color of his eyes, his general intellectual capacity and abilities, his talents, and many other physical and mental characteristics. In short, they constitute his heredity.

After nine months of sheltered prenatal life, during which every need of the growing fetus is supplied by the mother's body, the baby emerges from the uterus into a world that begins to make demands on him immediately and continues to do so throughout his life, but a world which, if he has developed normally, he is well designed to live in and adapt to.

Environment

The world, or that portion of it reflected by his parents and their home, is the child's environment, and it causes him to react to a multitude of new situations and to other human beings. His personality forms as the result of the interaction of his environment and his heredity.

Under ordinary circumstances, a child lives with, depends upon, and follows the examples that his parents set for him. While the inheritance of certain physical characteristics is important in the building of personality (stature, intelligence, strength, beauty), the effects of the outside world upon the child are equally important.

Developmental Stages

Just as our bodies go through successive stages of physical development until they reach adulthood, so, too, our personalities normally undergo developmental stages until they reach maturity. Harmful influences may interfere with the normal physical growth and functioning of a tissue, an organ, or the entire body. Similarly, early disturbing experiences and unsatisfied emotional needs may lead to an arrest or fixation of the normal growth pattern of the personality and can result in personality distortions and immaturities.

It is considered that a wholesome mother-child relationship is essential for the normal growth and personality development of the child. The child must have the feeling that he is wanted, loved and enjoyed by his parents, and especially by his mother or the mother-figure.

If the child feels that he is loved and cared for, a desirable sense of security will follow. If, on the other hand, he experiences rejection, harshness, and frustration, his personality will be characterized by anxiety and insecurity, and he may develop hostile and aggressive tendencies. The emotional experiences of early years leave permanent imprints on the personality, although they may no longer be a part of the individual's consciousness.

One of the most important processes in influencing personality development is called **identification**. Through this process, the child, because of his love for and his wish to be like the parent, particularly the parent of the same sex, molds himself after that parent and adopts his characteristics and his attitudes. This is not a conscious imitation, but is automatic in its occurrence. If the parent is an emotionally mature and well-adjusted person, this process may contribute greatly to a desirable development of the child's personality.

As the personality continues in its growth, it is influenced and molded by many factors. Many arise from emotional problems that involve security, love, aggression, and dependence. Some of the child's experiences will stimulate his personality growth; others will block or distort its development. As he begins to strive for independence, he encounters many difficulties in meeting the new responsibilities that independence entails. Sometimes, new problems and contradictory urges result in emotional turmoil, and sometimes in healthy, adaptive behavior.

Emotional development often progresses fitfully. But, if early identifications have been healthy, and if most conflicts have been successfully resolved, the personality should eventually emerge into adulthood.

We think of someone with a mature personality as one who has achieved a harmonious adjustment to his environment and has reached that place where he can meet life's inevitable stresses realistically and effectively.

In order to understand deviant personality, we must first understand how a normal personality develops. For our purposes, personality does not mean personal charm and distinction; rather, it is the total person, including his strengths and weaknesses, his attributes, aspirations, and drives—in fact, the sum total of all his individual tendencies—which determines his adjustments to his material and social environment. As one writer puts it, "It is the inward organization of an individual as he interacts with the outward organization of his environment." Another says, "Personality consists of patterns of behavior which are characteristic of an individual in a variety of situations."

Personality is always in a state of flux. It is always in the process of becoming something else, yet it retains a continuity that makes it ordinarily identifiable from situation to situation, from year to year, from birth to death.

Although definitions of personality vary greatly, most theorists agree on the following six points:
1. Personality can be thought of as a relatively enduring organization of patterns of behavior characteristic of the individual.
2. Dynamic forces underlie behavior (i.e., behavior is caused).
3. Some of these dynamic forces are unknown to the individual (i.e., there exist unconscious determinants of behavior).
4. All theorists agree on the total complexity of heredity and environment, though some think the biological forces are more important, while others feel the psychosocial factors are more important.
5. All theorists agree on the importance of childhood in forming and organizing relatively enduring patterns of behavior characteristics of an individual.
6. Behavior, both in its outward and inward manifestations, is a function or expression of personality.

References

Duvall, E.: Family Development. ed. 4. Philadelphia, J. B. Lippincott, 1971.
Erikson, E. H.: Identity and the Life Cycle. New York, International Universities Press, 1967.
Salk, J.: Man Unfolding. New York, Harper & Row, 1972.
Scheinfeld, A.: Heredity in Humans. Philadelphia, J. B. Lippincott, 1972.
Thomas, A., Chess, S., and Birch, H. G.: The origins of personality. Scientific American, 1970.
Waechter, E. H., Blake, F. G., and Lipp, J. P.: Nursing Care of Children. ed. 9 Philadelphia, J. B. Lippincott, 1976.

Learning

Behavioral Objectives

The student successfully attaining the goals of this chapter will be able to:

- Describe the 4 steps that lead to learning.
- Explain the main factor that causes a person to forget something he or she has learned.
- Define the term extinction in relation to learning.
- Explain the role of reinforcement in the learning process and give examples in which reinforcement can result in immediate learning and examples in which learning requires frequent reinforcement.

Human beings are amazingly versatile. Under differing environmental situations they can learn to paddle canoes skillfully through churning rapids, to build fires by rubbing two sticks together, or to make an atom bomb and drop it from the heavens with amazing accuracy. They can learn to be enthralled with the chanting and tom-tom rhythms in an African village or the music of a symphonic orchestra; to build crude shelters or steel and glass skyscrapers against a city sky. They can learn to equate beauty with white, bronze, or black skins. They can be trained to be cruel, warlike, and treacherous or to be gentle, peaceable, and trustworthy. They can be taught to plow the soil with a primitive tool or to fly beyond earth's gravitational pull and land on the moon, or other planets.

Processes of Learning

Few fields have been as fully studied as the field of animal and human learning. Yet, much remains to be understood about how learning occurs. Psychologists studying the processes of learning, have encapsulated learning into four steps:

1. We must first want something (the drive, the need, or the motivation).
2. We must then notice something (the stimulus or the cue).
3. We must then do something about the stimulation (the response).

4. We must then get something (the reward, the reinforcement, or the need reduction).

These four steps of learning are, of course, much oversimplified. Learning is a process with each of the steps capable of infinite elaboration. For example: A newborn baby becomes hungry and his tissue needs impel him to restless activity. Mother offers food; he sucks and the hunger pangs subside. He becomes comfortable and drowsy. Here are all the ingredients of a learning situation—a need (hunger), a stimulus (the feel of a nipple in his mouth), a response (sucking), and reinforcement (relief from hunger pain). And learning will take place. At birth, a baby will actively seek the nipple, turning his head from side to side and making sucking responses if his cheek is stroked when he is hungry. He then learns that food (nipple plus sucking) brings relief. After a few weeks, the learning has extended to include other elements of this sequence. Now he may stop his hungry crying upon being picked up. New cues have been tied in or associated with the food-brings-comfort pattern. Soon baby will smile when mother bends over him, even when he is not hungry, which indicates that the original food-brings-comfort learning has been elaborated into "mother is something good."

A little later, baby may learn to associate the sound of the opening and closing of the refrigerator door as a cue to mother's getting his bottle of milk, and he will wriggle with anticipation.

The greater the reinforcement, the stronger the learning. The reinforcement may have to come in succeeding episodes or, if strong enough, a single reinforcement may result in fixing the pattern of learning. For instance, the process of toilet training or of learning to convey food from the plate to the mouth by fingers, and, later, by spoon, becomes effective only after repeated efforts followed by the reinforcement of praise.

On the other hand, a single experience that is very painful or surprising, such as a burnt finger or tumbling down several stairs, will usually result in a clearly remembered learning experience. The baby will avoid the hot object and refuse, even when coaxed, to try the stairs again until his coordination is much better.

When the pattern of learning no longer serves the need, reinforcement ceases to operate. When this happens the learning process progressively decreases and finally ceases altogether. We call this **extinction,** or in ordinary language, forgetting. While lack of reinforcement is just one cause of forgetting, it is the chief one. Many things that were highly important to us as children ceased to be important to us as we matured, and lack of reinforcement caused a progressive decrease in the sharpness of the mental image, and memory finally ceased.

However, something once well-learned is never fully forgotten. It is stored in our subconscious mind, and it can be brought back to immediate awareness.

Sometimes this remembrance may be immediate; sometimes we must concentrate quite a bit on a dim memory before it emerges clearly to our view. The learning of many activities, such as learning to play a piano, to type, or to tie an intricate knot, improves with reinforcement, but will fade away, or become extinct when the art is not used. But the relearning of a once-acquired skill is usually accomplished by a little practice, and the old skill returns again.

References

Bellugi, U. and Brown, R. editors: The acquisition of language, Chicago, University of Chicago Press, 1970.

Hall, E.: A conversation with Jean Piaget and Barbel Inhelder. Psychology Today, May 1970.

Havighurst, R. J.: Developmental Tasks and Education. ed. 3. New York, David McKay, 1972.

Sutterley, D. and Donnelly, G.: Perspectives in Human Development, Nursing Throughout the Life Cycle. Philadelphia, J. B. Lippincott, 1973.

chapter

3

The Needs of a
Human Being

Behavioral Objectives

The student successfully attaining the goals of this chapter will be able to:

- List the 4 childhood situations that are most important to development.
- Identify the 6 basic primary needs of the human organism and explain why they are important to life.
- Explain how love, status and recognition, achievement and identification each constitute a psychosocial or secondary need.
- Describe a concept of the ego-ideal.

The newborn infant shows a generalized response to all stimuli. Emotions develop as the baby reacts to his environment. For the infant, life is first of all a biological fact. He responds physiologically to the unpleasantness of hunger and cold and to the need to move his muscles. It soon becomes necessary for him to react to a multitude of new situations and to other human beings.

One ability which the infant possesses is highly significant—the unexplainable power of communication of emotional feeling tones (the power of **empathy**). The baby is able to sense and respond to feelings of approval and disapproval of the mother or mother-figure. Feelings of approval increase its sense of well-being, and the opposite feelings cause discomfort. This happens long before the baby is capable of understanding the meaning of either feeling.

Although all experiences are planted forever in the mind, at this time the infant has simply a vague association of them in relation to the mother-figure.

Satisfactions are achieved with the first magic tool, the cry, and comfort and discomfort are known but not understood. The baby's responses to comfort and discomfort begin to form a patterned behavior.

Situations in childhood that are particularly important in future development are:

1. The feeding situation in early infancy (especially weaning).

2. Toilet and cleanliness training.
3. Early sex training.
4. Training for control of anger and aggression.

Adjusting to these situations can be quite upsetting to the child, and it takes patience and understanding on the part of the parents to help him accept social rules and regulations. If they approve of him as a person, even when they may disapprove of his actions, he will usually accept their rules and values as his own and build them into his growing personality.

Physiological Needs

The growing child has many needs; some are physiological and some are psychosocial. The physiological needs are often called **basic** or **primary** needs because they are basic to physical survival. Six basic requirements are: oxygen, food, water, sleep, protection from temperature extremes (clothing and shelter) and excretion. Extreme deprivation of any one will result in death of the organism. To these six should be added a seventh—sexual activity—not because deprivation of this activity would result in death of the organism, but because, without it, the human race would become extinct.

If these physiological or biological needs were man's only concern, he would live on a very primitive level indeed. Brute force would determine his survival.

Psychosocial Needs

But the child acquires other very important needs as he interacts with other persons in a social milieu, and human societies have always found it necessary to evolve standards of conduct that protect their members. These **psychosocial** or **secondary** needs are learned through the interaction of the individual with society.

The psychosocial needs are very important factors in determining our patterns of thought, our attitudes, and our habits. Such needs vary from society to society and in degrees within the individual, depending on individualistic backgrounds. We shall discuss a few of the most important of these needs.

Love

Probably the deepest psychosocial need most of us have is the need for love or emotional security. Love is a complex feeling of trust, warmth, and understanding—of closeness, intimacy, and emotional give-and-take. All babies need a sense of emotional security; they need to be "mothered" regularly, held against the mother's body, stroked, caressed, cuddled, spoken and sung to, and rocked. So deep is this need that some psychologists place it with the seven basic needs. Man does not outgrow the need to love and be loved. He merely shifts it from the parental figure to peer figures (those of his own age level).

Status and Recognition

Two other psychosocial needs closely allied to the need for love are the needs for status and recognition. Status is our particular place in society; this place is allotted to us by virtue of our age, sex, abilities, vocation or profession, our parents' status, and our socioeconomic standing. Recognition is the approval, the acceptance, given the individual by society as he or she performs in keeping with the role society has accorded.

Statuses tend to be arranged in a hierarchical order, certain statuses having more prestige than others. For instance, professional persons such as lawyers and physicians have a higher status than, say, a common laborer or a small businessman.

Most of us seem to derive a vicarious pleasure in reading or hearing about those who move at a higher status level than we do. Members of "high society" belong to a prestige social group, their parties and social affairs are avidly read about, and their mannerisms and appearances are widely copied.

In America, although we have a so-called classless society (i.e., one without aristocratic titles), we do have criteria that substitute for aristocracy—success and money. The pressure to succeed, to achieve, to excel, begins very early in our lives. Power and possessions are two very important symbols of success.

The need for status and recognition is probably related directly to our need to belong—to the need for approval and acceptance—first by the family, and then by the group.

Achievement

Then there is the need to achieve, the need to accomplish and do. The little child will pull off the golden head of a dandelion and rush in to his mother to offer her his gift. Another, on hearing that daddy will soon be home, will rush to pick up his crayons and will scrawl wriggly lines on a paper which he will proudly offer to his father, saying, "Look at the picture I made!" Pride in doing is a very necessary ingredient in the making of a successful personality.

If the child's struggle to creep, stand, walk, talk, and master his environment is well rewarded by the approval of the significant figures in his life, he will learn the satisfaction of accomplishment and will build a healthy concept of himself as a "doer of deeds," a success. If he fails to earn the approval of those about him, if his small achievements are ignored or, worse yet, criticized severely, he will build up a picture of himself as "one who fails," and he will lose his pride in doing.

His rights and his limits should be clearly defined for him, and his rights respected by the family. Then he will learn to respect the rights of others.

Identification

There is a vital need in the child for self-development. He must gradually acquire a concept of *who* he is, *what* he is, and *what he can do*. By the time he is four or five years old, he tends to have an exaggerated self-concept. He deems himself able to do anything. But the lessons slowly learned from the environment tend to level off this concept to a more realistic one.

Still, some of this self-idealization remains in most of us. We have a strong tendency to see ourselves much closer to perfection than we really are. This is the **ego-ideal** Freud speaks of in his concept of personality development, and is a strong motivation to continued growth.

References

Ames, L.: Child Care and Development. Philadelphia, J. B. Lippincott, 1970.

Bernard, J. W.: Human Development in Western Culture. ed. 3. Boston, Allyn & Bacon, 1970.

Chin, P. L.: Child Health Maintenance. St. Louis, C. V. Mosby, 1974.

Vetter, J. J., and Smith, B. D., editors: Personality Theory. New York, Appleton-Century-Crofts, 1971.

Human Emotions

Behavioral Objectives

The student successfully attaining the goals of this chapter will be able to:

- Describe the physiological changes caused by emotions such as anger and fear and explain what is meant by the "fight or flight" syndrome.
- Explain 3 ways that a child may handle or repress his unacceptable feelings.
- Define the feeling which constitutes aggression.
- Describe how a small child expresses aggression and how he learns to control these feelings.
- Identify the ways aggression can be expressed outwardly and inwardly.
- Explain the relationship between aggression, guilt, and self-destruction.
- List several types of behavior that are forms of self-destruction.
- Explain the basis of treatment of people who suffer from self-destruction.

Emotions are **feeling states** that involve both physiological and psychological changes. If a need is satisfied, the resultant emotion tends to be pleasant. For example: baby is hungry, he makes his need known, he is fed; this leaves him in a satisfied, contented emotional state. But if a need is blocked, or ungratified, the resultant emotion is unpleasant. If a baby is not fed when he makes his need known, he becomes tense and frustrated, usually showing his frame of mind by loud, protesting, angry crying.

Physiological Response

Under emotional stress, whether it be pleasant or unpleasant to the individual experiencing the emotion, decided physical changes tend to accompany the feeling state. When angry, we have all experienced the speeding up of our heart and pulse rates, the flushing of our faces, the quickening of our breathing, the trembling of our hands. When struck by fear, we may show some of the above symptoms, or we may blanch or turn pale, our mouths may become very dry, our lips may tremble, the pupils of our eyes may dilate, we may hold our breath, our digestive tracts may slow down (peristalsis may actually reverse itself), and the small hairs on our bodies may stand erect.

Even when we experience a feeling of delight, we tend to experience physiological changes, although they are not usually as intense as those evoked by anger, hatred, or fear.

Cannon, in discussing the physical changes that occur in relation to the emotions of anger and fear, says the body is readying itself either for active aggression or for escape from that which is terrifying it (hence, the name, "the fight or flight" syndrome). The adrenal glands pour out adrenalin into the bloodstream and extra strength or power is available for quick action.

Both pleasant and unpleasant emotions are the lot of all mankind. We are always involved in trying to fulfill our needs. Some needs can be met, others cannot. Man is a creature torn between many conflicting emotions. He runs the gamut between the extremes of love and hate; from childlike trust to paranoid suspiciousness; from heights of self-sacrificing bravery to the depths of cowardice. Furthermore, emotions are very powerful motivators of our behavior.

Control of Emotions

One of man's major struggles is the effort he must make to learn to control his emotions, and learning must take place, even in early childhood, in the way in which he may express his emotions or must repress them. Some emotions are acceptable in a social group, others are not. Each culture has its own standards of behavior and, to be socially accepted, one must conform to these standards. Some cultures impose more control over emotions than others. As an example of this, contrast the emotionalism of an American Indian child with that of a southern European child, say an Italian child. The Indian child is taught to repress all expression of emotion, to become stoical. This is not to say that he is unemotional. He has the same strong urges to express joy, love, hatred, and fear as any other human being. But his social acceptance depends in part upon his learning how to control all expression of emotion, and tribal custom demands of him a "deadpan" facial expression and fierce controls of any show of intense fear, joy, or pain.

The Italian child grows up in a highly emotional atmosphere. He is encouraged to express his likes and dislikes freely; he is highly verbal and laughter and tears may succeed each other quickly in him. Surging anger often results in aggressive behavior. Perhaps he is better off emotionally than the Indian child, for when emotions are too sternly repressed, they tend to finally result in explosive behavior when tensions mount too high.

All too often, a child learns that the expression of some emotions is unacceptable and, since he feels these emotions (such as jealousy, hatred, anger, fear, and aggression), and since he is often punished for showing them, he must learn to repress them in one way or another. He may "swallow" them (i.e., bury them in his unconscious mind); he may displace them on toys, pets, or belongings (i.e., he may break or destroy his possessions or mistreat his pet); or he may turn them inward upon himself. He tends to accumulate guilt concerning these forbidden feelings and desires.

We have come to believe that healthy, enlightened parents will encourage their children to feel whatever they feel, to verbalize these feelings when it is appropriate, and help them to find ways of expressing these feelings in society in ways which damage neither society nor the child.

Aggression

Just what is aggression? Menninger in his book, *Man Against Himself*, defines it as an emotion compounded of frustration and hate or rage. It is an emotion deeply rooted in every one of us, a vital part of our emotional being which must either be projected outward upon the environment, or be directed inward, destructively, upon the self. Freud, in attempting to explain the dual emotions of love and hate, postulated that there exist, in every human being, from the very beginning of life, dual impulses toward self-preservation and self-destruction. He called the constructive impulse **Eros** (love or life), and the destructive impulse **Thanatos** (hate or death). He conceived these forces as ever antagonistic, ever present, ever striving. He said that we do not truly live until we love; that in the end we are undone by our own hate and that Thanatos wins since death is the final end for all of us.

Menninger likens hate to an ugly, grey stone wall which is softened in time by love, which is like a creeping mantle of green ivy that covers the ugly starkness of the stone, turning it into a thing of beauty. He postulates that hate and frustration appear first in personality growth, followed by the appearance of love as we mature. But hate never completely disappears. It shows itself in various aggressive disguises, and even, on occasion, in frank form when our controls slip.

Aggression becomes apparent in the infant very shortly after birth. In the child's prenatal life, all of its needs are met, but with the advent of birth, its comfort is violently shattered, and it is this birth trauma that supposedly sets the pattern for all subsequent frustration anxieties.

As the infant becomes hungry, cold, wet, and uncomfortable, he exhibits his rage by crying, stiffening, and contracting his muscles. His skin flushes a deep red in color, and he may hold his breath. As he grows older, he exhibits increasing rage when his needs are not met. He may have temper tantrums, scream, hold his breath, scratch, strike out, throw and smash toys and other articles within his reach, bite, pinch, kick, whine, refuse to comply with instructions or admonitions, and, still later, run away, use angry, abusive language, spit at you, soil himself intentionally. The child is narcissistic and wants his own way. This is common, frequently encountered behavior in the normal small child. It is a display of frank, uninhibited aggression.

Progressively, these manifestations of aggression will be met by controls from without, as parents and other family members start curbing temper tantrums and destructive behavior. The child bitterly resents the restrictions and demands that are made upon him, and his hostility builds. This feeling of hostility is accompanied by, or succeeded by, a deep feeling of guilt. In addition to guilt feelings, he fears the loss of love and approval from the persons who are significant to him. There is also the factor of expected punishment when he is disobedient. And so the small child learns to modify his behavior to conform to the demands of his family and, later, to conform to the expected norms of society.

Slowly he learns to build up his own inner controls (his **ego strength**), and, as his own self-punishing system (**superego** or **conscience**) develops in him, he learns to differentiate between right and wrong.

Since our social laws deny us permission to commit bodily assault on other persons, or to wantonly destroy their property, we must learn to channel our aggression into sports, games, politics, business, hobbies, wit and humor, and many, many other forms of socially acceptable activities. We may also displace it on non-retaliative objects or sublimate it. But we must remember that hate and violence, whether controlled or not, remain as strong catalysts in the personality balance of all of us throughout our lifetime. Sometimes we manage to bury hate deeply, but often, when we least expect it, our controls slip and we demonstrate our rage in a very frank manner, if only for a few brief seconds, and then often to our great dismay!

The child, then, as he matures, learns to control his emotions. Slowly, but steadily, his behavior turns from a frank expression of his anger to more veiled forms of aggression such as lying, stealing, defacing property, forgetting, denial, sarcasm, silence, rejection, truancy, bullying, swearing, refusing to work up to his potential.

Up to this point we have been discussing the outward expression of hostility, the directing of a person's wrath upon the environment. We have subdivided it into frank, overt, or direct aggression, and into veiled, covert, or indirect aggression.

Now we shall speak of another form of aggression, that which is inwardly directed upon the self.

The turning of aggression in upon one's self appears in many forms. It is a strong underlying force in self-debasement or ego-flagellation and many other forms of self-destructive behavior. Suicide is, of course, the final form of self-destruction, but there are many degrees, or levels, of self-destruction before this final, violent form.

In medical practice, physicians are becoming increasingly aware of, and interested in, self-directed aggression as being a causative factor in *organic* diseases. The part it plays in hysterias, neuroses, and psychoses has long been known, but the line between the so-called organic diseases and the psycho-logical diseases is becoming difficult to assess.

The fear of (and wish for) punishment seems to be very prominent in most of us. Self-destruction tends to have both psychological and physical expression. When we have uncontrollable and, at the same time, inadmissible hate, we tend to develop physical symptoms as well as psychological ones. Love and hate are very often combined in our feelings for the people about us (ambivalence). Hopefully, the need to love and to be loved will become sufficiently well-developed in most of us so as to dominate our relationships with our families and our friends.

But because we so often hate the very people we also love, and because we cannot bear to acknowledge this hate, even to ourselves, and fear to expose it to others, we try to disavow it and often succeed in repressing it into our unconscious mind.

Inwardly directed aggression is primarily based on strong guilt feelings that are inadmissible to our egos. When hate is turned inward, our life-instincts must battle our self-destructive tendencies and arrive at some form of compromise. These compromises, while handicapping our personalities, often severely, do enable us to focus our self-destructive impulses so as to prevent suicide in its crude, immediate form.

In some neuroses, we see the effects of inwardly directed aggression ap-pearing in the wish to suffer. The extraordinary fact that a person should enjoy suffering or should prefer pain to pleasure is difficult for the average, normal person to accept. Yet, the neurotic enjoys ill health. The masochist frequently does violence to his body. The psychologist sees alcohol and drug addiction as forms of self-destruction due to a need for punishment from a sense of guilt related to aggressiveness. It is, in a sense, self-destruction accomplished by means of the very device used by the sufferer to relieve his pain and his sense of inadequacy.

Criminality, anti-social behavior, and sexual perversion are all based on self-destructive tendencies. Frigidity and sexual impotence are very common forms of self-directed aggression.

Self-mutilation, malingering, compulsive polysurgery, and unconsciously purposeful accidents are all forms of self-destruction. Biting of fingernails, biting of fingers, hands, arms, and legs; the scratching and digging of flesh; the plucking out of hair; the rubbing of skin to the inflammation point; head banging; self-slapping or pounding—these are all commonly seen forms of self-mutilation. Is it too difficult for us to see these forms of *local* self-destruc-tion as forms of *partial* suicide to avert total suicide?

The psychological needs for love and acceptance seem to be the chief causative factors in self-mutilation. There may also be contributing factors of mechanical, physical, and chemical pathologies. The treatment of emotionally deprived persons must be based in part on our ability to convince them that they are wanted and loved. For an individual overwhelmed by his own hostility and other emotional conflicts, even the tacit assurance that somebody loves him enough to listen to him and to try to help him is, of itself, a tremendous reassurance. These self-punishers must first learn to trust and hope in personal relationships before any other therapy can be effective. The importance of personal relationships is suggested in this quote from Freud: "A strong egoism is a protection against disease, but, in the last resort, we must begin to love in order that we may not fall ill, and must fall ill if, in consequence of frustration, we cannot love."

References

Mayeroff, M.: On Caring. New York, Harper & Row, 1972.
Menninger, K. A.: Man Against Himself, New York, Harcourt, 1956.

Communication

Behavioral Objectives

The student successfully attaining the goals of this chapter will be able to:

- Define the word communication in its broadest terms.
- Compare verbal and nonverbal communication.
- List the 4 components of verbal communication.
- Explain why the skill of listening is so vital in the care of sick people.
- List 10 types of behavior which constitute nonverbal communication and give 2 examples of each—one that conveys a negative message and one that conveys a positive message.

What is meant by the word **communicate?** The dictionary definition is, "To communicate means to share; to impart; to transmit; or to give and receive information, signals, or messages in any way."

Communication actually includes all the ways in which people influence each other. The field of communication is usually divided into two sections, *verbal* and *nonverbal*.

Verbal Communication

Most of us think of communication as being primarily concerned with speaking, listening, writing and reading. These are all parts of verbal communication. While much communicating does center around the spoken and written word, there are numerous other ways in which we communicate with each other daily. These other ways involve all five of our special senses and we term them nonverbal ways of communicating.

First, let us discuss verbal communication. Two of its forms, talking and listening, are parts of a two-way process. He who talks must have a listener or listeners. Listening, then, is the other half of talking.

The ability to talk, to use a well-developed language, is one of man's greatest achievements. Other forms of life also communicate, and, like man, some species such as the dolphin appear to have the ability to use a system of phonetic symbols to convey thought and feeling. Man's speech has been built upon this use of symbols, and the basic unit of speech is the word. A word is not a thing in itself. It is only a symbol of a thing, and it actually stands for our conception of that thing.

Language makes it possible for us to accumulate knowledge, wisdom, and skill; it enables us to profit from the experiences of others, even from persons and races who lived long ago.

Not all groups of men have a written language, but all men have a well-developed spoken language.

, We use our language to convey meanings. However, meaning is a very personal thing. The meaning of a word can differ from person to person, area to area, and from language to language.

Our dictionaries attempt to convey the precise meaning of words to us, but sometimes a word has more than one meaning and how it is interpreted will depend mainly on how it is used in a sentence. Sometimes, a word of the same sound may be spelled differently and the way it is spelled will determine its meaning. As an example, let us look at the words "eight" and "ate"; they are pronounced exactly the same but have very different meanings. If we say, "There are eight apples in the bowl," and "Joe ate all the apples in the bowl," we hear what seems like the same word used quite differently. When we look at these two sentences in written form, it becomes apparent to us that the difference in spelling determines the meaning of the word.

In order to communicate with words, the word must have some degree of uniformity in meaning to both the speaker and the hearer, to the writer and the reader.

Pronunciation varies greatly in different areas and even at different social levels within the same area. As an example of area differences, the Bostonian pronounces the letters "aw" like the Chicagoan pronounces "ar." The former says he enjoys "rawr ersters," while the latter says he enjoys "raaw oisters." Each has to adjust to the pronunciation of the other.

Culture and communications are deeply interrelated. America has a special language problem in this area because it is the melting pot of so many cultures and races. And now, with the frontiers of our world shrinking daily, due to extensive travel and to mass communication, we not only have to adjust to differences in culture within our own boundaries, but to the cultures and value systems of many foreign countries.

We find that one of the basic problems in understanding culturally deprived groups today rests mainly upon the difference in the value systems of persons from disadvantaged groups as compared to those who are being raised in an affluent society. The communication barrier between the child of the inner city and the child of our well-to-do suburban society may be so great that effective understanding between them may be most difficult. Our familial, social, intellectual, and ethnic backgrounds vary markedly. Our frames of reference, and especially our feelings about things may be so divergent that communication may not take place.

If we are to understand each other, we must make an effort to understand how the other person feels about a situation rather than how we feel about it. We must try to put ourselves in his position and look at the situation from his point of reference.

Now let us consider listening. The statement was made earlier that listening is the other half of talking. To listen well is often much more difficult than to speak well. The speaker is concentrating on putting his thoughts into words that will convey his mental images to his audience. The listener usually has much more difficulty in concentrating on the words of the speaker. He tends to be easily distracted by his own ideas and feelings and must make a conscious effort to attend to the auditory stimulation reaching his ears. To become a good listener requires the concentration of all of our mental faculties.

In the field of healing, being able to listen well is a tremendous asset and a skill worth developing. Troubled, disturbed, unhappy, or fearful people need to be able to ventilate their feelings to someone who will really listen to them. As a listener, we do not always have to agree with what the speaker is saying. The important thing is to allow him to say what he is feeling and thinking.

Communication is usually facilitated when there is free feedback between persons. When we feel free to ask questions of a speaker, we can arrive at a better understanding of what he is trying to convey to us.

Writing and reading also come under verbal communication, for writing and reading also involve the use of words. During man's early history, he communicated some of his thoughts and feelings by drawing pictures in the sand and upon the walls of caves. Later, he chiseled thought pictures on stone or traced them on tablets of clay or wax. The pictures gave way to hieroglyphics and these, in turn, to words. The Phoenicians gave us our alphabet. Here, at last, man had a tool with which he could communicate the finest shades of his feelings and meaning to others.

Scrolls of parchment and silk were among the early materials on which man wrote and painted. Then came papyrus and the advent of manuscripts and bound books. But, for centuries, reading and writing were reserved for only a few—the scholars. Only men of wealth could afford to own books that were laboriously written by hand. Most of the writing during the Middle Ages was done by educated monks in the monasteries. Many of these manuscripts and books were beautifully illustrated with color and gold leaf.

Then came the printing press. Now books could be produced cheaply and they found their way into the homes of those who had learned to read. The need to become literate increased. All advancing countries stressed the need of children to learn to read and write.

In America, as the need to communicate has steadily increased, we have become one of the most literate people in the world. But, even here, not all of our citizens can read and write. There are pockets of illiteracy in isolated areas; there are illiterate persons in our disadvantaged groups, especially in the ghetto areas of our large cities. There are also large segments of foreign born persons who, while probably quite competent in the languages of their ethnic backgrounds, have not learned to communicate in the language of their adopted country.

We have entered a very busy technological age in which communication has become a vital part of our daily lives. Television has brought the whole world, even outer space, into our living rooms. Yet, in spite of all the advancement in the field of communication in our generation, man still is poverty stricken in the areas of self-knowledge and in truly understanding his own needs and those of his fellow man.

Nonverbal Communication

This form of communication includes every way in which people influence each other, exclusive of words. Though we tend to rely heavily on visual observation to affirm facts or truths, all of our senses are involved in picking up the real feelings of people. Dr. Edward Hall believes that we communicate our real feelings in our silent language—the language of behavior. Gestures, body movements, tone of voice, facial expression, posture, body appearance, touch, odor, evasion, and even silence, can each tell its own story to one who is keenly perceptive. Generally speaking, our ability to perceive is based on our own past learning and experiences. This means that we tend to differ widely in our ability to perceive. Sometimes the nonverbal message a person is sending out is stronger than the verbal one; sometimes it is weaker; and sometimes it strongly contradicts the words being spoken. We often hide our real feelings and meanings when we converse or write and reveal them only in subtle behavior. The doctor and nurse must become skilled in the nonverbal field of communication if they really wish to learn how a patient truly feels about things.

Gestures widely accompany speech. We are seldom aware of how much gesturing we do, as it is mostly an unconscious mechanism. A baby will understand your gestures before your words, and will unconsciously imitate them. If you hold out your arms to him, he will lift his in expectation of being picked up. If you wave to him as you leave the room, he will understand the meaning of the wave before he learns the meaning of "bye-bye," and will wave back at you. When someone makes a circle of his thumb and finger and gestures with it, we understand that "all is well" or "everything is O.K." The Roman citizens in the arena used to demand death for the contestants in their struggles by extending the thumb and rolling the four fingers into the palm, then pointing the thumb downward. This sign is still widely understood centuries later. The nodding or shaking of a head to indicate "yes" or "no" is commonly used.

Body movements can tell us much about feelings. A patient moving restlessly in bed, a child squirming in a church pew, someone impatiently tapping his fingers on his desk, all tell their story.

The tone of a person's voice is very revealing; for instance, one may speak in a cheerful, an impatient, an angry, a venomous, a feeble, or in an excited voice. One's tone of voice can also give some indication as to personality traits and even educational background.

Facial expression can reinforce words or nullify them. A smile, a frown, raised eyebrows, compressed lips, lowered eyelids, eyes that won't meet yours, eyes intently fixed on yours, all convey emotional states. The eyes are extremely expressive. The mouth may smile but if the eyes express boredom, disinterest, anger, irritation, fear, or hate, the keen observer will make his own judgment on the value of the smile. Tear-filled eyes tell us the individual is unhappy or in pain, or feeling joy.

Much information is conveyed by touch. The hands speak eloquently. A gentle touch can subdue anger, quiet fear, and relax tensions; a vigorous handclasp can convey enthusiasm, pleasure, and interest; a limp hand can convey shyness, coldness of emotion, lack of interest, or even dislike. The touch of a body against ours can convey a warning or express a shared attitude; the touch of a cheek on ours usually conveys tenderness or sympathy; the touch of lips can be very tender or roughly demanding.

A person's complete appearance can communicate much about his attitudes and his emotional state. His grooming, attire, the way he wears his clothing, his posture, and the way in which he handles his body, all contribute to the overall impression of his personality.

A person who has lost his self-respect usually neglects his appearance. He may be unshaven, wrinkled and soiled; his shoes may be unpolished, and his hands and nails unkempt. If he is mentally ill, his mental disorganization tends to reflect itself in disorganized behavior and disorganized physical appearance.

Even body odor conveys a message. A fresh scrubbed odor, the fragrance of soap, body powder, or cologne, tells us that a person wishes to be pleasing to others, as well as to himself. Someone reeking from perspiration, foot odors, bad breath, or discharges from body orifices, tells us he is insensitive to his own unpleasantness and has little concern for the esthetic needs of others.

And then there is silence. The "silent treatment" is one of the most upsetting of all forms of communication. When a person meets our greetings, questions, or statements with complete silence, we become very anxious. Is he deaf? Can't he understand us? Or is he rejecting us? Silence can indicate evasion, fear, uncertainty, anger, rebelliousness, and other negative emotions as well as rejection, but few of us can be comfortable in the presence of prolonged silence. Silence may also mean that the person is "far away," whether on drugs, or in the ecstasy of contemplation or meditation, or catatonic due to disease of the mind.

We communicate in a multitude of nonverbal ways with each other. Some of these ways are subtle and some quite frank in their expression.

A good nurse must explore her own feelings and behavior. After she has learned something about her own motivation, she must try to understand the motivations of her patients. In order to understand what her patients are experiencing and feeling, she must try to use their frames of reference and to feel what they are feeling from their points of view. To do this effectively, she must develop keen insight and skill in communicating.

References

Bateson, G.: Steps to an Ecology of Mind. New York, Ballantine, 1972.
Matheney, R. V., and Topalis, M.: Psychiatric Nursing. Ed. 5. St. Louis, C. V. Mosby, 1970.
Ruesch, J.: "Communication and Psychiatry" in Comprehensive Textbook of Psychiatry, ed. 2. Baltimore, Williams & Wilkins, 1975.
Ruesch, J. and Kees, W.: Noverbal Communication, ed. 2. University of California Press, Berkeley, 1972.

Discussion Questions

THE SITUATION:

You are a student nurse in the hospital. Joey, a nine-year-old Caucasian boy, is admitted on your ward. He presents the "battered child syndrome." He is covered with bruises and welts, and there is a section of one cheek that has a raw, infected wound on it. You undress him and put him to bed. He sullenly and slowly obeys your requests but does not answer you when you speak to him. When he lifts his eyes to yours, they are hostile and hot with hate and fear. When you touch him, he shrinks from your touch.

You go out to where his mother has just been giving information to an intern concerning Joey's history. Mrs. Adams is a large, obese woman with bleached hair, soiled clothing, and the smell of stale beer on her breath.

You learn, upon reading the history, that Joey is the fifth of nine children. Mother and children are on "Aid to Dependent Children"; the father's where abouts are unknown. He left his family ten years ago. A succession of common-law husbands have fathered at least six of the nine children. The family lives in the inner city. Living conditions are very crowded; the children are often cold and hungry; the older ones attend school sketchily, due—among other things—to inadequate clothing. The festering wound on Joey's cheek was caused by a rat bite; the bruises, lacerations, and welts are due to a severe beating with a heavy leather belt and buckle last night by an intoxicated "father" whom Joey had "sassed." The mother complains that Joey gives her more trouble than any of her other children. He is disobedient; "sasses" her and her "husband," quarrels with his brothers and sisters and all the neighborhood children; lies and steals; rarely attends school.

When questioned as to whether or not she approves of such a physical punishment for a small boy, she retorts that it is the only way you can handle the child. She would not have brought him to the hospital, battered though he was, had not the social worker called today, and, upon seeing Joey, insisted he be brought in to the hospital for treatment.

QUESTIONS:
1. Do you think that Joey's environment is conducive to healthy growth and personality development?
2. Do you think there is a wholesome mother-child relationship evidenced in this history?
3. How secure do you think Joey feels?
4. Who does Joey have to *identify* with?
5. How would you assess Joey's need for status and recognition?
6. How would you assess Joey's ego-ideal, or self-concept?
7. How would you assess Joey's feelings of security and acceptance in his family?
8. What do you feel are Joey's greatest emotional needs right now?
9. How might you go about conveying to Joey that you are a friend and not a foe?
10. How might you win his confidence?
11. How will you handle your own feelings if you are unable to win his confidence?

Personality
Development

Introduction to Concepts of Personality Development

Behavioral Objectives

The student successfully attaining the goals of this chapter will be able to:
- List several factors that can influence a child's personality.
- Explain the heredity theory of personality development.
- Describe the biochemical theory of personality development.
- Name 4 people who have developed theories of personality development.

Why are people seemingly so different? Why is one man angry, aggressive, and ready to fight at the slightest provocation while another is passive and gentle, always willing to compromise and bend in order to seek a peaceful solution?

The differences in basic personality set and energy level are apparent in any newborn nursery. One-day-old infants vary greatly in the amount they move about, the vigor with which they cry, the strength with which they suck, the tolerance they show for discomfort. Any mother with more than one child will readily admit that there were definite differences in the way each child went through the neonatal period and infancy. One child was weaned easier, one got toilet trained "automatically," and so forth.

One can observe that even with the same parents, the genetic make-up of each sibling is different. One may "take after" his mother and the other "lean to his father's side of the family." One child may be significantly brighter than another. Literature is full of references to "the beautiful sister" and "the ugly sister" or the son who is "the dreamer" and the son who is "the doer."

Another obvious factor is the order of birth. The first child is born into a home where childrearing is a new experience for the parents. Not only is the infant new at the job of being an infant, but also the parents are new at the job of being parents. The second child is born into a different situation.

His parents have had some experience at being parents. They are, perhaps, better at limit setting. They have, perhaps, made the house more "child proof" so that the second child is less likely to break valuable things and get into situations of physical danger.

The first child is an "only child" until his brother or sister is born. He has his parents' full attention until suddenly the parents have a new baby and he is an only child no longer. The second child is never an "only child."

Parents, although they often deny it, have preferences among their children. The father may like boys or more aggressive children, while the mother may like quiet, obedient children more. Often the reverse is true, the mother favoring her sons and the father favoring his daughters.

With all of these variables, it is little wonder that a great number of theories (also referred to as "belief systems") have evolved regarding the issue of how personality development occurs. That genetic factors play a part is virtually beyond dispute. The most universally accepted belief about heredity is that it is the background, the "set" on which environmental factors play to form the personality.

For example, it is believed by some (although by no means proved) that an infant with a genetic predisposition to schizophrenia may develop in one family as a quiet, sensitive, artistic youth, in another as a person with a schizoid personality (See pp. 117-118), in yet another as a latent schizophrenic (See p. 105), and in still another family as an acute schizophrenic (See p. 105) with a clearly defined psychosis. Studies on identical twins (who have of course identical genetic structures) show that there is a very high likelihood of each twin developing the same mental disorder even though they are separated at birth and reared in different families.

Related to the heredity-as-cause belief system, but containing some of its own special concepts, is the biochemical (or neurotransmitter) theory. There are subtle but distinct biochemical differences between persons with no mental disorder and persons with major mental illness. Which comes first, the biochemical disorder or the mental disorder, is still under dispute but this area of investigation is among the most promising in psychiatric research today.

Most belief systems, however, have little to do with heredity or biochemistry. They are concerned with one facet or another of the individual person's development from birth on, and focus on the various forces that impinge on the child (father, mother, siblings, family, society) and/or the intrinsic developmental forces (the child's initial dependence and growth toward independence, the development of language, the development of motor skills, and bowel and bladder control).

That there is no belief system that has, as yet, "the answer," should be well understood by the student at the outset. At the same time, there is no place for a negative attitude which says "since nobody knows, there's no reason for listening to anybody." Each belief system has some element of truth in it, and it's all we have to work with at this time.

Sigmund Freud focused on the erotic nature of the patient-therapist relationship and on the importance of early sexual traumas as causative elements in neuroses.

Carl Jung emphasized concepts of the collective unconscious, the idea of individuation (becoming an individual), and on introversion and extroversion.

Harry Stack Sullivan believed that the individual could be studied only in relation to his interaction with others. Sullivan developed four basic postulates which underlie his theories: (1) Biological Postulate. This belief states that man (as an animal) differs from all other animals in his cultural interdependence. (2) Man's Essentially Human Mode of Functioning. This refers to those characteristics which distinguish man from all other animal life. (3) Significance of Anxiety. This belief refers to the central role of anxiety in human development. (4) Tenderness Postulate. Sullivan states that "the activity of an infant which arises from the tension of his needs produces tension in the mothering one which is felt by her as tenderness." Man has a growing capacity for tenderness.

Erich Fromm's theories reflect the orientation of the social scientist. He emphasizes the role of society in mental disorder rather than the classic psychoanalyst's concern with the individual. Fromm believes that "self-love" is really self-affirmation, which is the basis of the capacity to love others.

Alfred Adler influenced child psychiatry a great deal and began by considerations of "organ inferiority" and "nervous character," later becoming preoccupied with educational, social, and political issues in the genesis of mental illness.

Wilhelm Reich made a valuable contribution to the understanding of the development of the character.

Otto Rank was primarily concerned with the application of psychoanalysis to mythology and literature.

Eugen Bleuler published a comprehensive study of schizophrenia (his term).

Hermann Rorschach (who developed the ink blot test) was a pioneer in the elaboration of projective testing.

Other names of significance are **Adolf Meyer** (psychobiology), **Sandor Rado** (adaptational psychodynamics), **Melanie Klein** (play therapy with children), and **Arthur Janov** (primal therapy).

The concepts of Freud and Erickson will be explored more thoroughly in Chapters 7 and 8.

References

Berne, E.: What Do You Say After You Say Hello? New York, Grove Press, 1972.

Hale, N. G.: Freud and The Americans: The Beginning of Psychoanalysis in the United States, 1876–1917. New York, Oxford University Press, 1971.

Jung, C. G.: Psychological Types. Princeton, Princeton University Press, 1971.

Kelman, H.: Helping People: Karen Horney's Psychoanalytic Approach. New York, Science House, 1971.

Senesco, R.: "Sandor Rado." in Comprehensive Textbook of Psychiatry, ed. 2. Baltimore, Williams & Wilkins, 1975.

Shereshefsky, P. M.: Rank's Contribution to the Psychology of Women. New York, Rank Association, 1972.

Sullivan, H. S.: Personal Psychopathology. New York, W. W. Norton, 1972.

Wilder, J.: Alfred Adler in Historical Perspective. American Journal of Psychotherapy, 24:450, 1970.

Wyckhoff, J.: Wilhelm Reich, Life Force Explorer. Greenwich, Conn., Fawcett, 1973.

The Freudian Concept of Personality Development

Behavioral Objectives

The student successfully attaining the goals of this chapter will be able to:
- Identify the name of Sigmund Freud and explain why he is so important in the study of personality.
- List the 7 phases in personality development as described by Freud and indicate the age range of each.
- Define the word empathy and explain its importance in a child's development by noting the effects when empathy is present and when it is not.
- Describe the best age and method for toilet training a child and indicate the adverse effects which may result if attempts are made to toilet train a child too early.
- Explain the adverse effects on a child's personality if he is punished or scolded for masturbating, and indicate what steps should be taken when a child masturbates.
- Describe the feelings which are associated with an Oedipus complex and an Electra complex and explain how adults who have such complexes might behave.
- Define the term sibling and give three examples of sibling rivalry.
- List 5 characteristics of a child in the latent phase of development.
- Describe the type of physical changes that occur during puberty and explain how children can be helped to adjust to these changes.
- List 3 types of stress encountered by the adolescent.
- Describe the characteristics of an adult personality.

Sigmund Freud (1856–1939) was a Viennese physician who made important contributions to our understanding of personality development. The contributions are a part of the system of psychology to which he gave the name psychoanalysis.

Freud gave a predominant place to an aspect of the personality which he termed **sexuality.** His selection of this term to express the pleasure-seeking component of the personality was unfortunate, since it erroneously carried the implication that all forms of pleasure seeking were associated with genital sexuality and pleasure. But, if we can bear in mind that Freud's use of the term sexuality is quite broad, we can trace a step-by-step development of the psychosexual aspect of the personality from its earliest expression in the baby to maturity.

Freud divided the growth and development of the human body into phases. From birth to adulthood, he listed them as: (1) The Oral Phase; (2) The Anal Phase; (3) The Genital Phase; (4) The Latent Phase; (5) Puberty; (6) Adolescence; (7) Adulthood.

The Oral Phase

This phase lasts from birth to about the end of the first year. It terminates in weaning. Before birth, the infant is fed through the maternal bloodstream and has never experienced the satisfying pleasure provided by the gratification of this instinctual need. With birth, however, a biological need for food arises, and he receives satisfaction through nursing. Not only is the discomfort from hunger relieved by sucking, but, as other tensions arise, the infant turns to the most available substitute as a source of security and satisfaction and sucks his thumb. The mouth becomes, therefore, the part of the body in which interests, sensation, and activities are centered and through which gratification is secured. Breast feeding not only supplies the infant's physical needs for food and warmth; it also supplies an emotional need—providing security. As the baby is cradled in his mother's arms and held against her body, he feels comforted and secure. Not all mothers can breast feed their babies, but, even when the child is bottle fed, he should be held and fondled during the feeding process so as to give him this needed sensation of security. If a baby is seldom held and loved, and is left lying untended for long periods of time, often uncomfortable at not being turned or changed, or if he is allowed to go hungry beyond his first hunger pangs, he will have definite feelings of discomfort and he will tend to become insecure. This early insecurity may present problems for him later in his ability to cope with life. If he does not feel the overtones of love from the mother figure, he will sense that something is not right in his environment. This ability to sense or feel the feeling tones of others is called *empathy*. The child is able to sense the presence or absence of loving feeling on the part of others long before he is able to understand language or to communicate with others. The baby should have his mother, her comforts, her caressing, and her satisfying of his basic needs as much as possible during this vital first year.

We speak of this first year of a child's personality development as being the first stage of psychosexual development.

The Anal-Expulsive Phase

This phase starts about the end of the first year. At that time, the mouth begins to share its pleasure-giving role with the organs of elimination. The child becomes as much interested in his excretory functions as the mother is in controlling them. This period covers the toilet training stage and usually terminates early in the third year. The small child does not have the same feeling of revulsion for excreta that adults have. The process of elimination is pleasure-giving to him. In our culture, toilet training is begun very early and is usually rigidly enforced. Some parents begin this training in the ninth or tenth month of a child's life. It is thought that conscious control of the rectal sphincter is not fully developed until after brain and nerve fibres make standing and walking possible Toilet training is not possible until necessary development of the nervous system has taken place, and until the child has acquired a sign language with which to make his wants known. If the mother, unmindful that the child may find pleasurable elements in elimination, attempts to enforce toilet training by punishment, if she whips or severely reprimands him when he soils himself, the child is going to feel bewildered and puzzled and sure that his mother does not love him. In retaliation, he may withhold his feces, or he may soil himself purposely. He may even smear feces on himself and his surroundings. Thus are aroused many conflicting emotional factors which may harmfully influence the developing personality. On the other hand, if the mother does not rush the child, if she carefully observes the usual time of a child's bowel movements and, just before they are due, places the child on the toilet and carefully indicates what she expects of him, he will slowly but surely learn to accomplish this task successfully, especially if she supports him with her warmth and patience and praises him upon completion of the task. If this plan is followed through regularly for several months, the child can usually be toilet trained by the end of the second year. True, he may still soil himself occasionally, but, for the most part, he will accept his responsibility, knowing that this is the way in which he can please his parents.

The Genital Phase

This phase is characterized by the child's growing awareness of the differences in the male and female bodies. This stage usually extends from late in the third year or early in the fourth, until the sixth or seventh year. At this stage of personality development, there is an increasing interest in the genitalia and the child discovers that he achieves a pleasurable sensation when the genitalia are handled or rubbed. As he fondles himself, he is not at all aware that he is doing something that is socially unacceptable—that he is masturbating—and it is only when parents become upset at seeing his actions and express their displeasure that it assumes an abnormal significance to the child. Up to this point, he has only followed the normal pattern of curiosity about his own body and discovered the pleasurable sensations he can derive from it. Seeing the importance his parents attach to his actions, and being unable to understand why they are angry with him or punishing him, he feels threatened or frightened. He becomes confused, unhappy, and ashamed. Because of the confused emotions, he will often resort to the new, pleasurable activity with increased attention in his desire to feel comforted. Thus, punishment tends to reinforce the activity.

Masturbation is not physically harmful in any way, but it does pose an emotional problem when conflicts set in. If the child becomes unhappy enough, he will resort to masturbation in secret, and this will increase his guilt feeling and isolate him even further from his parents.

Obsessive masturbation can be avoided by a wise and tolerant attitude on the part of the mother and father, and by a program bent toward diverting the child's interests and energies. Parents should try to spend more time with the child during this period; they should offer him interesting games, play with him, and not let him spend too much time alone. Genital cleanliness, frequent vigorous activity, mixing with neighborhood children in supervised play, and a wholesome attitude in the home toward the human body will help the child pass through this phase with a minimum of difficulty.

Now, during this same period of genital interest, another problem frequently arises. According to psychoanalytic belief, each child goes through a stage of strong attraction to the parent of the opposite sex, accompanied by jealousy of the one of the same sex. Thus, a boy has a feeling of great tenderness for his mother, wants all her love and attention, and has mingled feelings of jealousy, hate, and fear for his father. Freud gave the term **Oedipus complex** to this situation because of the legend of the Greek King Oedipus, who, moved by forces over which he had no control, and without knowledge of his parents' identity, slew his father and married his mother. The corresponding situation in which the little girl prefers her father is known as the **Electra complex.** Ordinarily, with further maturing of the personality, this stage of psychosexual development is outgrown. The son tends, unconsciously, to take over the adult characteristics of his father's personality, and the daughter tends to identify wholesomely with her mother.

If this situation is not handled with understanding by the parents, it can result in a permanent attachment for the parent of the opposite sex. This will be observed in the case of a daughter who will continue to be deeply devoted to her father and will stay home and care for him in his old age in preference to mating and establishing a home of her own. Or, if she marries, she will choose a much older man who in some way resembles her father. Also we see sons who exhibit very tender love for their mothers. They will continue living at home and do not exhibit normal interest in girls of their own age. If they marry, it may be to an older woman.

Another problem that is frequently met with in children between three and seven years of age, although this problem can also occur earlier and later in a child's life, is **sibling rivalry.** A sibling is a brother or a sister who is the offspring of the same parents. This problem most often becomes notable when a new brother or sister is born. When a new baby arrives, the older child is bound to feel dislodged from his previous secure position in the family circle. The parents, especially the mother, must necessarily spend much time with the new arrival, and her unceasing care of it makes the older child feel neglected, unwanted, and jealous. He may actively hate the newcomer. He may even try to get rid of the baby. He is resentful toward his mother because of her limited attention to him and he will resort to all kinds of attention-getting devices to gain attention. If these fail, he may resort to infantile behavior, such as thumb sucking or bed wetting. He may develop stuttering or he may lose his appetite. He often misbehaves in the presence of company. Sibling rivalry can occur at any age. It often is seen reversed; the younger child is resentful and jealous of the older brother who seems to be allowed more privileges and adult companionship with the parents. If a plain child is compared unfavorably with more handsome brothers and sisters, or a slower learner criticized for not being as bright as his siblings, the less favored child may either develop a severe inferiority complex or it may develop deep feelings of hostility and rivalry. Parents who can perceive these difficulties appearing in their children and can understand the causes will be sure that each child receives his full share of attention and praise and will divide their love equally among their offspring.

The Latent Phase

The latent phase is the term applied from the seventh to, or through, the eleventh year. This is a period of comparatively quiet personality growth. The child identifies more and more strongly with the parent of the same sex. This is desirable, since it helps to establish appropriate masculine or feminine traits and ideals. Children are busy, interested in school and other learning experiences. Boys tend to form gangs and enjoy rough play. They have little, if any, appreciation for neatness and cleanliness. They speak disparagingly of girls and look upon them as sissies and as generally useless individuals. Little girls play at being mothers; they sew, cook, and play with dolls and think of little boys as rough, dirty, and mean. This period of personality development is often spoken of as the homosexual stage, one which is often outgrown during adolescence when an interest in members of the opposite sex appears. Stereotype sex roles are being criticized today and there is much discussion about the place of rigid sex roles in our society.

Puberty

Puberty is the term applied to the fifth phase of personality development. It occurs between the tenth and thirteenth years and is characterized by profound physical changes that result in considerable personality change. With the physical changes, there is a growing awareness of sex and of sexual attraction toward others. This is a particularly trying and significant time for girls, since it includes the onset of menstruation. The secondary sex characteristics start making their appearance, and sexual urges arise. Children need the close support of their parents during this time, and they especially need a full and frank explanation about the many changes taking place in their bodies and in their emotions.

Adolescence

Adolescence, or the final transition from childhood into adulthood, stretches from about the thirteenth year on up to about the eighteenth year. As a rule, adolescence manifests itself later in boys than in girls. It is an acute period of transition fraught with many physical and emotional problems. Caught between the dependency of childhood and the independence of adulthood, the teenager is strongly ambivalent in his desires and emotions. He is torn between a desire for emancipation from parental controls and a fear for the consequences of his own acts and judgments. He desires responsibilities, but is not ready for them. He craves reassurance from peers and adults alike, but slowly the scale moves more and more toward the set values of his own age group. He is tremendously uncertain about his own status. He is awkward physically, due to the rapid changes taking place in his body. His emotional state fluctuates from ecstasy to deepest despair, from gaiety to moodiness, from overconfidence to underconfidence.

This is a trying period for both child and parents. It is hard for most parents to accept the complete separation of their child from them. They do realize that he must become a fully independent human being, but it is difficult for them to help him cut the strings that bind them together.

The adolescent must, in addition to separating the parental bonds, bring about a satisfactory relation with the opposite sex. He must also decide on a vocation and start preparing for it, and he must develop a sense of mature responsibility for himself and others. No wonder the teenager is under such stress and beset with such a multitude of anxieties.

Adulthood

Adulthood normally follows adolescence, and this mature phase of personality extends over many years, in fact, up to the onset of senility.

We consider a person as adult when he is capable of assuming the full responsibility for his own actions, and when he is able to consider the needs of other human beings as being as important as his own. During this period, his personality should be characterized by maturity, flexibility and stability. He should be able to achieve a healthy sexual adjustment. He should be able to establish a family, if he wishes, under conditions which provide the security and independence necessary for the rearing of children.

These are the successive stages of development of personality as they are psychoanalytically conceived. As this development or unfolding of the personality proceeds to successively higher phases, characteristics appropriate to lower, less mature levels should be left behind. The individual should progressively replace previously acquired behavior patterns, relationships, ideas, and feelings with new ones appropriate to his age. To fail to do so means that he is compelled to meet life handicapped by habits of feeling, thinking, and behaving that should have been outgrown. Such immaturities and arrests of personality leave one poorly equipped to achieve successful interpersonal relations. As a result, an individual so handicapped may fail to adjust to the stresses of life successfully.

References

Robinson, A.: Working With The Mentally Ill. ed. 4. Philadelphia, J. B. Lippincott, 1971.

Saul, L. J.: Emotional Maturity: The Development and Dynamics of Personality. ed. 3. Philadelphia, J. B. Lippincott, 1971.

Zetzel, E. R. and Meissner, W. W.: Basic Concepts of Psychoanalytic Psychiatry. New York, Basic Books, 1973.

Erikson's Concept of Personality Development

Behavioral Objectives

A student successfully attaining the goals of this chapter will be able to:
- Identify the name of Erik Erikson.
- Discuss the role which developmental tasks play in Erik Erikson's theory of personality development.
- List the 8 stages of personality growth described by Erikson and identify and explain the development task in each stage.
- Indicate the type of care an infant must receive if basic trust is to develop.
- Describe the kind of personality which will result when basic trust is present in an infant's upbringing and the kind of personality which develops when basic trust is missing.
- Explain the child's struggle for autonomy in early childhood and identify the characteristics of a person who has successfully achieved this stage.
- Compare and contrast the features of later childhood and adolescence and explain how parents and adults can help children through both periods of growth.

Personality development as conceived by Erik Erikson does not stress the psychosexual aspect of all the stages of development as Freud does. Erikson compares the evolution of the personality to the evolution of tissues in the early stages of embryonic development. He feels that there is a "timetable" inherent in the dvelopment of various specialized tissues, organs, and systems in the physical body. He proposes that during each stage of development there is a **developmental task** to be accomplished, and that each developmental task not only contributes some vital attribute of personality, but lays the groundwork for the next task. Upon this concept he builds the theory that a whole or partial failure at one step means that the personality will be deficient in the trait which should have arisen at that particular time. If succeeding stages are developed on too faulty a foundation, the total personality may suffer as a result. Erikson points out that these successive stages of personality development should not be thought of as arising at exact time periods, but rather at approximate age levels, with considerable individual variation, and that the developmental tasks of each stage overlap.

The following outline is a brief description of the periods into which he develops personality growth.

Infancy

This period is characterized by **basic trust.** The child is completely help-less and at the mercy of adults. If he is warmly accepted, wanted, and loved, he comes to feel that the world is a nice place and that the people in it are friendly and helpful. He develops a cheerful confidence that his wants will be met.

If, on the other hand, the baby feels unloved and unaccepted, he will develop a diffuse anxiety, a distrust of his small world. He may become pre-occupied with his own needs because of the constant uncertainty that they will be met. Being given so little opportunity to respond positively to others, his relationships are likely to become demanding, fearful, hostile, or simply cold and withdrawn. Basic trust is the necessary foundation for the capacity to love. The history of our largest group of mentally ill patients, the schizo-phrenics, all have a remarkable sameness—the feeling of being unloved and unwanted in childhood. They have all felt so unloved that they failed to develop the basic trust that enables them to build binding ties with one another. The schizophrenic is afraid to love, afraid to invest affection in an-other human being. Thus, he lives in a world of isolation.

Early Childhood

This period is characterized by **autonomy.** Between the ages of 2 and 4 years, the baby comes into contact with increasing restrictions. He must adapt himself to the family and its practices. He must learn to adjust himself to social and moral norms. He becomes fiercely rebellious at all these restrictions. His favorite word is "no." He is impatient with routines and regulations. But, because he is still very dependent upon the very adults he defies, and because he desires their love and their approval, he usually will build a fine and pre-carious balance between independence and conformity.

This negative stage seems to last for about two and a half years. Dur-ing this time, the child repeatedly pits his will against the will of his parents as a vital and necessary contribution to his personality growth. If the child-parent interaction is a constructive one, the successful outcome will be the independence of spirit so highly prized in our culture. The child develops a concept of the dignity and worth of himself as an individual, as well as the worth of others.

Ages Four and Five

This period is characterized by **initiative.** As trust represents the first phase and independence the second, so is the third characterized by an outstanding attribute of personality, that of initiative. This is the period in which the child expands his imagination. He starts "trying on" the role of the parent of the same sex. The boy unconsciously adopts the mannerisms and attitudes of his father, the girl adopts her mother's.

Later Childhood

This period is characterized by **industry** and **accomplishment.** It is equivalent to the *latent* stage in Freud's classification. Children between 6 and 11 years of age stage have much energy that needs channeling into constructive accomplishments. The child is in school, and he learns to compete with his peers in many areas. Pride in doing develops as a result of praise and attention to his efforts. Group projects become absorbing; interests develop into hobbies. These are the peaceful, joyous, exciting years of childhood, between seven and eleven years, when the child learns to work beside and with others, when he begins to learn the skills, both intellectual and mechanical, that will be necessary to his future as a citizen in a complex society. It is the lull before the storm of adolescence.

Adolescence

This period is a stormy one, characterized by a search for **identity.** The young boy or girl is usually ill prepared for the tremendous physiological and emotional changes that must occur before the body becomes ready for reproduction and the emotions become stable enough for the assuming of the responsibility of a family. The new surging sexual feelings, the striving for independence from the restrictions of the family, the self doubts of one's abilities and a terrific feeling of ambivalence all unite to confuse and upset one. Then there is the need to choose a vocation or career. Often the teenager has qualms over the selection of his life's work. He may be bewildered by the vast array of possibilities before him and uncertain of what course he really wishes to follow. Sympathetic and understanding parents and teachers can do much to lighten the emotional burdens of the adolescent. They must understand his need to reject their standards and ideals temporarily; he finds his security in identifying with the gang, in strictly adhering to their modes of manners, dress, speech, and activities. If he feels that he is well loved and that his parents stand as safe ports in a storm, to which he can retire temporarily when the going gets too rough, he will emerge from the turmoil with a renewed sense of identity and a reasserting of good fundamental human values. His reasserted identity will be based upon an inner integrity which, in turn, is based upon his inner conviction that he is truly himself, a person worthy of respect and of a place in the adult world.

Young Adulthood

The period of adulthood is characterized by what Erikson calls **intimacy.** It is the time to select a life partner. The marriage relationship is a most intimate one, involving not only sexual fulfillment, but also a mutual trust and respect. It demands love, freely given and freely accepted, and may involve, on the part of both partners, a joyful acceptance of the responsibilities of parenthood. It demands shared enterprise and shared recreation. To fulfill this state properly, one must be a mature and responsible adult. It implies a successful journey through the stages of the past and a wholesome acceptance of the future.

Middle Years

This period is characterized by **generativity.** We begin to look at what we have generated, or helped to generate. This period of life is characterized by concern for the legacy we leave to future generations.

Old Age

This period is characterized by **integrity.** To Erikson, integrity sums up our ability to live out the later portion of our life with dignity and an assured sense of order and meaning in the total scheme of life. Serenity, a continued joy in living, a sense of accomplishment, of things well done, an anticipation that there are still worthwhile things to be accomplished, these are the facets of the integrity of the later years.

References

Coles, R.: Erik H. Erikson: The Growth of His Work. Boston, Little Brown, 1970.

Erikson, E.: Childhood and Society. New York, Norton, 1968.

Saul, L. J.: Emotional Maturity: The Development and Dynamics of Personality. ed. 3. Philadelphia, J. B. Lippincott, 1971.

Sutterley, D. and Donnelly, G. Perspectives in Human Development, Nursing Throughout the Life Cycle. Philadelphia, J. B. Lippincott, 1973.

9

The Structure
of Personality

Behavioral Objectives

The student successfully attaining the goals of this chapter will be able to:
- Name the three parts of the personality identified by Freud and briefly describe the function of each.
- Identify the 3 parts of the mind described by Freud and briefly define each.
- Explain the role of defense mechanisms as a means of dealing with conflict and anxiety.
- Explain the similarities and the differences between fear and anxiety.
- Describe the type of behavior which may result from too much anxiety.

According to Freud, the personality, which is formed by the interaction of environment and heredity, consists of three basic parts whose internal conflicts and maintenance of balance are the factors that produce what we call behavior. He has called these three components of personality the **id**, the **ego**, and the **superego**.

The Id

At the time of birth, the child is all **id.** The id, therefore, is that part of the personality with which we are born—ruled only by the **pleasure principle.** (The concept that man instinctually seeks to avoid pain and discomfort and strives for gratification and pleasure.) It is the raw stuff of presonality, consisting of the body's primitive, biological drives and urges, which are concerned only with striving after satisfaction and pleasure.

Within a very short time, the baby is faced with frustration by the thwarting of immediate satisfaction of its needs. It wants to be fed and must wait a while, it wants to be moved or turned over and is not, it is wet or soiled and fails to achieve quick changing by its crying. The cry is its first protest and is used as a tool to achieve its needs. And so the second component of personality comes into being—the **ego** or **reality principle.**

The Ego

The ego is that part of the self most closely in touch with reality. It develops to mediate between the strivings of the id and the demands of the environment so that satisfaction may be achieved in a manner which coincides with physical and social reality. It is roughly equivalent to what is meant by conscious awareness, or the self. As it develops, the reality principle, or ego, supersedes, or operates in concert with the id, or pleasure principle, in guiding behavior. By the time the average child is three years old, he has learned that there are many things he may not do and many things that he must do. He is also learning to defer immediate satisfactions for anticipated or delayed satisfactions. During this time, the child has learned to accept the attributes and standards of his parents as his own. He is not yet able to understand the reasons behind behavior, but readily accepts his parents' judgment about what is right or wrong to do or say.

The Superego

Slowly, the child begins to make judgments within himself as to the "rightness" or "wrongness" of things and to regulate his conduct on the basis of this judgment. By the time the child is seven years old, this judgmental process should be integrated into the personality fairly well. Freud calls it the **superego** and labels it as being social or cultural in origin. It is roughly equivalent to what we call our **conscience**—that inner voice that tells us whether our thoughts and actions are good or bad.

The id, ego, and superego are involved in constant conflicts. These conflicts and frustrations give rise to our behavior and result in emotional growth. Without conflict and frustration, there would be no personality growth.

Some of our conflicts are apparent to us. We are aware of them and are consciously involved in them. But we are unaware of many of our conflicts. They go on at a deeper level and, because we are unaware of them, we cannot resolve them. They act as strong motivators of our behavior.

Levels of Consciousness

One of Freud's greatest contributions to an understanding of human behavior was his popularizing of his concept of the **unconscious.** He presented the mind to us as though it consisted of three overlapping parts. These he labeled, in descending order, the **conscious mind, the subconscious mind,** and the **unconscious mind,** likening them to the parts of an iceberg.

The **conscious mind** refers to that part of the mind that is immediately focused in awareness (the part of the berg that is above the water level, freely visible). The **subconscious mind** refers to that part of the mind just below immediate awareness that is the storehouse for memories. These memories are either those which have ceased to be important to us or those which are mildly uncomfortable and which we have suppressed. They can be brought back into awareness at will. (This is the part of the berg below the water level that can be perceived by peering down into the water.) The **unconscious mind** refers to that part of the mind that is closed to immediate awareness. It is that vast reservoir of memories, experiences, and emotions which cannot be recalled. (This is the part of the berg which cannot be perceived at all and which may extend a great distance down and out into the water, completely unknown to the observers above it.)

Conflict

Conflicts between the three parts of the personality may result in behavior which is wholly conscious, partly conscious, wholly subconscious, or wholly unconscious. *But the important aspect of behavior is that it does resolve conflict.* Faced with an upsetting situation, people ordinarily do one of three things: (1) They will become aggressive and oppose the situation. (2) They will flee from it. (3) They will compromise with it. This last way of handling a situation seems to be the most realistic one and the one most likely to resolve the conflict or anxiety.

Conflicts are resolved through the use of certain methods of thinking and acting which either eliminate the conflict or reduce its severity. These methods, commonly called **defense mechanisms** or **mental mechanisms,** are not always clear cut; in fact, they often overlap or may be used simultaneously. Many defense mechanisms have been identified. We shall only describe a few of those most commonly used (See Chapter 10).

Since adaptation is one of the most fundamental characteristics of life, it is not strange that man has evolved mental mechanisms that increase his sense of security, protect his self-esteem, or solve his emotional dilemmas. The self-conscious personality, with its intense need for security and self-esteem, evokes mental defenses of a protective nature as instinctively as self-preservation prompts protection against physical harm. Anxiety is with us from the cradle to the grave. We all employ defense mechanisms to a greater or lesser degree to supply comfort and to provide defense against anxiety. A study of these mechanisms is essential to our understanding of human behavior and should lead us to a clearer recognition of the forces operating in each of our lives.

Some defense mechanisms, if employed within certain limits, may help to promote a sound personality, but, if used imprudently or excessively, may lead to a distortion of the personality. Other mechanisms progressively disorganize the personality. Because of this, we say that some of the mechanisms, properly used, are wholesome, while others are unwholesome.

We all have conflicts. A civil war, as it were, exists in most personalities, which must be handled satisfactorily by compromising conflicting wishes and strivings. Frequently, we are unsuccessful in our efforts and our anxiety is not resolved, but most of us handle our conflicts sufficiently well so that we are not seriously hampered in our adjustment to our environment.

Anxiety

Let us, for a moment, examine the word **anxiety** and see how it differs from the word **fear.** In psychiatric terminology, anxiety means a condition of heightened and often distressing tension accompanied by a vague but very disquieting feeling of apprehension of impending harm. Anxiety and fear have much in common, both being responses to threatening danger. However, fear is a response to an actual, present, external danger. As soon as this danger is no longer present (either because we have forcibly overcome its source or have escaped from it), the fear is resolved. Anxiety, on the other hand, is a response to threats from repressed, prohibited impulses deep within the personality, or to repressed feelings striving to re-enter the consciousness. It may also arise from feelings of frustration, dissatisfaction, insecurity, or hostile feelings toward a significant person in the environment. It is characterized by a persistent feeling of dread, apprehension and impending disaster.

Each person has a level of intolerance as far as stress and nervous tension are concerned. When this tension is not released, or some solution worked out to care for it, behavior reactions of a neurotic or psychotic type usually appear. It is the function of defense mechanisms to resolve, or at least lessen, anxiety.

References

Bischof, L. J.: Interpreting Personality Theories. ed. 2. New York, Harper & Row, 1970.

Fromm, E.: The Anatomy of Human Destructiveness. New York, Holt, Rinehart and Winston, 1973.

Maslow, A. H.: The Farther Reaches of Human Nature. New York, Viking Press, 1971.

Defense or
Mental Mechanisms

Behavioral Objectives

The student successfully attaining the goals of this chapter will be able to:
- Name and define the 16 defense mechanisms discussed.
- Explain the similarities and differences between suppression and repression.
- Define the term neologisms as it relates to mentally disturbed patients.
- Explain the meaning of over-compensation or reaction formation.
- Note the difference between conversion and conversion hysteria and give examples of each.
- Explain how playing or watching a football game may be a form of sublimation.
- Give 3 examples of aggressive behavior.
- Explain how criticism of others may be a form of projection.
- Identify the basic stimulus for dreams and hallucinations.
- Explain how alcoholism and drugs are forms of defense mechanisms.

Mental mechanisms or defense mechanisms do not actually change the situation; they merely channel off some of the anxiety the situation produces. They are used so frequently by all human beings at some time or another that many of them are considered essential to our personality growth. We shall describe several of the most important or most commonly used mechanisms.

1. **Denial** is an unconscious method used at all stages of personality development to reduce anxiety. It is simply a refusal on our part to face things as they really are. A child knocks a vase off a table and it breaks. Mother comes into the room and sternly inquires if the child broke the vase. The child, filled with guilt feelings, and apprehensive of punishment, denies being responsible. A soldier in training makes his first parachute jump from a plane. When asked if he experienced fear, he denies it, for to admit fear would be damaging to his ego. For each of these examples to be denial in the psychiatric

sense of the word, the person would have to **believe** that what he said was true. Conscious lying is not denial as used here.

2. **Suppression** is a conscious pushing away from awareness of certain unwelcome ideas, memories, or feelings. We merely push them into the background (into our subconscious mind, which is our memory storehouse) where they are accessible to us whenever we wish to remember them. Into this realm also drift memories that have ceased to be important to us.

3. **Repression** should not be confused with suppression. The two words are very similar and there is similarity in their action. Repression consists in excluding from one's field of awareness unbearable ideas, experiences, and impulses and of forcing them down into the unconscious and of keeping them there.

Repression is a wholly unconscious mechanism. It is not produced by a deliberate and conscious effort of rejection on the part of the self. Rather, it is an involuntary process of denial or repudiation that serves to blind one to what is going on inside.

If it operates smoothly and prevents feelings of anxiety, it may help to promote a well-adjusted life. However, it is a sort of "burying alive" mechanism. The repressed material is always active and heavily charged emotionally. It seems to be constantly seeking for expression. Since this material is denied direct, conscious, frank expression, it tends to break through and obtain expression in a disguised form (i.e., in symbolic form). We therefore find that the content of hallucinations and dreams is a meaningful, symbolic expression of mental material from the unconscious. It might be said that symbols are the language of the unconscious.

4. **Symbolization** is a mechanism of both the unconscious and the conscious. It is the using of a meaning-bearing sign to represent, or stand for, an idea, quality, or object. We use symbols constantly, almost unconsciously. A symbol we are all acquainted with is our country's flag. Intrinsically, it is only a bit of cloth with a particular arrangement of color and design. In itself, it is of little value; as a symbol, it stands for our country and arouses sentiments of respect, loyalty, and love, and its value is limitless. Much of our adaptation to our culture occurs in the learning and use of symbols. "W-o-r-d" is only four printed letters, but it means one of the tools of language. A small child learns that the sound "mama" represents the important person who cares for him. Later, it learns that the letters m-o-t-h-e-r represent both the sound "mama" and the figure represented by this sound. A single gesture or expression can symbolize, or hold the entire meaning of a complex situation.

With the mentally ill individual, symbolism often becomes distorted. Sometimes, a psychotic patient will construct new words of his own, or he will give specialized meaning to words (**neologisms**). In many retardates, the ability to symbolize is poor. Their perceptions tend to be more concrete and less abstract than those of normal persons.

5. **Rationalization** is a mechanism used frequently by persons of all ages. It is said to be the joy and delight of the average human being and is self-deception at its subtle best. It is simply finding a logical reason for the things one wants to do, or a reason (or excuse) for not doing what one should do. John's wife insists that he go out and mow the lawn after breakfast. John wants to go fishing. He explains that the motor of the mower didn't sound just right and that he feels he should take it to the shop to have it checked over before he uses it again. He goes fishing. His wife buys an expensive dress she does not need and rationalizes its purchase by saying that it had such quality and style that she couldn't afford not to buy it; she could use it for years as a basic garment in her wardrobe, and in the end it would save John money.

6. **Identification** has two slightly different meanings in psychology. First: it is a method of vicarious achievement and enjoyment through another person or through a group of people, such as clubs or fraternities; or it may be vicarious emotional identification derived from a movie or from reading a story. For instance, an unpopular child may enjoy a popular child's interpersonal triumphs by becoming a loyal friend; a child lacking in physical attraction will attach herself to one who is pretty and attractive and thus share in her successes; the person who identifies with the characters in a play or a book will laugh with them in their joys and weep with them in their sorrows.

Second: it is accepting persons, ideas, or ideals outside the self, feeling with them as though they were part of the self, and finally integrating them into one's own personality. All children identify with their parents, copy their behavior, and pattern their identities after them. A little girl watches her mother dress and feed the baby. She picks up her doll and copies her mother, imitating each step. A little boy watches his father making a table in the workshop. He is not content unless he may handle the same tools (or toy duplicates) and will go through the motions of sawing, planing, and sanding a piece of wood. Many of the learning processes of childhood take place through identification. As we become a little older, we identify with our teachers, legendary figures, heroes, and idols. We play at being soldiers, astronauts, cowboys, and film stars. Even after we are adults, we tend to copy the actions and mannerisms of people we admire immensely. If the object with which we identify is good, the effect on us will be constructive; if it is bad, the effect can be destructive.

7. **Compensation.** Just as nature compensates for disease or defects in our bodies (as when a blind person develops extraordinarily keen hearing or remarkable tactile perception), so we develop personality traits and beliefs about ourselves as a means of compensating for various inadequacies. The little man will often try to compensate for his lack of stature by being loud and

blustering or pompous in manner. A hostile person may act excessively sweet and polite under any and all circumstances in order to conceal from others, and especially from himself, his hostility. When carried to excess, such compensation is called **over-compensation** or **reaction formation.** The person using this form of compensation usually makes the listener feel uncomfortable. Another frequently seen form of compensation is that of a mother who is over-protective of, and over-indulgent to a child whom she unconsciously rejects. Her inner rejection and hostility toward the child is unacceptable to her conscious self and so she develops an outward attitude of deep concern and solicitude for the child in order to prevent any conscious awareness of these inner feelings. However, simple compensation can be very helpful to the personality when used to develop a constructive quality to take the place of a destructive one, or a missing one, or one which the person has not been able to use successfully. For instance, a plain girl who cannot compete with her more beautiful sisters may determine to develop her mind or some talent to compensate for her lack of physical beauty. Rivalry often leads to compensation.

8. **Regression** is a retreat from the present pattern to past levels of behavior. When a person's environment or actions react on the self so as to make it feel intensely uncomfortable and anxious, the self tends to seek a lower level of adjustment and of expression (behavior), to retreat to an earlier level of behavior, where it finds less conflict and, hence, less anxiety.

Some persons regress to childish behavior because childhood was a time when their problems were comparatively few and little was expected of them. They instinctively seek that level of their past behavioral experience which has proven least traumatizing to them. Thus, one person may regress only a few years; another will start behaving on the five-year-old level, and occasionally, one may regress so profoundly that he will curl up in the fetal position and remain in it without moving.

Regression is not a wholesome mechanism of adjustment and does not promote a desirable adaptation. Extreme forms and degrees of regression result in a serious disorganization of personality.

A simple and often seen form of regression occurs when an adult temporarily reverts to childish behavior in order to achieve a certain result (e.g., a person failing to have his or her own way, may burst into tears if that person has discovered at an early age that tears usually produce results).

9. **Conversion.** Conversion is a mechanism or process by which an emotional conflict is expressed as a physical symptom. We have all had our anxiety result in a headache. A college student, studying for an exam and very anxious about his ability to pass it successfully, may develop a severe headache. A woman, invited to a party which presents an upsetting situation to her, may develop gastrointestinal symptoms which will justify her calling her hostess

to be excused on the grounds of illness. Usually, when the hour has passed when she would have been obliged to attend, her symptoms resolve themselves.

Conversion hysteria is the converting of strong emotional conflicts into such physical symptoms that the very helplessness of the victim will resolve the conflict; for instance: a soldier on the battlefield may be deeply upset at the prospect of having to kill or be killed. He cannot admit his cowardice to himself for this is too damaging to his ego. As a result of a very slight injury to his foot, he is brought into the hospital for treatment. While in the hospital, the leg becomes paralyzed. The doctors can find no reason for this sudden paralysis. The patient is not malingering (the term we use for conscious "faking"); he cannot move his leg. He is quite unaware that the paralysis has developed as a result of his fear of returning to the battlefield. While his leg is paralyzed, it is physically impossible for him to do so. Thus, his conflict is resolved. During World War I, many men developed paralyses which kept them from returning to the trenches. When the armistice was announced, these soldiers were suddenly able to use completely paralyzed arms or legs. It was this experience that convinced the Army doctors that some paralyses were unconscious defense mechanisms.

Another example of this mechanism would be that of a small boy who hated his father so deeply that he wished to strike and hurt him. If fear held him back from acting out this impulse, he could suddenly develop complete paralysis of that arm, which would do two things for him, (1) resolve the conflict (he could not strike his father even if he wished to) and (2) bring him a great deal of attention and sympathy.

But, returning to the less dramatic and more common form of conversion, in which anxiety is eased by being channeled into various physical symptoms, these persons express their symptoms freely (like to talk about them) and seem to be attached to them. They are not pretending to feel ill—they really do feel miserable— but doctors can find no basis for their aches and pains. Their illness seems to be a substitute for unacceptable emotions or obligations, and they will resist any real effort to help them since they are unconsciously using these ills to escape from the consequences of their own actions.

10. **Sublimation** is a mental mechanism that is usually constructive in nature. Essentially, it is the channeling of a strong and socially unacceptable drive, or urge, into a form that is acceptable to society; for instance, an artist may have a very strong sexual drive. To express this drive in promiscuity could be damaging to his reputation. If he channels it into another form of expression, that of painting seductively nude women, it seems to be quite an acceptable expression of eroticism, and he will not only be accepted by society, he will be acclaimed and honored if his paintings are really good. Aggressive impulses may be sublimated into sports and games which are not only highly acceptable, but which can also help the audiences channel their aggression.

11. **Withdrawal** is a protective device by which an individual prevents further hurt and damage to his security by withdrawing from people and avoiding all close interpersonal relations. It may occur only as a temporary or seldom used pattern, or as a form so complete that the person seems completely unaware of, or indifferent to, his surroundings. When withdrawal dominates a pattern of behavior, loneliness ensues. A lighter form of it is seen in the persons who make only a superficial contact with many different persons. They make no real friends because they fear to become deeply emotionally involved. We say they are "cold" emotionally.

Withdrawal is one of the dominant personality traits of the schizophrenics. These patients not only have an inability to relate well with people emotionally, they also use another defense mechanism in conjunction with withdrawal—the defense mechanism of **regression.** Schizophrenia afflicts the largest group of psychotic patients and is also the only form of mental illness frequently found in children. The mental mechanism of withdrawal is also of special interest to us when studying retardation.

12. **Aggression** may be an expression of hostility. Hostility may be expressed openly or symbolically. Open aggression, such as striking another person, tongue-lashing him, or abusing him in any way, is sure to call forth retaliation. Retaliation, in turn, carries a threat to security. And so the outward expression of open aggression may end in disastrous consequences.

Some persons, unable to refrain from expressing their hostility, but fearing retaliation, will turn their hostility in upon the self and express it by striking, biting, or otherwise punishing themselves. This form of self-punishment is fairly common among the profoundly mentally retarded.

A more subtle form of open aggression is the constant use of sarcasm or ridicule. The frequent forgetting of names and appointments may also be indicative of hostility.

Aggression may also be displaced upon the environment, and an individual may be quite destructive of material objects. We have all heard of, or met the person who has a continual "chip on his shoulder" or the short-tempered person who breaks into aggressive action with the slightest frustration. We also are aware that certain persons, under the influence of alcohol, become very aggressive. These particular persons may be mild-mannered, friendly, kindly, responsible people when sober, but when their inhibitions are released under the influence of alcohol, repressed hostility flares out and they will often want to fight and break up the furniture.

A form of aggression rarely understood for what it is by the average person is severe depression. The severely depressed person is exhibiting a form of self-aggression, or self-punishment. And so we see that aggression can be open or symbolic. Whichever expression it takes, it is a very common defense mechanism.

13. **Projection** is blaming someone else for your own faults, shortcomings,

or failures. A student comes home and bitterly complains, "I got flunked in my history test just because my teacher has it in for me!" A clerk blames his wife because of his failure to succeed at his work; one government blames another for broken promises, bad ethics, or suspiciousness; the mentally ill person will say, "All these people in this place are crazy! I have to get out of here or I'll go crazy, too!"

It is not uncommon to observe persons who severely criticize in others the very faults which are the weak points in their own personalities, utterly failing to recognize that they, themselves, possess these qualities. Persons always suspicious of the motives of others are usually untrustworthy themselves; those always complaining of gossiping friends do not recognize or acknowledge their own vicious tongues. What the projector sees in others is a mirror image of his own self. By attaching his own rejected qualities and tendencies to others he escapes self-reproach and any sense of guilt. By criticizing and condemning undesirable qualities in others, he is made more comfortable in the presence of his own. In effect, he accuses others of his own wishes. Results of the mechanism are that persons come to feel that others are responsible for their misfortunes. This often leads to criticism, prejudice, intolerance, hatred, brooding, unreasonable jealousy, and unjustified suspicions and accusations. When the need for self-protection against disowned impulses and motives becomes very great, they may be projected in the form of delusions, particularly delusions of persecution; or in the form of imaginary perceptions (hallucinations frequently take the form of voices which accuse or threaten the person.)

14. **Displacement** is the transference of emotion from one object, situation, or idea to another. The boss loses quite a sum of money in the stock market. He takes his frustration and anger out on one of his employees at the office. The employee, fearing to talk back or defend himself, seethes with anger all day and comes home at night to meet his wife with sharp criticism that dinner is not all ready for the table. The wife, smarting under this unjust rebuke, slaps her five-year-old son for shouting in the house, and the child runs outside, slamming the door behind him, and kicks his dog who has run up to him affectionately.

Some of our unreasonable fears and phobias are also displacements or transferences. For instance, an intense fear and hatred of cats (**ailurophobia**) is usually a displacement of hostility and fear from a person to the animal. Afraid to acknowledge and express openly the hostility we feel toward a person who can retaliate, we can safely transfer it to the cat who cannot retaliate. If we transfer a strong feeling of love from one person to another, we call this *positive transference*; if the emotion is hate, we call it *negative transference*.

15. **Ritualistic behavior** is uniform and repetitive behavior used to control the environment and the self. It is found extensively in normal persons,

such as in our habits of doing certain things always in the same way. This reduces the necessity for making decisions and guarantees to some extent that the same results will be achieved. If this type of behavior becomes exaggerated to an abnormal degree so that it becomes **compulsive behavior** (i.e., if an irresistible impulse to say, do, or think some one thing almost constantly interferes markedly with our work or living habits), it can seriously interfere with our social effectiveness. (The actual term used for this is pathological compulsiveness.)

Ordinary ritualistic behavior serves the purpose of lowering our anxiety level, but anxiety that is discharged through compulsive behavior is only temporarily relieved, since the anxiety builds up again and the compulsive act must be indulged in repeatedly.

The various forms that compulsive behavior may take all have in common an irresistible urge to do, say, or think some one thing, which the individual usually resists with mounting anxiety and then indulges in, gaining temporary relief from the anxiety.

Antisocial compulsions are fairly common. Compulsive stealing (**kleptomania**) is more understandable if we realize that the person who steals articles for which he has no use or desire is only lowering his anxiety level by such stealing. Obscene or vulgar comment, indecent exposure, or other sexual aberrations, are compulsions of this same type.

All phobias have in common a deep-seated fear of some person, object, or situation which the victim, himself, usually cannot explain but which produces panic if he is forced into the situation he fears. (See Chapter 16.)

16. **Props that blur reality** are, in effect, defense mechanisms that are used as crutches to help us cope with life. Alcohol and drugs are often used in this way. They are toxic substances which, when taken in excess, so blur our consciousness that they reduce self-criticism and judgment to such a degree that anxiety vanishes. In this way, they produce a comfortable feeling of self-confidence and sureness. Under their influence, with anxieties banished, or at least greatly reduced, the victim becomes uninhibited in thought, speech, and action and is able to express his true feelings and desires. (The "props" will be discussed in more detail in Chapters 21 and 22.)

And thus we learn that all of us, children as well as adults, are beset by anxiety and frustration from the cradle to the grave, and that how we adjust to these situations will determine the personalities we will form. Our behavior, in turn, will indicate the facets of personality development that have occurred in us.

References

Kyes, J. and Hofling, C. K.: Basic Psychiatric Concepts in Nursing. Philadelphia, J. B. Lippincott, 1974.

Morgan, A. J. and Moreno, J. W.: The Practice of Mental Health Nursing: A Community Approach. Philadelphia, J. B. Lippincott, 1973.
Peterson, M.: Understanding defense mechanisms. Amer. J. Nurs., 72:1651 (September) 1972.

Discussion Questions

THE SITUATION:

A male patient is admitted to the surgical ward at 2:00 P.M. He is scheduled for removal of his gall bladder at 8:00 A.M. tomorrow. The student nurse reads his chart. He is fifty-two years old, married, the father of three children, and he is a teller at a local bank. He has had increasing gastrointestinal distress for the past three years. Tests made last week indicate stones in the gall bladder.

The young student nurse sees the light above his door come on, and she goes to answer it. Upon opening the door, she sees Mr. Schulte sitting in his pajamas on the side of his bed, scowling fiercely at her. She smiles pleasantly and says, "Good afternoon, Mr. Schulte. I am Joan Miller, a student nurse on this ward. What can I do to help you?"

Mr. Schulte growls, "Close that damn window; it's cold enough in here to catch pneumonia!" The nurse closes the window, then turns to the patient and says, "You don't look comfortable sitting there on the edge of your bed. Let me help you back in; I can raise the head of the bed for you if you prefer sitting up." Mr. Schulte barks back at her, "I don't need help to get into this bed. It's full of wrinkles and I'm going to sit in that chair."

The student smooths out the bed and says, "You are permitted to walk around and to sit in a chair today if you wish, Mr. Schulte." He does not answer her but gets down from his bed and sits in the chair. The student asks if he would like a paper to read. He snarls an abrupt "No!" at her and looks out of the window. The student moves the light switch over to his chair and says, "Do put your light on if you want something else, Mr. Schulte." He mutters an unintelligible reply and the nurse goes out.

At the desk, she comments on the unpleasant manner of Mr. Schulte, and the nurse who admitted him replies, "That man hates the whole world! How I detest having to look after a disgruntled sourpuss like that! And after his surgery, he'll be a bear cat!"

A few minutes later Mr. Schulte's light goes on again. He is back in bed pounding his pillow. He demands another pillow, saying, "This one is as hard as a brick!" The nurse cheerfully brings him another pillow, plumps up the first one and places the second one on top of it, remarking, "There, now, that should feel better, Mr. Schulte."

The patient grunts, turns his back to the nurse, and lies there in silence as she leaves him.

Five minutes later, he puts his light on again. He wants a fresh glass of water this time.

The Questions:

1. Why do you think Mr. Schulte's behavior is so difficult?
2. What is he trying to accomplish with his behavior?

3. What *needs* are being expressed by his behavior?
4. What part of his personality do you think is dominating his behavior?
5. Do you think the student nurse was responding to the patient in appropriate fashion?
6. What else might she have done that might have reduced the patient's obvious tension?
7. Which defense mechanism, or mechanisms, was Mr. Schulte probably exhibiting?

Three

Mental Health and Mental Illness

Human Behavior and Mental Health

Behavioral Objectives

The student successfully attaining the goals of this chapter will be able to:

- Define the term behavior and explain the difference between normal, neurotic, and psychotic behavior.
- Explain the meaning of mental health and give the characteristics of a mentally healthy person.
- Describe the type of behavior that reflects a mentally ill personality.

The word behavior implies an acting out of a thought or a feeling that can be observed by others. In other words, our behavior is what we do about how we think or feel. Actually, the field of behavior is divided into the three categories of *thinking, feeling,* and *acting,* but it is the action that is most commonly meant when we use the word behavior. We class behavior (or our actions) as normal, neurotic, or psychotic, also as appropriate or inappropriate to a given situation.

Normal Behavior

Normal behavior is that course of action which is adapted to reality. The normal person is able to *modify* his behavior through the learning process (or experience). He has *insight* into cause and effect. For example, if he dreams, when he awakens he is aware that his experience was a dream. He knows it was unreal or a phantasy. A normal, conscious person is oriented as to time, place, and person (i.e., he knows who he is, where he is, and what he is doing). He may or may not be fully aware of why he behaves as he does at all times.

Neurotic Behavior

Neurotic behavior is less adapted to reality. It tends to express more of the unconscious motivation of persons than true reality. The neurotic person is still well oriented as to persons, places, and things, but he lacks insight into the why of his behavior. He cannot modify this behavior at will. If a neurotic person dreams, his dream tends to seem half real to him or he may feel the dream has real significance or magical connotations. Most people show some neurotic tendencies.

Psychotic Behavior

Psychotic behavior is unrelated to reality. There may be complete loss of insight. To the psychotic, a dream may seem wholly real. He is unable to differentiate between the real and the unreal.

Mental Health

Normal behavior is a complex balance between conscious and unconscious striving, drives, and feelings. The mind and the body are so united that when one is affected the other shows changes also. When a person suffers a prolonged physical illness, it is quite common for the nervous system to also become so involved that the patient may evidence neurotic or even psychotic behavior. Likewise, when a person is mentally ill, his body functioning may become so involved that he will develop definite physical symptoms.

Mental health can be defined as the ability to adjust to new situations and to handle personal problems without marked distress, and still have enough energy to be a constructive member of society.

The mentally healthy person must value those attributes that are needed to hold society together. He must be well-integrated and stable and must be able to see, not only himself, but also the people about him, as he and they really are. He should have positive qualities of idealism, understanding, humanitarianism, honesty, courage, justice, morality, and optimism.

One's degree of mental health fluctuates from day to day and from situation to situation, yet tends to have a certain continuity and consistency.

Certain types of maladjustment seem to be more socially acceptable than others. Types of behavior that are "bizarre," "strange," or "queer," or that violate cultural standards which have a strong emotional impact are usually labeled as symptoms of mental illness, and society feels impelled to take action in regard to such conduct. For example, a person who flagrantly violates sexual standards (perhaps by exposing himself in public) calls for prompt attention. He is quickly categorized as mentally ill or bad. Other types of behavior which also indicate a maladjustment may be ignored or accepted. Consequently, a person who is withdrawn and avoids relationships with others may be regarded as "a little odd," but is seldom recognized as being as "sick" as he is; a person channeling all his mental anxieties into physical symptoms and constantly dwelling on his indigestion, fatigue, or headaches, may be considered a social bore, but most persons would not consider him mentally ill.

It is important for health professionals not to mirror society's moral model of categorizing people. All of the patients described above as "bad" or "odd" or social "bores" are entitled to be called sick and derive the benefits of patienthood and medical care.

Anxiety

Anxiety, that intense sense of personal disorder, is a profound motivator of behavior. It occurs when the individual is threatened from the outside, or the inside, in his self-esteem. The situations that evoke anxiety are usually the result of past experience. Some of us are made anxious by love, some by hate, and some by the indifference of those with whom we come in contact. The method of resolving the conflicts produced, and reducing the anxiety, is largely that of previous patterns. The elements of newness or uniqueness in any situation may bring about a change in the pattern of behavior. The greater the sense of security an individual possesses, the more this is apt to occur.

Mental Illness

Actually, the behavior of maladjusted persons does not differ in kind from the so-called normal; it differs mainly in degree. For instance, we all project* at times, but a mentally ill person will use projection as a major technique in relieving his anxiety. Again, a degree of shyness in a person is not considered too great a deviation from normal, but when this form of withdrawal intensifies so that the withdrawn person sits alone in one position, head down, never speaking and seemingly unaware of his surroundings, we recognize that his behavior is far from normal.

When behavior or feelings deviate sufficiently from the normal so as to indicate disorganization of the self, we say that person is mentally ill. There are many degrees of such disorganization, from the mildly neurotic to the profoundly psychotic.

Mental health is closely related to the awareness of one's motivations as balanced by the depth of stresses to which the individual is exposed. In other words, a mentally healthy person must have an intellectual insight into his strengths and weaknesses and must also have an emotional acceptance

---

* "To project" means to ascribe to others feelings that are our own. When we "project" we cloud a clear and realistic perception of the other person and see him as "better" or "worse" than he really is.

of that insight. He must be able to live comfortably with his weaknesses and be able to use his strengths constructively.

The World Health Organization speaks of mental health in these broad terms, "Mental health is the presence of physical and emotional well being."

Kolb says, "A mentally healthy adult shows behavior which confirms an awareness of self or personal identity coupled with a life purpose, a sense of personal autonomy, and willingness to perceive reality and cope with its vicissitudes; the capacity to invest in (i.e. care about) others, to understand their needs, to achieve a mutually satisfying heterosexual relationship, to be active and productive, have persistence and endurance in pursuing tasks to their accomplishment, to respond flexibly in the face of stress, to receive pleasure from a variety of sources, and to accept his limitations realistically."

In the decade since Kolb wrote this definition, a number of psychiatrists have come to believe that heterosexual behavior is not necessary for mental health. Celibacy or homosexuality or bisexuality can also be found in mentally healthy persons. In addition, a mentally healthy person shows creativity, a sense of humor, and continued growth and evolvement throughout life.

References

Laughlin, H.: The Ego and Its Defenses. New York, Appleton-Century-Crofts, 1970.

Mereness, D.: Essentials of Psychiatric Nursing. ed. 9. St. Louis, C. V. Mosby, 1974.

Mental Illness
and Its History

Behavioral Objectives

The student successfully attaining the goals of this chapter will be able to:

- Describe the characteristics of mental illness and give 6 terms that are used to describe this condition.
- Briefly summarize the general attitudes that existed toward the mentally ill up to the 20th century and compare these attitudes with the attitudes today.
- Compare the kind of treatment a mentally ill patient would have received in a mental institution in the first half of this century with the type of treatment available today, explaining the advances which have brought about this change.

Major mental illness is a disorder characterized by a disequilibrium, derangement, or unbalanced condition of the mental processes. Such a derangement results in unrealistic thinking and behavior. A person sees things "out of focus" and his reasoning and consequent behavior becomes strange, odd, and even bizarre to others. Until his thinking and behavior return to normal, he is just as sick as if he were suffering from a physical illness. Other commonly used names for this condition are dementia, derangement, psychoses, madness, lunacy, and craziness.

Men have suffered from mental illness at least since the advent of recorded history, and evidences of crude operations upon skulls from very early excavations indicate that it existed even in prehistoric ages.

In the early ages of man's existence, the preservation of life was each man's own responsibility; the tribal member who could not care for himself must, of necessity, have been cast out. Probably the first tribes banished those afflicted in mind or body from the group, leaving them to the mercy of the cold, storms, wild beasts, or starvation. Today, on our own continent, isolated Eskimo groups are still following the age-old custom of placing their deformed, crippled, defective, and aged tribal members on ice floes and towing them out into the Arctic waters where they abandon them to die of exposure and hunger.

As we survey the course of physical and mental illness down through the centuries, we note fluctuations of attitudes toward suffering. Though civilizations have at times viewed the ill with compassion, most of them have been indifferent to suffering. The Greeks showed compassion for their suffering members during the "Golden Age." They built beautiful temples for the care of the physically infirm and the mentally ill, and their priests ministered to these patients tenderly.

The Old Testament evidenced concern for the physically ill but tended to consider the mentally ill to be possessed by devils. This same attitude is seen also in the New Testament, and the belief in "possession" continues today. During these ages, the mentally ill were often greatly feared and avoided; they were thrown into damp, foul prisons, chained to the walls, starved, cruelly beaten and tortured; they were even burned at the stake, on the assumption that only the most drastic means could drive the evil spirits from their bodies.

The religious orders offered the mentally ill haven in their monasteries, but the monasteries could care for only a small number of patients, and conditions remained appalling for most sufferers of mental illness.

Insane asylums were eventually set up in Europe to care for them, but the conditions in these institutions were not too much better than those in the prisons.

An interesting word in the English language evolved from one such asylum. An insane asylum called "St. Mary's of Bethlehem" was erected outside of London in 1547. Here, on Sundays, for a small fee, people were allowed to view the inmates. They came from far and near to watch these wretched people on their foul straw mats, chained to the damp stone walls—much as we go to the zoo today to see the caged animals perform. The Cockney pronunciation of "Bethlehem" was "Bedlam." Our modern word bedlam is defined as a condition of unutterable confusion.

The picture was essentially the same in other asylums of the time, and even in the last century here in our country, our jails and almshouses presented much the same state of affairs.

But there were increasing numbers of people who, motivated by attitudes of kindness, pity, and humility, tried to help the so-called insane and to improve their condition.

Two physicians, Dr. Pinel in France and Dr. Tukes in England, realizing that mental illness was a sickness of the mind, and not a sin, and feeling that it was the responsibility of the community to improve the conditions under which these patients lived, attempted to bring about change.

To Pinel is given the credit for "removing the chains from the mentally ill" in the 1790s. Now, two centuries later, we are still working to remove all restraints from the patients in institutions for the mentally ill.

Miss Dorothea Dix, a New England schoolteacher with deep humanitarian principles, is credited with instituting a one-woman reform of institutions in America. In the late 19th century, appalled by the conditions she found in our jails and poorhouses and recognizing that many of the persons dwelling there were not petty criminals but mentally sick people who needed help, she set out to inform the public of existing conditions. She attended legislative sessions in state after state and convinced our lawmakers of the need for better facilities and care for these people. One by one, our states began to construct special institutions for the care of the mentally ill or to improve those already in existence.

Following closely on Miss Dix's work came a book entitled, A *Mind That Found Itself*, written by Clifford Beers. Beers had been hospitalized for some time with mental illness but recovered and wrote this book on his experiences. The book helped people to understand the needs of the mentally ill. In 1908, Mr. Beers founded "The National Committee for Mental Hygiene." This association, now known as "The National Association for Mental Health," is very active today in every state, educating the public to the problems of the mentally ill and working for the improvement of our mental hospitals.

Years ago, when a person was mentally ill, he was cared for at home as long as he was not harmful to others or to himself, but when his behavior became too bizarre or too dangerous, he was committed, involuntarily, to an institution. Here, for the most part, he remained a prisoner behind barred windows and locked doors, cared for physically, but with few provisions made for his mental rehabilitation. When he became resistive or hyperactive, he was laced into a "strait jacket" or chained to his bed by wrist and ankle cuffs. Attendants would immerse him in a cold bath or forcefully spray him with cold water to break his will or subdue him. Such treatment was still common in the 1940s in various private and public institutions.

The past three decades have seen a rapidly changing picture in the field of mental health. Many new facilities have come into being for the protection, treatment, and rehabilitation of the mentally ill. These include rehabilitative care of the patients on the wards of state hospitals, the establishment of psychiatric units in many community hospitals, the setting up of mental health clinics all over the country, and the shortening of psychiatric episodes by electroconvulsive treatment, new drugs, and psychotherapy. And, most important of all, hospital personnel are being trained to establish a safe and comfortable milieu on the wards so as to reduce the patient's anxiety and enhance the reintegrative process.

Another very important factor in today's picture is the changing attitude on the part of the public toward mental illness. The family's feeling of shame and embarrassment at a member's "different" behavior is diminishing somewhat. Instead of trying to cover up peculiar behavior, many families are now able to discuss the situation objectively and to seek help for the patient.

Newspapers, magazines, films, television, and radio have all helped to decrease the ignorance and fear that used to surround the subject of mental illness. More and more people are accepting the idea of a "sick mind" as well as a "sick body" and are turning more and more to the trained personnel in the mental health field for help.

And, best of all, many troubled people, realizing they need help with their problems, are voluntarily seeking this help in community mental health centers, or are voluntarily seeking admission to a psychiatric facility before reaching the point of breakdown.

But, though acceptance and understanding have come far in the field of mental illness, much remains to be done. We are greatly in need of sheltered workshops and of halfway houses for patients who have been hospitalized and are now ready to leave the protective, accepting atmosphere of the hospital, but who may not as yet be fully able to return to their families and society. They and their families usually need psychotherapeutic help to enable them to see each other's problems and to adjust to these problems together. The family needs to understand how it may have contributed to the patient's illness, if this indeed is the case.

References

Havens, L. H.: Approaches to the Mind: Movement of the Psychiatric Schools From Sects Toward Science. Boston, Little, Brown, 1973.

Rumbaut, R. D.: The First Psychiatric Hospital of the Western World. Am. J. Psychiatry. 128:1305, 1972.

Abnormal Patterns
of Behavior

Behavioral Objectives

The student successfully attaining the goals of this chapter will be able to:

- List the 7 patterns of abnormal behavior which may be used to allay anxiety and briefly explain how each works.
- Explain the basic purpose of withdrawal as a defense mechanism and give 3 examples of unhealthy manifestations of this mechanism.
- Identify the relationship between hostility and aggression and give examples of symbolic aggression.
- Indicate the emotional basis of manic-depressive conditions.
- Explain how paranoia may be related to projection.
- Note that each of the abnormal behaviors discussed are forms of defense mechanisms and explain the protective purpose of each.
- Give 3 examples of obsessive-compulsive behavior.
- Describe the basic character disorder in an antisocial person.

In the normal person, behavior is constantly changing, yet there is an identifiable pattern about it. Our behavior changes as we mature; we are not expected to behave at fifteen as we did at five, nor at fifty as we did at fifteen. In addition, accepted behavior differs from generation to generation and from culture to culture; it even differs at different social levels within the same culture.

But when we speak of abnormal patterns of behavior, we refer to none of these normal changes in accepted behavior. By abnormal patterns of behavior, we refer to a serious disorder of personality which is socially unacceptable.

An abnormal method of handling anxiety is an individual thing, but roughly speaking, it tends to fall into one of seven patterns. These patterns are:

1. Withdrawal
2. Aggression
3. Projection
4. Use of physical disability

5. Use of ritualistic behavior
6. Use of props that blur reality
7. Failure to integrate

It must be remembered that the establishment and use of these mechanisms is out of the conscious control of the person. The patient does not "will" to be abnormal.

Withdrawal

Withdrawal is a common method of handling problems of interpersonal relationships. Its purpose is protective. By withdrawing and avoiding relationships, further damage to security is avoided. The danger of such a pattern is that it results in deep loneliness. Withdrawal has many degrees of expression. One person may avoid all contact with all other people on every possible occasion. (We see this happening to recluses who live isolated lives, shunning all but the most necessary contacts with others.) Another may make frequent contact with many different people, but with all relationships kept on a superficial level. Another may express a withdrawal pattern by the cynical rejection of people as worthless. If the pattern progresses sufficiently, complete regression may develop. If there are sufficient positive attitudes within the conscious self, and if there is enough motivation, this process may be reversed.

In the schizophrenic, withdrawal is a dominant pattern of behavior.

Aggression

The pattern of aggression is another way of handling problems of interpersonal relationships. It is the pattern used by persons who are predominantly hostile. Hostility is, to some extent, common to all of us. But when it dominates a personality, difficulties inevitably follow. Open aggression, while undeniably discharging pent-up energy, does call forth retaliation which carries a further threat to security, and thus a vicious cycle is set in motion. Because of this, many people turn to other ways of expressing hostility.

Symbolic aggression is more subtle. It includes the sarcastic remark, ridicule, unfavorable comments relayed "for your own good," forgetting names and appointments, or silence. Hostility is often disguised in this way because the person who feels it fears retribution.

This same fear may cause an over-compensation, or reaction-formation, in which the person develops the opposite attitude of the one he feels. This is a compensatory protective device.

Another person, afraid that his hostility may find its way into outward expression and bring retaliation upon him, may turn that hostility upon himself. This is one of the reasons for suicidal behavior.

Aggression may also be displaced onto the environment and an individual may be quite destructive with material objects, consciously or unconsciously.

In the mentally ill person, a pattern of hostility may explode into impulsive, uncontrolled, aggressive behavior. However, even in this syndrome, the fear of retribution may be seen in episodes of depression.

Aggression and depression may occur in combination or one may follow the other. It is as though the patient, directing his aggression outward, feels he has gone too far and, fearing serious retribution, then directs his aggression inward to avoid the consequences. This alternation between aggression and depression may be seen in manic-depressive conditions where, it appears, there is a genetic and/or biochemical defect.

Projection

The third pattern of handling the problem of insecurity in interpersonal relationships is projection. It is a protective technique commonly used to protect one's sense of security by attributing to others one's own feelings. In psychoanalytic terms, the "I hate you" is an unacceptable feeling. It gets changed to, "It is not I who hate you, it must be you who hate me." This then becomes, "Not only do you hate me, but you are out to get me."

These happenings may combine into an organized conspiracy against the person. "A foreign power is out to get me!" "Enemy agents completely surround me!" The individual may then develop elaborate ideas about what an important person he is in order to compensate for his actual derogatory or critical attitude toward his "self." The paranoid person uses projection extensively.

Use of Physical Disability

The use of physical disability is another method of attempting to attain security. The individual develops physical symptoms that then cause him to avoid the types of situations that produce anxiety and this causes a reduction in society's demands on him. In addition he secures a certain amount of sympathy because of the physical illness. It is also a weapon with which to demand the attention of others. This pattern of behavior is usually related closely to early experiences. If a child finds that physical aches and pains are the only method of gaining any sign of affection from parents, this is the pattern apt to be followed in any crisis thereafter. If experiences outside the home confirm the child's impression that he is important to others only when he is sick, the pattern becomes fixed.

Anxiety is both a physical and an emotional phenomenon. Emotional stress will very often produce a headache or a gastrointestinal upset. Most of us, at some time or another, have developed physical symptoms of distress over an unpleasant experience. In addition, most of us have used these physical complaints as a means of evasion. The mentally ill person may develop a chronic complaint that he can use as a protection in any situation which carries a threat to his security.

The use of such behavior may produce paralysis of a hysterical nature, which can be used to force an entire household to organize itself around the patient's needs.

Amnesia, or a circumscribed memory loss, may also be used in place of physical ailments as a means to evade and excuse, but always on the unconscious level.

Use of Ritualistic Behavior

The use of ritualistic behavior is still another means of handling the problems of interpersonal relations. The person uses rigidly ritualistic behavior in an attempt to retain control over a situation and keep anxiety at a minimum. It appears to the patient as though obsessive-compulsive acts *must* be done, regardless of how foolish they may seem to the doer. The individual responds to a compulsion to do something which seems to give him control over the situation which causes his anxiety. This obsessive-compulsive behavior has many expressions. Usually, obsessive ideas precede the compulsive act. For example, some persons, having locked a door when leaving home, *must* unlock it and go back and check the furnace, or empty the ash trays; others, at bedtime, *must* go back and hang up a toothbrush to dry, or they cannot sleep. Fundamentally, these are "magical" operations which dispel a threat by keeping the situation in a known sequence, which is a form of control over the environment; one is, thereby, "in control" and therefore secure.

With the mentally ill individual, these episodes may constantly recur and may progress to a severe and prolonged ritual which will severely handicap the person in his activities of daily living. For example, the elaborate ritual of handwashing displayed by a very compulsive patient who must wash his hands every time he touches something. He may wash his hands 60 to 200 times a day until they are red and sore. Little time is left for any other activity.

Use of Props That Blur Reality

Another method of handling personal problems is to blur reality with some outside influence that either changes the nature of reality or increases one's sense of ability to handle it. Alcohol and morphine produce in an individual a delightful sense of well-being and of security. For persons who lack security due to difficulties in personality development, this artificial sense of well-being can become an all-important prop for them to lean on. When the effects of the drugs wear off, the sense of insecurity is greatly increased and this leads to a renewal of and dependence on their use. People who use this pattern to reduce conflicts have a low tolerance for frustration and anxiety. We say they have a low ego-strength. (See Chapters 21 and 22.)

Failure to Integrate

The final method of the abnormal handling of anxiety is probably the least understood of all. This consists of failing to integrate experience so that the individual neither profits from past experiences nor takes account of future consequences. This person is called an antisocial personality. Verbally, he may be fluent and he is often superficially charming, but depth and duration of emotion are alien to him. He lives purely for the moment, reaching out to satisfy his needs with little concern for enduring personal security. We do not know what causes a person to develop a character disorder, but some authors describe "super ego lacunae"—a defect in the "conscience." Behavioral modifications principles (See Chapter 32) may be profitably applied in the correction of this disorder. A number of chronic offenders in penal institutions can be diagnosed as having "character disorder."

Although this pattern of behavior is seen by some to indicate that the person has little, if any, unresolved anxiety, this is not true. (See Personality Disorders, Chapter 19.)

References

McDonnell, C., et al.: What would you do? Amer. J. Nurs. 72:296 (February) 1972.

Solnit, A.: Aggression: A view of theory building in psychoanalysis. J. Amer. Psychoanalytic Assoc., 20, 3:435, 1972.

Storr, A.: Human Aggression. New York, Bantam Books, 1970.

Symptoms of Mental Disorders

Behavioral Objectives

The student successfully attaining the goals of this chapter will be able to:

- List the 9 symptoms of mental disorder and briefly describe each.
- Compare and contrast illusions, delusions, and hallucinations and give examples of each.
- List the types of hallucinations which may exist and note the physical causes which may produce visual hallucinations.
- Define the terms "word salad," neologisms, flight of ideas, and incoherence as expressions of thinking disorders.
- Explain the meaning of delusion and list and explain 8 types of delusion.
- Note the 4 types of consciousness disorders, describe each, and note the causes of each.
- Demonstrate how to test a person's orientation level.
- Explain how each of the following terms may be described as a feeling disorder: euphoria, elation, exaltation, tension, panic, depression, apathy, inappropriate emotionality, and ambivalence.
- Define the term conation and list 7 such disorders along with a brief definition of each.
- Compare and contrast the 2 types of attention disorders.
- Define amnesia and confabulation and indicate the possible physical causes of such disorders.
- Describe how a paranoid person might demonstrate retrospective falsification of meaning.
- Note the physical causes of dementia and the type of behavior which results.

Some symptoms of physical conditions such as impairment of memory in old age, or confusion in a toxic delirium, or psychotic behavior caused by a brain tumor, are the results of physiological disturbance of brain cells. But, in most mental disorders, there seems to be no known disturbance in the anatomy or physiology of the brain, although recent research on the chemistry of the brain and nerve cells indicates that a disorder in the **neurotransmitter** mechanisms, i.e., a **biochemical defect**, may lie at the base of the major mental illnesses such as schizophrenia and endogenous depression. Neurotic symptoms appear to be **psychogenic** in origin; they seem to derive from the person's inability to deal with such problems as troublesome instinctual drives, with difficulties in family relationships, with feelings of guilt or of insecurity, or with disturbing memories from past experiences. Symptoms have, therefore, cause and meaning. Sometimes a person's symptoms indicate clearly the nature of the problem. Sometimes symptoms appear in disguised forms. In order to effectively treat the neurotic person, we have to try to identify his problems through his symptoms so as to help him resolve them. This way of understanding mental disorders is called the **psychoanalytic model.**

The symptoms of mental disorders may be grouped as follows:

1. Disorders of Perception
2. Disorders of Thinking
3. Disorders of Consciousness
4. Disorders of Orientation
5. Disorders of Affect or Emotion
6. Disorders of Motor Aspects of Behavior
7. Disorders of Attention
8. Disorders of Memory
9. Dementia

Let us discuss each group of disorders briefly but in sufficient detail so as to help us understand the major symptoms of each group.

Perceptual Disorders

The dictionary defines the verb **perceive** as "the act of comprehending or of grasping mentally"; it defines the noun **perception** as "the mental awareness of things, or data, through the medium of the senses."

The process really consists of two successive steps; the first step involves a sense organ and the nerves associated with it; the second step involves the sensory cortex of the brain and the large association areas of the brain where "understanding" takes place.

Not infrequently, patients with mental disorders suffer from disturbances of perception. The most common form is called **imperception,** a condition in which perception is difficult or impossible. This condition is often found in toxic states, and in degenerations such as senile dementia and cerebral atherosclerosis. The sensory picking up and carrying of the impulses to the brain is normal, but the sensation is not assimilated into consciousness (i.e., the sensory part is completed but the mental interpretation is lacking). In this case, objects and events seem indistinct or incomprehensible. The patient is perplexed, bewildered, or confused. He does not "grasp" what is presented to his senses.

When a misinterpretation of **sensory impulses** occurs, such an incorrect, falsified interpretation, this is known as an **illusion.** The word illusion comes from the Latin word *illudere* which means "to mock." An illusion is a misperception of something in reality. It is as it were, "faulty seeing."

On the other hand, "faulty believing" is called a **delusion.** The word delusion comes from the Latin word *deludere* which means "to deceive." A wisp of smoke seen out of the corner of the eye may seem like a person moving, or heat rising from the desert may seem like water (a mirage)— these are examples of illusions. The belief that one was Napoleon would be an example of a delusion.

While normal people may misinterpret what is perceived, the error is soon recognized and does not persist. In the mentally ill, misperceptions tend to persist, are strengthened by anxiety and fear, and may give rise to compelling behavior.

In mental disorders, a frequent and more serious disorder of perception consists of experiencing sensations that have no basis in fact. There is no special stimulation of the senses, yet the psychic interpretation in the brain presents pictures to the self that arise from within and which seem very real to the patient. Such imaginary perceptions are known as **hallucinations.** The content of a hallucination carries a meaning. The images visualized represent emotional needs, wishes, daydreams, or repressed or rejected impulses.

There may be hallucinations of any of the senses; thus, there are as many types of hallucinations as there are special senses: auditory (hearing), visual (sight), tactile (touch), olfactory (smell), gustatory (taste). However, the auditory and visual varieties are the most common.

Auditory hallucinations (hearing "voices") are the most frequent type of perceptual disturbance. The patient may hear a single word spoken to him or a complete sentence. These words or sentences may vary from a whisper to loud conversation. Their content may be comforting in nature, but is frequently unpleasant, derogatory, obscene, or accusing.

The patient may or may not realize that the voices are unnatural, but if he realizes they are unnatural, he may fear he will be considered "crazy" if others learn of his experiences. Therefore, he will persistently deny their existence. He may attribute the voices to the radio, to dictaphones, to persons concealed in the wall, or may try to explain them to himself in other ways.

If such a person is carefully observed, his behavior will often betray the fact that he is hallucinating. He may be observed with his head inclined in a listening attitude; his lips may be moving soundlessly, or he may be talking aloud to himself; he may have his ears stopped with cotton in an attempt to keep the voices out.

Visual hallucinations occur, but are much less frequent than auditory hallucinations. They occur most typically in the deliria of acute infectious diseases (brain fevers) and in toxic psychoses (such as the delirium tremens of acute alcoholic psychosis). The most common cause of visual hallucinations today is the ingestion of **hallucinogenic chemicals,** including LSD, mescaline, peyote, amphetamines, and cannibus in high dosages.

Thinking Disorders

Normal thought is usually orderly and directed by, or in tune with, the real world about us. In certain mental disorders, especially in schizophrenia, thought is disorderly and unrealistic or irrational. It seems to wander without order, and to be attuned to wishes and desires that lie below conscious awareness. Such thought is termed **autistic.** The dictionary defines autism as "a state of mind characterized by daydreaming, hallucinations, and disregard of external reality."

The **schizophrenic,** when expressing himself in words, often shows this loss of orderly thought progression by using unconnected words which we call "fragmentation" or "word salad." He also may coin new words that have no meaning to the listener (neologisms).

The **manic patient,** on the other hand, has a different type of thinking disorder. His words on a subject, as far as they go, evidence orderly thinking, but his stream of thought is very distractible, and he flits from one idea to another so rapidly that he rarely seems to reach his goal. The result is a rapid succession of superficially related ideas and this is known as **flight of ideas.**

Flight of ideas is usually accompanied by distractibility of attention. The mind is in too much of a hurry and sentences are rarely completed before a new thought takes over.

In occasional patients, progression of thinking becomes so disorderly that one idea, or fragment of an idea, shifts into another so that there seems to be no logical sequence. The resulting disjointed sentences or phrases are known as **incoherence.**

Beliefs that have strong feeling-tones tend to dominate thought content. When an idea has an extreme feeling-tone connected with it, it indicates an inner need for such a belief. The person tends to select only those observations and memories which will confirm this idea and to deny into consciousness any that conflict with it. All of us are prone to develop comforting fiction to afford support and security for our personalities, but we continue to make our beliefs conform to reality to a degree that permits us to maintain a working adjustment with our world and our fellow man. Sometimes, however, the demand for the satisfaction of some inner need may be so insistent that reality is disregarded and an unfounded belief or delusion is created. A delusion is often defined as a false belief which cannot be corrected by reason or logic. Delusions come into being to deal with the special problems that confront an individual. Frustrated hopes, thwarted urges and drives, feelings of inferiority, unattainable desires, and deep senses of guilt, or the need to defend one's thoughts or actions, are among the most common causes for the building of delusions. The patient seems to utilize or employ the particular defense mechanism that will meet his special need.

Delusions are often sub-classified according to similarity of type. Here are a few of the most commonly occurring types:

Delusions of grandeur. The patient develops an expansive delusion of his own status, or ability, to compensate for feelings of inadequacy, inferiority, or insecurity. He sees himself as a person of power, influence, wealth, tremendous abilities.

Delusions of self-accusation. This type is believed to arise when the defense mechanism of repression weakens and nonacceptable desires or drives threaten to engulf the patient. Fearing that these forbidden tendencies may be indulged in causes feelings of guilt to arise and these lead the patient to develop ideas of self-accusation.

Delusions of persecution. The patient projects his own hostility and aggression onto the environment and believes that persons and things are setting up elaborate traps to injure or harm him. Delusions of persecution permit a shifting of responsibility and serve to relieve a guilty anxiety. In a society where phone tapping and electronic surveillance are commonplace, the patient may not be delusional, merely persecuted. It may be important to consider whether the patient is actually being persecuted to some degree.

It is common to find that a person has delusions both of persecution and grandeur, since they both serve to make him feel more comfortable with himself; they actually supplement each other. By the grandiose delusion, the patient builds up his self-esteem, and by his ideas of persecution, he disavows the feelings and thoughts that threaten this self-esteem.

Ideas of reference. The patient directs remarks he overhears, which in fact have no relation to him, to himself and thinks that others are talking about him or acting against him.

Depressive delusions. This is a condition many people are afflicted with when emotional pain from repressed memories becomes very disturbing and gives rise to a feeling of hopelessness and melancholia.

Hypochondria. In hypochondria, the patient is also depressed, but his attention is abnormally concentrated on his own body; he becomes preoccupied with some organ or tract which he is convinced is incurably diseased. This is sometimes found in the psychosis named **involutional melancholia.**

Obsessions. Thoughts that persistently thrust themselves into consciousness against our wishes are known as obsessions; they cannot be dispelled and are uninfluenced by logic or reasoning. Obsessive thoughts are closely related to compulsive acts.

Phobias. Phobias are obsessive fears and are closely related to obsessive ideas. There are a wide variety of phobias. Very often the thing feared is symbolic of another fear the patient cannot consciously acknowledge. Thus, he channels this impossible-to-think-about fear into some other person, place, or thing (this is a form of transference or displacement).

Some patients become so tormented by these fears and the compulsive acts that so often follow them, that they cannot continue at their work.

Disorders of Consciousness

A "clear" mind is one that functions well and is keenly aware of its surroundings.

Confusion is a disturbance of consciousness in which the powers of recognition and interpretation are impaired. The patient is perplexed, bewildered, and disoriented; he has difficulty in associating ideas. Confusion frequently occurs in toxic or infectious states, high bodily fevers, brain injuries, and often after an epileptic seizure; sometimes it accompanies hysteria.

Clouding of consciousness is a condition in which a patient appears to be in a "mental fog." The patient's grasp of his environment is incomplete and inaccurate. We see this in toxic states such as uremia. Often the patient must be shaken or shouted at in order to get his attention. Following the "clouding" there is a memory loss of the events that occurred during this time.

Stupor is characterized by an extreme dulling of consciousness. It takes great effort to rouse a person from a stupor, if it can be done at all. Sometimes the patient will respond partially to your efforts for a moment, then lapse again into unconsciousness. Stupor occurs in some toxic states, in some organic diseases of the brain, in certain psychogenic mental disorders (i.e., those that are emotional in origin), and often following grand mal attacks of epilepsy.

Delirium is a syndrome (i.e., a group of associated symptoms). It is characterized by clouding of consciousness, bewilderment, disorientation, incoherent or dreamlike thinking, illusions and hallucinations, restlessness or stupor, and at times it is accompanied by extreme fear. The patient's activity may vary from mild restlessness to intense and uncontrollable activity.

Delirium is usually due to toxins acting on the brain. We see its occurrence in patients suffering from acute infections accompanied by high fever, from the use of certain drugs, from uremia, and from chronic alcoholism.

Disorders of Orientation

Orientation is a function by which we apprehend or grasp our environment and locate ourselves mentally in it. A person is said to be oriented if he knows *who* he is, *where* he is, and *what he is doing*. He is also expected to know the current year, month, day, and the time of day.

Another way of saying this is to say that we should be oriented as to *person, place,* and *time.*

Disorientation in one or more of these spheres frequently occurs, both in toxic-organic diseases and in psychogenic disorders. Thus, a person may know where he is and what time of the day it is, but may insist he is Napoleon Bonaparte; or he may say he is Napoleon Bonaparte and insist he is in France and marshalling his troops for a dawn attack and insist you get up and march with him.

Disorders of Feeling or Affectivity

The word **affect** has substantially the same meaning as the word "emotion."

Every mental experience is accompanied by affectivity or feeling. Feeling penetrates and colors all of our mental life, and there are many variations in our feeling or emotional state. Intensity of feeling, duration of feeling, and appropriateness of feeling all enter into variations of affectivity.

Deviations in intensity of feeling are in the direction of pleasure or of pain—of an elevation or a dejection of spirits. Here are some of the varieties of feeling tone:

In **euphoria** the patient evidences a marvelous sense of well-being and his attitude is positive and optimistic.

In **elation** there is a still greater raising of spirits and the patient evidences great happiness, enjoyment, and self-satisfaction.

In **exaltation** the patient experiences ecstasy. He may have religious fervor and mystical experiences.

In **tension** the patient feels restless, dissatisfied, and has a sense of discomforting expectancy. Tension tends to arise in emotionally charged situations and when a person is torn between contradictory desires and strivings.

In **panic** the patient has a sudden, overpowering feeling of terror resulting from prolonged tension and a sense of impending danger. The patient usually attempts to escape from the terrifying condition he believes exists, or that does indeed exist.

Depression is a feeling-tone of sadness that may vary from a mild downheartedness to complete stupor. In the milder depression, the patient is usually quiet, restrained, pessimistic, discouraged, has a feeling of inadequacy and hopelessness, and loses interest in his usual activities. Some depressed persons are irritable and distrustful.

In deeper depression, the patient is dejected, fearful, and deeply hopeless. His initiative is lost, decision-making becomes very painful, and he feels rejected and unloved. Attention, concentration, and memory may become impaired. Ideas of guilt, unworthiness, and self-accusation are common. Suicidal thoughts are often entertained. Fear is frequently expressed.

Apathy is a condition in which a pathological dulling or absence of emotional feeling occurs. The face shows an emptiness of expression, and all drive and interest seem to disappear.

Inappropriate emotionality is frequently observed in schizophrenia, especially of the hebephrenic type. In a situation that should normally evoke sadness, the patient will respond with an inappropriate elevation of spirits; in one that should evoke pleasure or happiness, the patient will respond with sadness or tears.

Ambivalence is the simultaneous feeling of opposing emotions for the same thing or person. Such feelings as love and hate for someone may coexist in normal states, but a patient is often confused by this awareness.

Disorders of Motor Aspects of Behavior

Action tendencies are considered the striving aspects of the personality, and are technically known as **conation.**

Increased psychomotor activity is a speeding up of all activities. This increased activity may range from mild increase of energy and zeal to severe activity that is quite unrestrained and even destructive. In the manic phase of manic-depressive psychosis, this hyperactivity is quite characteristic; thinking (flight of ideas), talking, and actions all speed up tremendously and the patient will become hoarse from almost constant chattering, and exhausted from constant moving about.

Decreased psychomotor activity is characterized by a distinct slowing up of all motor expression. The patient speaks and acts slowly. In extreme cases the patient becomes mute and motionless. Two forms of mental illness exhibit this extreme hypoactivity—the depressive phase of manic-depressive psychosis and the catatonic type of schizophrenia.

Stereotypy is the repetition of some activity for an indefinite period of time. It is a persistent, aimless repetition of activity found in some forms of mental illness, especially in schizophrenia and some organic disorders. For instance, a patient may pick at clothing or skin for hours at a time.

Catalepsy is the constant maintenance of immobility of position. The patient's body is usually rigid, and the breathing and heartbeat slow down until they may be imperceptible. Death has sometimes been pronounced on these people when the physical examination was very sketchy.

Mannerisms are common in schizophrenics. They usually are individual, distinctive expressions of activity that are often odd and bizarre.

Compulsions also fall under aspects of motor behavior. We have discussed them earlier, under defense mechanisms. They are basically irresistible urges to perform certain acts. The patient realizes that a habit is abnormal but feels unable to resist the impulse. Compulsions range from simple acts, such as touching certain objects, to complex rituals, such as constant handwashing.

Compulsions even include destructive behavior such as pyromania (setting fire to objects) and kleptomania (compulsive stealing). Sexual compulsions are not uncommon.

Waxy flexibility is a state in which a patient's extremities may be flexed or extended by another person, and these extremities will be maintained in this position for an incredibly long time. Then they will very slowly return to the normal position. This odd positioning is seen in catatonic schizophrenia.

Disorders of Attention

Distractibility is a flitting of the attention from one matter to another, with the patient unable to hold a focus of attention. We find this condition in various types of mental illness, but it is particularly noticeable in the manic phase of manic-depressive psychosis.

Tenacity of attention is the very opposite of distractibility. It is usually found in profound depressions. The depressed patient refuses to respond to stimuli that are not related to his depressive mental content. His attention cannot be diverted from his own misery.

Disorders of Memory

Memory is the function of storing of data so that it can later be summoned to consciousness again. We think of this process as consisting of three successive steps: (1) the registration of a mental impression; (2) the retention of the impression; (3) the reproduction or recalling of the impression.

Emotional attitudes toward a subject tend to promote or to interfere with memory relative to that subject. The most important disorders of memory are amnesia and falsification of memory.

Amnesia is a loss or impairment of memory. It may be due to destructive or toxic disturbances in the brain cells (organic cause), or it may be due to emotional influences which interfere with the recall of impressions that are damaging to one's self-esteem (psychogenic causes).

Confabulation is one form of falsification of memory. In this disorder, the patient abruptly forgets what he is thinking and talking about and hastily fills the gap with fabrications. These "fill-ins" are false and he hurriedly talks about anything that enters his mind in order to cover up his memory lapse. This symptom is often seen in an advanced form of alcoholism (**Korsakov's syndrome**).

Retrospective falsification of memory is an embroidering of the truth as we retell a happening. Actually, we may or may not be aware of the fact that we are coloring the truth; most normal persons tend to do this to some extent. We do it for various reasons, such as a desire to have others think more highly of us, to forget our unworthy acts, or to fill our emotional needs and forget whatever is not in harmony with our self-esteem. In a patient with a paranoid psychosis, we see an abnormal intensification of this memory disorder. The paranoid person often misinterprets an actual event and, without any conscious attempt to deceive, will relate experiences that have little basis in fact.

Dementia

True dementia is permanent and irreparable. It is caused by degeneration or destruction of brain cells in the higher centers of intellect. Such organic diseases as cancer of the brain, syphilitic gummas of the brain, or atherosclerotic blood vessels in the brain, cause a degeneration of nerve cells that results in defective memory, judgment and reasoning; the patient becomes progressively confused and disoriented and often violent in his actions.

Psychogenic symptoms often reveal clues that make possible the discovering of problems that are troubling the patient and indicate the way he is trying to meet him.

References

Freud, S.: On Aphasia. New York, International Universities Press, 1953. (Translated by Stengel.)

————: Psychopathology of Everyday Life. New York, Norton 1966. (Translated by A. Tyson.)

Horney, K.: Our Inner Conflicts. New York, Norton, 1945.

Manfreda, M. L.: Psychiatric Nursing. ed. 9. Philadelphia, F. A. Davis, 1973.

Matheney, R. V., and Topalis, M.: Psychiatric Nursing, ed. 5. St. Louis, C. V. Mosby, 1970.

Mereness, D.: Essentials of Psychiatric Nursing. ed. 9. St. Louis, C. V. Mosby, 1974.

Classification of Mental Illnesses

Behavioral Objectives

The student successfully attaining the goals of this chapter will be able to:
- List and define the 5 types of mental illness.
- Differentiate between psychosis and neurosis.

As in the case of defense mechanisms, many attempts have been made to classify and catalogue mental illnesses. We should remember that mental illnesses seldom appear as clear-cut as a case of pneumonia or appendicitis. Labeling the neurotic and psychotic maladjustments is an artificial device we resort to in an effort to fit them into various behavior patterns. However, no two individuals behave exactly alike, and no two persons, sick or well, ever exactly duplicate each other. But we tend to separate mental disorders into the following categories: (1) the psychoses, (2) the neuroses, (3) the personality disorders, (4) the psychophysiological disorders, and (5) transient situational disturbances.

The psychoses are more severe forms of mental illness. Here, the patients deviate further from normal behavior, and their contact with reality is more severely impaired than in other forms of mental illness.

The neuroses are the mild forms of mental illness, with the patient usually in good contact with reality and able to get along fairly well in society.

The personality disorders are characterized by maladaptive patterns of behavior which are deeply ingrained in the individual. These are often life-long patterns which may begin even before adolescence.

The psychophysiological disorders (physical disorders of presumably psychogenic origin) often involve one body system which is usually controlled by the autonomic nervous system.

The transient situational disturbances include mental disorders of any degree of severity (including psychotic reactions) which occur in persons who apparently have no underlying mental illness and whose disturbance is a response to overwhelming environmental stress.

These categories are further subdivided according to the American Psyhiatric Association's *Diagnostic and Statistical Manual,* second edition, DSM-II), seventh printing incorporating July 1974 changes in nomenclaure. The subdivisions will be discussed in separate chapters of this book and ιre presented here for reference only.

PSYCHOSES ASSOCIATED WITH ORGANIC BRAIN SYNDROMES

Senile and pre-senile dementia (290)*
  Senile dementia (290.0)
  Pre-senile dementia (290.1)
Alcoholic psychosis (291)
  Delirium tremens (291.0)
  Korsakov's psychosis (alcoholic) (291.1)
  Other alcoholic hallucinosis (291.2)
  Alcohol paranoid state (Alcoholic paranoia) (291.3)
  Acute alcohol intoxication (291.4)
  Alcoholic deterioration (291.5)
  Pathological intoxication (291.6)
  Other (and unspecified) alcoholic psychosis (291.9)
Psychosis associated with intracranial infection (292)
  Psychosis with general paralysis (292.0)
  Psychosis with other syphilis of central nervous system (292.1)
  Psychosis with epidemic encephalitis (292.2)
  Psychosis with other and unspecified encephalitis (292.3)
  Psychosis with other (and unspecified) intracranial infection (292.9)
Psychosis associated with other cerebral condition (293)
  Psychosis with cerebral arteriosclerosis (293.0)
  Psychosis with other cerebrovascular disturbance (293.1)
  Psychosis with epilepsy (293.2)
  Psychosis with intracranial neoplasm (293.3)
  Psychosis with degenerative disease of the central nervous system (293.4)
  Psychosis with brain trauma (293.5)
  Psychosis with other (and unspecified) cerebral condition (293.9)
Psychosis associated with other physical condition (294)
  Psychosis with endocrine disorder (294.0)
  Psychosis with metabolic or nutritional disorder (294.1)
  Psychosis with systemic infection (294.2)

* The numbers in parentheses following each condition are used by medical record librarians and are often entered after the diagnosis in patient charts. They are included here for reference use only.

Psychosis with drug or poison intoxication (other than alcohol) (294.3)

Psychosis with childbirth (294.4)

Psychosis with other and undiagnosed physical condition (294.8)

PSYCHOSES NOT ATTRIBUTED TO PHYSICAL CONDITIONS LISTED PREVIOUSLY

Schizophrenia (295)
  Schizophrenia, simple type (295.0)
  Schizophrenia, hebephrenic type (295.1)
  Schizophrenia, catatonic type (295.2)
  Schizophrenia, paranoid type (295.3)
  Acute schizophrenic episode (295.4)
  Schizophrenia, latent type (295.5)
  Schizophrenia, residual type (295.6)
  Schizophrenia, schizo-affective type (295.7)
  Schizophrenia, childhood type (295.8)
  Schizophrenia, chronic undifferentiated type (295.90)
  Schizophrenia, other (and unspecified) types (295.99)
Major affective disorders (296)
  Involutional melancholia (296.0)
  Manic-depressive illness, manic type (296.1)
  Manic-depressive illness, depressed type (296.2)
  Manic-depressive illness, circular type (296.3)
  Other major affective disorder (296.8)
Paranoid states (297)
  Paranoia (297.0)
  Involutional paranoid state (297.1)
  Other paranoid state (297.9)
Other psychoses (298)
  Psychotic depressive reaction (298.0)
  Reactive excitation (298.1)
  Reactive confusion (298.2)
  Acute paranoid reaction (298.3)
  Reactive psychosis, unspecified (298.9)

NEUROSES

Neuroses (300)
  Anxiety neurosis (300.0)
  Hysterical neurosis (300.1)
    Hysterical neurosis, conversion type (300.13)

Hysterical neurosis, dissociative type (300.14)
Phobic neurosis (300.2)
Obsessive compulsive neurosis (300.3)
Depressive neurosis (300.4)
Neurasthenic neurosis (300.5)
Depersonalization neurosis (300.6)
Hypochondriacal neurosis (300.7)
Other neurosis (300.8)
Unspecified neurosis (300.9)
Personality Disorders and Certain Other Non-Psychotic Mental
Disorders
Personality disorders (301)
Paranoid personality (301.0)
Cyclothymic personality (301.1)
Schizoid personality (301.2)
Explosive personality (301.3)
Obsessive compulsive personality (301.4)
Hysterical personality (301.5)
Asthenic personality (301.6)
Antisocial personality (301.7)
Passive-aggressive personality (301.81)
Inadequate personality (301.82)
Other personality disorders of specified types (301.89)
Unspecified personality disorder (301.9)
Sexual disorders (302)
Sexual orientation disturbance (Homosexuality) (302.0)
Fetishism (302.1)
Pedophilia (302.2)
Transvestitism (302.3)
Exhibitionism (302.4)
Voyeurism (302.5)
Sadism (302.6)
Masochism (302.7)
Other sexual deviation (302.8)
Unspecified sexual deviation (302.9)
Alcoholism (303)
Episodic excessive drinking (303.0)
Habitual excessive drinking (303.1)
Alcohol addiction (303.2)
Other (and unspecified) alcoholism (303.9)
Drug dependence (304)
Drug dependence, opium, opium alkaloids and their derivatives
(304.0)

Drug dependence, synthetic analgesics with morphine-like effects (304.1)

Drug dependence, barbiturates (304.2)

Drug dependence, other hypnotics and sedatives or "tranquilizers" (304.3)

Drug dependence, cocaine (304.4)

Drug dependence, Cannabis sativa (hashish, marihuana) (304.5)

Drug dependence, other psycho-stimulants (304.6)

Drug dependence, hallucinogens (304.7)

Other drug dependence (304.8)

Unspecified drug dependence (304.9)

PSYCHOPHYSIOLOGIC DISORDERS

Psychophysiologic disorders (physical disorders of presumably psychogenic origin) (305)

Psychophysiologic skin disorder (305.0)

Psychophysiologic musculoskeletal disorder (305.1)

Psychophysiologic respiratory disorder (305.2)

Psychophysiologic cardiovascular disorder (305.3)

Psychophysiologic hemic and lymphatic disorder (305.4)

Psychophysiologic gastro-intestinal disorder (305.5)

Psychophysiologic genito-urinary disorder (305.6)

Psychophysiologic endocrine disorder (305.7)

Psychophysiologic disorder of organ of special sense (305.8)

Psychophysiologic disorder of other type (305.9)

TRANSIENT SITUATIONAL DISTURBANCES

Transient situational disturbances (307)

Adjustment reaction of infancy (307.0)

Adjustment reaction of childhood (307.1)

Adjustment reaction of adolescence (307.2)

Adjustment reaction of adult life (307.3)

Adjustment reaction of late life (307.4)

References

Diagnostic and Statistical Manual of Mental Disorders. 2nd ed. Washington, D.C., American Psychiatric Association, 1974.

chapter
16

The Neuroses

Behavioral Objectives

The student successfully attaining the goals of this chapter will be able to:

- Explain why neuroses are considered minor mental illnesses.
- List and describe the 8 types of neuroses mentioned, noting the symptoms and treatment of each.
- Describe the feelings prompted by a phobic neurosis and explain how this episode is distinguished from an anxiety attack.
- Note the differences between a conversion hysteria neurosis and a dissociative hysterical neurosis.
- Describe the relationship between an obsession and a compulsive behavior as manifested in an obsessive-compulsive neurosis.
- Compare the symptoms in a neurasthenic neurosis and a depressive neurosis.
- Explain the differences between a hypochondriacal neurosis, a psychotic depression, and an hysterical neurosis.

In general, people with neurotic disturbances are said to have "minor" mental illnesses as compared to the psychoses, which are "major" mental illnesses.

In the neuroses the personality is not grossly disorganized nor does the patient tend to distort or misinterpret external reality (except possibly in hysterical neurosis in which some workers believe hallucinations and other psychotic-like symptoms may be seen).

The cardinal symptom of neurosis is anxiety, interpreted by Freud as a painful "signal" that unconscious, repressed material is threatening to break forth into conscious awareness. Commonly associated symptoms are depression and phobias (fears).

The neuroses are classified according to the primary symptom that is seen. Among the sub-groups are the following.

Anxiety Neurosis

This condition is marked by anxious over-concern which may reach panic proportions. There are often somatic symptoms associated with anxiety neurosis (palpitations, shortness of breath, stiff neck, perspiration) or there may be feelings of dread. The anxiety may occur under any circumstance, and is not restricted to specific situations or objects as in phobic neurosis (See below). Fear or terror in realistically dangerous situations is considered normal and not a manifestation of anxiety neurosis. Treatment of anxiety neurosis is psychotherapy and minor tranquilizers.

Hysterical Neurosis

Much more common at the turn of the century than at present, this neurosis is marked by a loss or disorder of function caused by the unconscious mind. Symptoms are symbolic of the underlying conflicts and usually begin and end suddenly in emotionally charged situations. The symptoms can usually be modified by suggestion or hypnosis. There are two types: (1) **Conversion type,** in which the special senses or voluntary nervous system are affected causing anesthesias, paresthesias, paralyses, blindness, deafness, ataxias, akinesias, and dyskinesias. The patient often shows a remarkable lack of concern over the symptoms, which is called *belle indifférence.* "The paralysis just came on suddenly, nurse, but it's nothing to worry about. It really doesn't bother me. I'm just brave I guess." Conversion hysteria must be carefully differentiated from psycho-physiologic disorders (mediated by the autonomic nervous system); from malingering (which is done consciously); and from neurological lesions. (2) **Dissociative type,** in which the patient's identity or state of consciousness is altered, producing amnesia, somnambulism, fugue, and multiple personality (as in the books *Three Faces of Eve* and *Dr. Jeckyll and Mr. Hyde*).

The treatment for hysterical neurosis is psychotherapy, hypnotism, and major or minor tranquilizers.

Phobic Neurosis

This condition is marked by immense fear of a situation or object which the patient clearly recognizes as not really dangerous to him. There are a wide range of phobias described, such as fear of open places (agoraphobia), fear of closed places (claustrophobia), fear of dirt, and fear of flying. Most of them have Greek names associated with them which are interesting but unnecessary to learn.

When exposed to the fearful object or situation the phobic person experiences fear, faintness, fatigue, palpitations, perspiration, nausea, and tremor. This reaction must be differentiated from an **anxiety attack** which is not so closely related to a specific situation.

The treatment of phobic neurosis is behavior therapy (See Chapter 32) or dynamic psychotherapy and/or minor or major tranquilizers.

Obsessive-Compulsive Neurosis

The treatment of phobic neurosis is behavior therapy (See Chapter 32) of unwanted thoughts, urges, or actions which the patient is unable to stop. The word *obsessive* refers to the repetitive thoughts that the patient may have (for example, a man may have the intrusive and unwelcome thought that he must kill his wife). The word *compulsive* refers to the repetitive, stereotyped act that the patient finds himself unable to resist performing (for example, the man may need to wash his hands every time he has the thoughts about killing his wife in order to "neutralize" the thought). The obsessive-compulsive patient in these examples could find both the thoughts and the actions repugnant, but any attempt to stop the pattern would result in extreme anxiety.

If started early enough in the neurotic process, psychoanalytic psychotherapy may help. Treatment of fully developed obsessive-compulsive neurosis is quite difficult. In some refractory cases, prefrontal leukotomy has been successful but this drastic measure does not meet with universal assent among the psychiatric community.

Depressive Neurosis

This condition is marked by an excessive reaction of depression following the loss of a cherished possession or love object or after an internal conflict. It must be distinguished from unipolar manic-depressive illness—depressed type. This is usually possible through the psychiatric history. Patients complain of lassitude (low energy level), fatigue, difficulty in sleeping (especially early morning awakening). They tend to depreciate themselves and feel they are worthless. These patients look and sound sad and often show **psychomotor retardation** (a slowing down of movements and lack of bodily vigor).

Treatment of choice in depressive neurosis is the use of the tricyclic antidepressants and psychotherapy. Group therapy often helps.

Neurasthenic Neurosis (Neurasthenia)

This condition is marked by easy fatigability, chronic weakness, and sometimes exhaustion. The patient's complaints are genuinely distressing to him and there is no evidence of secondary gain (differentiating it from **hysterical neurosis**).

The course of the illness is chronic and the attending depression is moderate (differentiating it from **depressive neurosis**). Physical conditions to be ruled out are chronic brucellosis and thiamine deficiency. Treatment of neurasthenic neurosis is difficult unless begun early. Psychotherapy should be tried.

Depersonalization Neurosis

This condition is marked by subjective feelings of unreality and of estrangement from the self, from the body, or from the surroundings. Brief episodes of depersonalization are not uncommon and do not necessarily signify an emotional illness. The symptom of depersonalization occurs in various neurotic and psychotic states such as depressions, obsessional states, hypochondria, hysteria, and acute schizophrenia. When it is the predominant symptom in a neurotic person, the classification **depersonalization neurosis** is used.

Treatment is dynamic psychotherapy.

Hypochondriacal Neurosis

This condition is marked by the patient's preoccupation with the body and with his fear of presumed disease of various organs. These fears persist despite reassurance but do not reach the delusional quality that they do in **psychotic depressions.** There are no actual losses or distortions of function in this condition as in **hysterical neurosis.**

Intensive psychotherapy is the treatment of choice, but is minimally successful, especially if an obsessional quality is present in the patient.

References

Lewis, H.: Shame and Guilt in Neurosis. New York, International Universities Press, Inc., 1971.

Linder, Robert: The Fifty Minute Hour. New York, Holt, Rinehart, and Winston, 1955.

Mereness, D.: Essentials of Psychiatric Nursing, ed. 9. St. Louis, C. V. Mosby, 1974.

Mickens, P.: The influence of the therapist on resistive silence. Persp. in Psych. Care, 9, 4:161, 1971.

Toffler, A.: Future Shock. New York, Random House, 1970.

Psychoses Associated with Organic Brain Syndromes

Behavioral Objectives

The student successfully attaining the goals of this chapter will be able to:

- Identify the basic causes that underlie organic psychoses.
- Explain the difference between acute organic psychoses and chronic organic psychoses.
- Describe the symptoms of senile and presenile dementia and note the age difference for each type of dementia.
- List the symptoms associated with the following forms of alcoholic psychoses: delirium tremens and Korsakov's psychosis.
- Explain how each of the following infections affects the brain and nervous system and causes psychoses: syphilis, meningitis, systemic infections, chorea, and pork tapeworm infestation.
- Indicate how blood flow to the brain is affected by cerebral arteriosclerosis and cerebral vascular accident and describe the physical and mental effects of each.
- List the 3 types of psychoses due to brain trauma and describe each.
- Explain how endocrine disorders such as myxedema, cretinism, exophthalmic goiter and diabetes mellitus each causes psychoses and describe the mental symptoms associated with each.
- Describe the psychoses caused by pellagra and pernicious anemia.
- Note the types of psychoses caused by drugs and lead poisoning.

Organic psychoses include those mental disorders that are caused by mechanical, thermal, or chemical brain damage. These psychoses may be **acute** (temporary, in which case the functioning of the brain tends to return to normal after a psychotic episode), or **chronic** (in which case the impairment is permanent and with a tendency to worsen with the passage of years). We shall discuss the various organic psychoses in the order in which they are listed in the outline in Chapter 15.

Senile and Pre-Senile Dementia

Senility is a degenerative process that involves both body and mind. The cause is largely unknown. Body cells are breaking down faster than they can be replaced, and general bodily enfeeblement is usually accompanied by a slowing up of the mental processes. The patient shows mental confusion, forgetfulness, disorientation, confabulation, and lack of ability to grasp mental concepts. He becomes untidy, tends to live in the past, and may not remember what was said to him a moment ago.

Presenile dementia includes a group of cortical brain diseases presenting clinical pictures similar to those of senile dementia but appearing characteristically in younger age groups. Alzheimer's and Pick's diseases are the best known forms, each of which has a specific brain pathology.

Alcoholic Psychoses

Delirium tremens is an acute psychosis which may be precipitated in the alcoholic by such factors as fever, infection, and exposure. As the name suggests, delirium and tremor (especially of the hands) are two outstanding symptoms. The delirium is preceded by an aversion for food, and by restlessness, irritability, and disturbed sleep. Visual hallucinations of a loathsome type may so terrify the patient that he may attempt to escape. These hallucinations are fleeting and changeable. Consciousness is clouded and the patient is usually greatly confused and disoriented. Amnesia occurs during this period. Delirium tremens usually runs an acute course, terminating in from three to ten days. Occasionally, the disorder terminates in death.

Korsakov's psychosis is a variety of chronic brain syndrome associated with longstanding alcohol use and characterized by memory impairment, disorientation, peripheral neuropathy and particularly by confabulation.

Other alcoholic hallucinoses commonly include accusatory or threatening auditory hallucinations which occur in a state of relatively clear consciousness.

Alcohol paranoid state is usually seen in chronic alcoholic persons. The paranoid state is characterized by excessive jealousy and delusions of infidelity by the spouse.

Acute alcohol intoxication includes all varieties of acute brain syndromes of psychotic proportion caused by alcohol which do not show the specific characteristics of the four previous categories.

Alcoholic deterioration includes all varieties of chronic brain syndrome of psychotic proportion other than the first four categories.

Pathological intoxication is an acute brain syndrome manifested by psychosis after minimal alcohol intake.

Psychosis Associated with Intracranial Infection

General paralysis (due to parenchymatous syphilis of the nervous system) and **psychosis with other syphilis of the central nervous system** (the chronic form due to gummata) are the two psychotic conditions attributed to intracranial infection with spirochaeta pallida.

Syphilis, if untreated, has, in its third stage, a penchant for involving the central nervous system. It may, and does, involve many tissues and organs of the body, but the spinal cord and brain are especially sensitive to the spirochete. They attack the delicate neurons and cause a breakdown of the nervous structure. **Gummas** form as the involved areas degenerate. This infection and subsequent breakdown of the nervous system is called **general paralysis.** The course of untreated general paralysis is usually one of progressive physical and mental degeneration. The patients often develop a maniacal form of psychosis, and most die in from two to five years after brain involvement becomes apparent.

Psychosis with epidemic encephalitis, with **other encephalitis,** and with **other intracranial infection** such as meningitis and brain abscess, are also seen.

In **meningitis,** the patient complains of severe headaches, his eyes ache, his neck becomes rigid, and he holds his head backward to relieve the deep ache in his neck muscles. There may be fever, vomiting, or convulsions, lethargy, clouding of consciousness, stupor, or delirium. Light is usually intolerable, and the slightest noise is painful. A large number of patients who have meningitis or encephalitis in a milder form recover. Those who have it more severely are more often left with a damaged brain and may evidence various psychotic symptoms.

Psychosis Associated with Other Cerebral Conditions

Psychosis with Cerebral Arteriosclerosis

The brain must receive a rich supply of oxygen in order to function normally. Anoxia, from whatever cause, can seriously affect the nervous tissue and result in brain damage.

Cerebral arteriosclerosis (hardening of the arteries of the brain) is a frequent organic brain disorder. The number of patients admitted to public mental hospitals with this disorder is exceeded only by schizophrenics. The onset of arteriosclerotic mental disorder varies widely but, in general, may appear between the years of fifty and sixty-five. Among the early symptoms are headaches, dizziness, inability for sustained concentration, short attention span, emotional instability, memory impairment, and episodes of confusion. Some patients develop delusions of a paranoid nature; some develop epileptiform convulsions; others show fluctuations in orientation and memory. When this disease becomes advanced, small thromboses may form in small intracranial blood vessels and the patient will have a series of small strokes. Following the rupture of such a vessel, and until the small bood clot is absorbed again, the patient will be confused, have difficulties in speech, his memory will ramble back into his youth, and perhaps he will show some small degree of muscular paralysis.

Psychosis with Other Cerebrovascular Disturbance

Included in this category are such circulatory disturbances as cerebral thrombosis, cerebral embolism, arterial hypertension, cardiorenal disease, and cardiac disease (particularly in decompensation).

When a large blood vessel becomes occluded by a large clot, or ruptures, the symptoms are much more severe, and we say the patient has had a **stroke** or a **cerebral vascular accident.**

In about half of these vascular accidents, consciousness is either lost or greatly disturbed. If a coma develops, it may range from a brief episode, or may terminate in death. Paralysis of the muscles on the opposite side of the body from the site of the cerebral hemorrhage usually results (**hemiplegia**), or there may be **monoplegia** (paralysis of just one extremity), **paraplegia** (paralysis of both legs), or **quadriplegia** (paralysis of all four extremities or the entire body). **Aphasia** (the inability to correctly say the words one is thinking) is frequently present; swallowing may be difficult or impossible, and bladder and bowel control may be lost.

Psychosis with Epilepsy

In certain patients with "idiopathic" epilepsy (See Chapter 26), the epileptic attack may take the form of an episode of excitement with hallucinations, fears, and violent outbreaks. Most commonly there is a clouding of consciousness before or after a convulsive attack, or instead of a convulsion the patient may show only a dazed reaction with deep confusion, bewilderment, and anxiety.

Psychosis with Intracranial Neoplasm

Tumors may develop in the brain and produce psychotic reactions. They may be benign or malignant. The benign tumors are usually encapsulated, and, if diagnosed before their growing pressure has done much damage, and if they are located in an area where surgery is feasible, they may often be successfully removed. Angiomas, or blood tumors, though benign, do not lend themselves well to surgical removal. Malignant tumors spread rapidly and usually result in severe mental unbalance. Surgery is of little avail, and although radiation therapy is usually tried, it merely slows down the spreading of the carcinoma. Chemotherapy may or may not help.

Psychosis with Degenerative Disease of the Central Nervous System

One example of this type of disorder is **Huntington's chorea,** a hereditary, sex-linked form of psychosis. It appears chiefly in men, usually makes its appearance in the early thirties, and progresses rapidly so that the patient "ages" mentally in a very short time and becomes helplessly psychotic in a few years.

Psychosis with Brain Trauma

Oddly enough, relatively few head injuries result in permanent brain damage. The brain tissue, though very delicate, is very well protected by its meningeal coverings and the bony case of the cranium. However, some injuries *do* result in extensive brain damage. In this event, scar tissue usually develops in the injured area.

Three types of acute psychoses due to trauma are **concussion, traumatic coma,** and **traumatic delirium.**

Concussion is very common as the result of a head injury. Its symptoms are amnesia (the patient will have a memory loss from just before the time of the accident up until his awakening from unconsciousness), unconsciousness (which may be momentary or continue for several hours), and nausea (he may vomit as he regains consciousness). He may regain consciousness suddenly, or he may pass through a variable period of clouded consciousness and confusion.

He usually recovers fully in a short time, but if the brain damage is more pronounced, he may pass into a coma, or the concussion may be followed by a chronic state of deterioration, personality change, or chronic neurotic invalidism.

Traumatic delirium may follow emergence from a traumatic coma or stupor. If the delirium is mild, the patient acts more or less bewildered, irritable, and restless. If it is severe, he may be noisy, belligerent, demanding, and verbally abusive. Delirium or coma of more than a month's duration usually indicates severe brain damage.

In the event the patient does not recover from his concussion (i.e., the brain damage becomes chronic), he may show mental enfeeblement accompanied by epileptic seizures, paralyses, and other neurological disturbances. He may develop a decided personality change, becoming unstable, aggressive, quarrelsome, and destructive; or he may become depressed, apprehensive, easily fatigued, and become a chronic, complaining invalid.

Psychosis Associated with Other Physical Conditions

Psychosis with Endocrine Disorder

This category includes complications of diabetes (other than cerebral arteriosclerosis) and disorders of the thyroid, pituitary, adrenals, and other endocrine glands.

Hyper- or hypoactivity of the thyroid gland often results in mental disturbances. If the secretion of the gland is insufficient, a condition known as **myxedema** develops. In addition to a well-known syndrome of physical symptoms (lowered blood pressure, temperature, pulse rate and respiration rate, chilliness of the body, especially cold hands and feet, slowed down physical activity, dullness of facial expression, etc.) such patients become slow in their thinking and in their ability to grasp ideas. Their memory becomes impaired and their speech becomes slow and listless. Some are irritable, fretful, fault-finding, or even paranoid in their ideas and attitudes.

Congenital insufficiency of the thyroid gland results in a condition called **cretinism**, in which there are decided defects in body and mind.

An overactive thyroid gives rise to a condition known as **exophthalmic goiter** or **Graves' disease.** The patient's symptoms are the exact opposite of persons suffering from insufficient thyroxin. The patient is nervous, high strung, irritable, very active, anxious, and apprehensive. In acute thyroid intoxication, he may go into acute delirium accompanied by incoherence, hallucinations, and great restlessness. This intoxication may lead to coma and death.

An undersecretion of the islands of Langerhans in the pancreas gives rise to a condition called **diabetes mellitus.** Diabetes is characterized by a hyperglycemia, or excessive amount of sugar in the blood, due to a deficiency of insulin to help the cells burn up sugars. When the hyperglycemia mounts too high, the patient goes into diabetic coma. He becomes irritable, anxious, confused, hallucinates, and may even become maniacal before reaching the convulsion state. Without treatment, coma usually results.

Psychosis with Metabolic or Nutritional Disorder

Pellagra and pernicious anemia are physical disorders, caused by vitamin deficiency, that tend to disturb mental balance.

While **pellagra** is not common today, it may occur in chronic alcoholics whose diet has consisted chiefly of alcohol over a period of several months, in poverty areas where residents are very restricted in their choice of foods, and in persons suffering from intestinal diseases which prevent the absorption of food. Advanced pellagra exhibits symptoms of mental confusion and delirious states. Irritability, distrust, anxiety, and depression are also common. The disorder is due to a lack of vitamin B (especially the nicotinic acid factor).

Pernicious anemia, while seldom reaching the frank psychotic state, does exhibit the milder symptoms of mental fatigue, memory loss, irritability, depression, and apprehension.

Psychosis with Systemic Infection

Systemic infections (pneumonia, typhoid, malaria, acute rheumatic fever) are very often associated with acute mental disturbances. Toxins produced by viral and bacterial invasion of the bloodstream may involve the central nervous system, and delirium is frequently seen. The higher the fever, the more intense the delirium usually is.

In **pork tapeform infestation,** if the eggs of the worms are deposited by the bloodstream in the brain, they will develop into encysted worms and these cystic masses will cause cerebral degeneration and psychoses.

Chorea, which is also known as **Sydenham's chorea** or **St. Vitus' dance,** is caused by a viral infection of the central nervous system. It occurs mostly in children and is characterized by involuntary, jerky movements, muscular incoordination, and facial grimacing. The child tends to be irritable, restless, disobedient, and quarrelsome. Delirious episodes may occur. Many children recover from this infection, but in some cases, a chronic inflammation results in behavioral problems and psychotic reactions.

Psychosis with Drug or Poison Intoxication (Other Than Alcohol)

Narcotic drug addiction may result in deterioration of the mental processes. Hallucinogenic drugs may result in acute psychotic episodes.

Cortisone and ACTH may produce a wide variety of mental disturbances.

The barbiturates may cause confusion, anxiety, delirium, and hallucinations, and are addicting, as are the amphetamines.

Lead poisoning, over a prolonged period of time, tends to permanently damage nervous tissue.

Psychosis with Childbirth

This diagnosis is rarely made today, and indeed should not be made unless all other possible diagnoses have been excluded.

References

Agate, J.: Ethical questions in geriatric care: Rights and obligations of elderly patients, part 2. Nurs. Mirror, 133:42 (November 12) 1971.

Antonini, F.: Why we grow old. World Health, 24 (April) 1972.

Browne, L. and Ritter, J.: Reality therapy for the geriatric psychiatric patient. Persp. in Psych. Care, 10:135 (July-August-September) 1972.

Chisolm, J.: Lead poisoning. Sci. Amer., 224:15 (February) 1971.

Cochran, A.: Recognizing minimal brain damage in the problem child. RN, 35:35 (May) 1972.

Driscoll, B.: Every two minutes someone gets V.D. Family Health, 4:31 (June) 1972.

Graef, J., et al.: Lead intoxication in children: Diagnosis and treatment. Post-grad. Med., 50:133 (December) 1971.

Gress, L.: Sensitizing students to the aged. Amer. J. Nurs., 71:1968 (October) 1971.

Goyer, R.: Head toxicity: A Problem in environmental pathology. Amer. J. Pathol., 64:167 (July) 1971.

Kolb, L. C.: Modern Clinical Psychiatry. ed. 8. Philadelphia, W. B. Saunders, 1973.

Psychoses Not Attributed to Physical Conditions

Behavioral Objectives

The student successfully attaining the goals of this chapter will be able to:
- List the 7 basic characteristics of schizophrenia and briefly describe each.
- Name the 10 types of schizophrenia and describe the personality characteristics of each.
- Define the terms echolalia and echopraxia and explain how each may be an expression of schizophrenia.
- Describe those aspects of a person's background which, according to the psychoanalytic theory, can lead to schizophrenia, and contrast this theory with the thinking of those who see a physical basis for this illness.
- Explain the behavioral pattern in involutional melancholia.
- Identify the 3 phases of a manic-depressive illness and briefly describe the behavior manifested in each phase.
- Describe the characteristics of a paranoid personality and list the main symptoms.
- Indicate the type of treatment which may be helpful for paranoid personalities.

The functional group of psychoses is divided into four types: schizophrenia, major affective disorders, paranoid states, and "other psychoses" (primarily psychotic depressive reaction).

While one's basic type of personality will be the predisposing factor as to which form of psychosis he will develop, should stress and strain precipitate this state, it does occasionally happen that a person with recurrent psychosis *may* show a different form than the one he evidenced earlier. However, as a rule, if psychosis occurs several times in the life of a person, it tends to follow the same behavioral pattern each time.

101

Schizophrenia

The behavioral patterns of the **schizophrenic** patient are characterized by much disorganization and discord of the personality. Schizophrenia comes from two Greek words—one meaning "to split," and the other, "mind."

Schizophrenia includes a large group of disorders characterized by disturbances of thinking, mood, and behavior. Disturbances of thinking are shown by changes in concept formation which often lead to misinterpretation of reality and, on occasion, to delusions and hallucinations. These delusions and hallucinations often appear to be psychologically self-protective. Accompanying mood changes may include ambivalent, constricted and inappropriate emotional responsiveness, and loss of empathy with others. Behavior may be withdrawn, regressive, and bizarre. In the schizophrenias the mental status is attributable primarily to a thought disorder. These states must be distinguished from the major affective disorders which are primarily disorders of mood. In paranoid states there is an absence of psychotic symptoms other than a narrow distortion of reality.

Today's researchers are probing into body and brain chemistry to see if there is, perhaps, some chemical substance affecting the nervous tissues of these disorganized persons. This new line of inquiry has been accelerated by several of the symptoms commonly appearing in the users of LSD (a hallucinogenic drug). There seems to be a remarkable similarity between some of the effects of LSD on the mind and the state of mind in schizophrenia. Should research bear out the theory that perhaps the schizophrenic has a chemical or physiological basis for his psychosis, we shall have to classify this large group of psychoses as organic rather than functional. Or perhaps we shall find that the schizophrenic has both a physiological and a psychological cause for his psychotic state.

According to psychoanalytic theory, the schizophrenic person appears to have a childhood deprived of meaningful relationships with the important persons in his family circle. An outstanding fact is that most of these persons have felt that as children they were unloved, unwanted, and unimportant to their families. This lack of good, firm interpersonal relationships at an early age results in immature adult personalities that find it difficult to adjust socially or to relate intimately with other persons.

When unresolved anxiety mounts too high, the schizophrenic person tends to meet his problems by turning away from the real world and withdrawing into a dream world of his own which is produced through fantasy, projection, delusions, and hallucinations. In other words, he becomes psychotic.

Although there are ten major subdivisions of schizophrenia, each with distinguishing characteristics, there are several *overall* characteristics seemingly possessed by all sub-groups. These are:

1. Disturbances of thought and speech (fragmentation) and activity
2. Inappropriate emotional responses
3. Lack of affect (cold emotionality)
4. Withdrawal
5. Regression
6. Delusions
7. Hallucinations

Disturbances of thought, speech and activity vary widely from patient to patient, but are usually evident to the observer. In thought, they tend to be disorderly, unrealistic, and often irrational. Autism is common. They disregard external reality to a large extent. When expressing thought in words, the schizophrenic shows a loss of orderly progression of thought by using unconnected words. This is termed "fragmentation," or "word salad." He may also coin new words that have no meaning to the listener. We call these new words "neologisms." His speech lacks unity, clearness, and coherence, reflecting the confusion of his mind.

The schizophrenic is often given to odd, unexplained, and sudden activities. Undirected restlessness, fitful behavior, and impulsive, apparently unpremeditated acts are frequent.

To sum up his behavior, we again use the word **autistic** (i.e., his actions, thoughts, feelings, ideas, and experiences are inappropriate, distorted, and not easily understood by other persons). He may laugh or show pleasure as the result of a painful experience or he may weep when the occasion would call for laughter (inappropriate emotional responses).

A **lack of affect** is a "coldness" of emotional response to others. The patient fails to relate to others in a meaningful way. We say he is emotionally "shallow," and whatever emotion he does evidence is often inappropriate.

Withdrawal is a progressive shutting out of the world. There is a reduction in interest, initiative, and spontaneity. Many patients seem to have withdrawn behind barriers which, if they could be penetrated, would reveal loneliness, hopelessness, hatred, and fear. The patient may defend himself by building a shell of indifference around himself. The withdrawal may vary from a mild degree of isolation to one so profound as to make the patient seem to be completely unaware of his surroundings. However, these severely withdrawn people, in spite of appearances, are sometimes acutely aware of all that goes on in the environment.

Regression varies in degree from slight to profound. There is a tendency for the schizophrenic patient to retreat to a more primitive and infantile level of thinking and behaving.

A **delusion** is a fixed, false belief based on a misinterpretation of fact. Since the ideas, or mental content, of the schizophrenic are so often delusional, and since the needs of the patient are so often disguised by symbolism, his thought content often appears complicated and difficult to understand. His delusions tend to center around themes of persecution, grandiosity, and sex. He dramatizes his problems, strivings, and conflicts in his fantastic delusional beliefs.

Another common symptom of schizophrenia is **hallucinations.** Hallucinations are sensory perceptions that have no basis in fact. They come, instead, from troublesome material from the patient's inner life. They are very real to him. Sometimes they are terrifying, sometimes accusing, sometimes pleasurable.

The **simple type** is chiefly characterized by withdrawal and regression. Hallucinations and delusions may be experienced but are not often noticeable. There is a progressive dulling of feeling, interest, and spontaneity, a withering of the personality. The patient becomes moody, irritable, and indolent. His appearance is that of passivity and emotional shallowness. Many people who live as recluses are simple schizophrenics. Some of them become vagrants, prostitutes, or delinquents.

The **hebephrenic type** has an insidious onset and usually begins in adolescence. The patient's emotions become shallow and inappropriate. He withdraws from social contacts, appears preoccupied, smiles and giggles frequently in a silly manner, and his speech becomes badly fragmented. Bizarre delusions and hallucinations, often of a pleasant type, if present, are transient and not well organized. He exhibits silly, giggling, childish behavior with fragmentation, often to the point of incoherence. Hypochondriacal complaints are frequent. There is more disorganization of personality and habits in the hebephrenic type than in any of the other types of schizophrenia, but it is rarely seen today because of early intervention, the use of the powerful phenothiazine drugs, and the end of the era of "warehousing" patients.

The **catatonic type** appears in two forms or phases. One phase is characterized by apparent stupor, immobility, mutism, and negativism; the other phase is characterized by unorganized, excessive, impulsive, and sometimes destructive behavior.

In **catatonic excitement,** the patient's behavior is characterized by impulsive and stereotyped activities, poorly coordinated, and often lacking apparent purpose. Hostility and feelings of resentment are common; unprovoked outbursts of violence and destructiveness may occur; hallucinations are frequent. The flow of speech may vary from mutism to a pressure suggesting flight of ideas. Some excitements are in the form of short panic reactions.

In **catatonic stupor,** or withdrawal, the patient shows no interest in his environment. His facial expression is vacant, he stares into space, his head is usually bowed, and he may lie, sit, or stand very still for long periods of time. He often must be tube fed when in this state, and given complete physical care. While apparently unheeding and insensible, his consciousness is actually very clear and after his recovery, he will often relate minute details of what went on about him. He lives in an unreal world and seems oblivious to his external environment. Occasionally, he may be seen whispering and smiling slightly to himself; at other times, he may use odd mannerisms and strange positioning of head and extremities. If someone raises his arm into an upright position, he will maintain this position an amazingly long time. The term **waxy flexibility** is used to describe this phenomenon. Two other peculiar mannerisms are occasionally seen: **echolalia**, in which the patient repeats all words or phrases directed toward him but offers no conversation of his own, and **echopraxia**, in which he mimics all actions of the person who is addressing him, but makes no answer at all.

The characteristic symptoms, then, of catatonia are *withdrawal, regression, repetitive stereotyped actions, odd mannerisms, strange positioning of parts of the body, waxy flexibility, mutism,* and *hallucinations.*

The **paranoid schizophrenic** adds suspiciousness, projection, and delusions of persecution to his other basic schizophrenic traits. Delusions occupy a prominent place in his mental concepts, and hallucinations are tied in with these delusions.

Voices command him from the air or out of the walls; he may refuse medications or food for fear of being poisoned. He is usually highly verbal and will tell you about the detectives who are following him everywhere, or about unseen instruments that are reading his mind. At times, he may become quite aggressive and even combative. At times, his utterances may become disconnected and fragmentary.

The other subdivisions of schizophrenia include the following.

Acute schizophrenic episode. The sudden onset of schizophrenic symptoms distinguishes this type from simple schizophrenia. The patient often recovers within weeks, but sometimes the disorganization becomes progressive. More frequently remission is followed by recurrence and over a period of time the patient may develop paranoid, catatonic, or hebephrenic characteristics (in which case the diagnosis would be changed).

Schizophrenia, latent type. These patients are clearly schizophrenic but lack a history of a psychotic episode.

Schizophrenia, residual type. These patients, formerly psychotic, have returned to a nonpsychotic state but continue to show signs of schizophrenia.

Schizophrenia, schizo-affective type. These patients show both schizophrenic symptoms *and* pronounced elation or depression (characterized as "excited" or "depressed").

Schizophrenia, childhood type. This category is used when schizophrenic symptoms appear before puberty. It has been noted in children as young as two years of-age, though it more commonly appears later.

Many psychologists still believe it to be psychogenic in origin and due to a disturbance in the mother-child emotional relationship. But, whatever the cause, the child becomes withdrawn, unsocial, and emotionally unable to relate to others. Such a child, projecting infantile autism, may pass for retarded. Hallucinations and delusions are seldom found in schizophrenics under the age of eight.

Schizophrenia, chronic undifferentiated type. This category refers to patients who show definite schizophrenic thought, affect, and behavior not classifiable under the other types of schizophrenia.

Major Affective Disorders

This group of psychoses is characterized by a single disorder of mood, either extreme depression or elation, that dominates the mental life of the patient and is responsible for whatever loss of contact he has with his environment. The onset of the mood does not seem to be directly related to a precipitating life experience and therefore is distinguishable from "psychotic depressive reaction" and "depressive neurosis."

The major affective disorders are divided into "involutional melancholia," "manic-depressive illness," and "other major affective disorders."

Involutional Melancholia

The behavioral pattern of the person suffering with involutional melancholia is characterized by worry, anxiety, agitation, and severe insomnia. Feelings of guilt and somatic preoccupations are frequently present and may be of delusional proportions.

This type of psychosis usually occurs in middle age. Many factors at this particular time tend to lead to discouragement, disillusionment, frustration, disappointment, and a sense of loss.

In a woman, loneliness due to the loss of her grown-up children, added to a fear of the loss of her physical attractiveness, may be contributing factors.

In a man, failure to achieve his goals of success and security, added to a fear that he may be losing his potency, can be important factors.

It is logical, then, that some disturbing experience which threatens one's life situation may precipitate a pathological type of depression, apprehension, and hypochondriacal delusions. Because life no longer seems worth living, many of these persons become preoccupied with death. They see no solutions to their problems and no possibility of living in anything but misery. They may try to kill themselves, and should be watched closely.

Those who show paranoid reactions have personality structures that, throughout their lifetimes, have been characterized by the traits of jealousy, secrecy, dissatisfaction, resentfulness, and suspiciousness. In involutional melancholia, we see a person who has been inclined to blame others for his or her failures and who has seen slights where none were intended. Such unhappy persons, given to nursing their grievances, will show paranoid tendencies during the involutional period. Some involutional-paranoid reactions are only temporary, while others are prolonged or even permanent.

Manic Depressive Illness

Manic depressive illness (manic depressive psychosis) is divided into three major subtypes: manic type, depressed type, and circular type.

The behavioral pattern of the **manic depressive** shows that this person has a lot of repressed hostility in his make-up. When he breaks down, this hostility shows up strongly, but usually in a disguised form.

Strong, exaggerated, cyclic mood swings characterize his behavior. All normal persons are subject to a moderate degree of mood swing. The form found in this type of mental illness is, however, a very exaggerated form lasting for weeks or months at a time. There is a slow, but steady, increase in mood acceleration up to a climax of frenzy, then a slow decrease in activity down to normal behavior again. Then, as a rule, the patient will start into the opposite cycle of hypoactivity, accompanied by agitated depression, only to slowly swing through this cycle and back to balance once more.

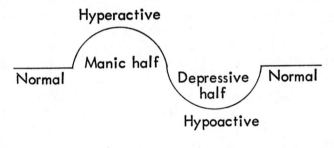

Fig. 18-1.

These episodes tend to recur several times within the patient's lifetime. It is not unusual for a patient to experience only one half of the complete cycle at intervals; in other words, he may show only the hyperactive (manic) phase of behavior, or he may show recurrent episodes of hypoactive (depressive) behavior. Whether he shows the entire cycle or only half of it, he will, even without treatment, return to normal. He may be normal for several years, then repeat the cycle (or half cycle) again. Modern therapy helps speed up the rate of recovery greatly.

Let us examine the patient's appearance and behavior when he is going into the hyperactive, or manic, phase of the cycle. His physical appearance becomes increasingly disheveled as he speeds up physically, mentally, and emotionally; he becomes increasingly restless and aggressive; his "id" seems to take over and his superego loses all control over the self; his thoughts speed up so that he becomes easily distractible. This gives rise to flight of ideas, as the patient's mind darts from subject to subject and his accelerated speech flits from one idea to another. His mood becomes euphoric, then shifts into exaltation, and finally, at the peak of the half cycle, into frenzy. The patient in this state sleeps and eats very little, losing weight rapidly. He frequently smashes or breaks things unintentionally. If crossed in something he wishes to do, he may become angry. But, because he is so easily distracted, he can usually be managed fairly well. As a matter of fact, he is usually happy-go-lucky, friendly, bossy, and highly verbal. He has delusions of grandeur and feels himself to be possessed of great charm, power, abilities, and wealth. If one or two of these hyperactive people are placed on a ward with a group of hypoactive patients, they actually have a stimulating effect on the latter by causing them to interact better. They tend to offend other patients on the ward, as their language and actions are often coarse, lewd, and suggestive. With the gradual subsiding of their hyperactivity, moral values again settle into place and behavior becomes more and more acceptable.

The hypoactive phase, or half cycle, which now usually sets in, sees a gradual slowing up of the entire personality. Speech becomes slow, halting, and anxious as the superego takes over and the patient becomes increasingly self-accusative. He paces slowly, later sits on a chair, rocking his body back and forth as he moans dejectedly. Finally, he takes to his bed or the floor, where he slowly and restlessly moves his body in a small circumscribed area. He is very dejected. He has a fixation about his worthlessness, the magnitude of his sins, and his need for punishment. He is directing all his aggression inward and eventually blames himself for all the sins and crimes in the world. His misery is very great. Just before, or immediately after he has reached the bottom of this cycle, he is very apt to try to commit suicide (when his activity reaches its very lowest ebb, he is usually too inert to carry out such a desire). He must be watched carefully during this period of self-destructive desire. Slowly he will return to normal balance again, acquiring more and more interest in life and its daily activities. It may be many years before another manic-depressive episode occurs, but it does tend to recur.

Paranoid States

There is considerable question as to whether the disorders in this group are distinct clinical entities or rather varients of schizophrenia, or paranoid personality. There are two major subdivisions of paranoid states. They are **paranoia,** an extremely rare condition, and **involutional paranoid state.**

The behavioral pattern in paranoia is characterized by a firm fixed system of delusion in an otherwise well balanced personality. This delusional system centers around feelings of persecution and grandiosity. The two major areas of activity most frequently involved are those of religion and politics. The delusional system slowly develops after a false interpretation of an actual occurrence. There are no hallucinations. The patient simply becomes convinced that a certain thing or situation is true, and he will accept no proof, regardless of how convincing it is, that he has a wrong concept of the thing or situation. Delusions of persecution are very common and he becomes increasingly suspicious of persons and situations. He feels that people are spying on him with intentions of harming him. He develops ideas of reference in which he assumes anything other people are talking about concerns him. As his persecution complex enlarges, so does his opinion of himself; he becomes grandiose. This self-importance is reflected in his statements such as "a foreign government is after me," or "an international ring is pursuing me."

If religion is his major problem, he may develop a preaching complex and strive to convert his friends and acquaintances alike. He is not able to discuss religion rationally. He may become convinced that he has been sent to save the world, and that he is even God, himself.

When institutionalized, his suspiciousness often involves food and medications, and persuading him to eat or take his medications often poses a real problem.

The interesting thing about a paranoid person is that he is well oriented as to person, place, and time, and that, outside of his special delusional system, he thinks, speaks, and acts rationally in all other areas. Thus, he frequently is able to convince his acquaintances that his "idea" is true and may be able to gather a group around him who become convinced that he is a great reformer, leader, or prophet until finally the fallacy of his claims becomes clearly evident to them and they turn away in disillusionment.

The outstanding symptoms of paranoia, then, are: a well-developed delusional system involving feelings of persecution and grandiosity, strong projection, and suspiciousness; there are no hallucinations. These persons may become dangerous. So great is their fear of being harmed by others that they may strike out first in self-defense. Therapy has not been especially effective in changing these delusional concepts. Phenothiazine medication and/or electroconvulsive therapy (E.C.T.) may be of help.

References

Aguilera, D.: Crisis: Moment of truth. JPN, 9:23 (May-June) 1971.

Benfer, B.: Mood swings. Nurs. '72, 2:28 (August) 1972.

Delaczay, E.: Loneliness. New York, Hawthorn Books, Inc., 1972.

Johnson, M.: Developing the Art of Understanding. ed. 2. New York, Springer Publishing Co., 1972.

Nolan, W.: What menopause is—and isn't. McCall's, 99:36 (May) 1972.

Oraftik, N.: Only time to touch. Nurs. Forum, 11, 2:205, 1972.

Parkes, C. M.: Bereavement. New York, International Universities Press, 1972.

Discussion Questions

THE SITUATION:

The student nurse comes on duty at 7:00 A.M. on the psychiatric ward of the community hospital. She finds a new patient on the ward, who accosts her with these words, "I know this is your dirty work! You've been plotting against me for a long time now, and had me forcibly brought here last night! Take off that nurse's outfit, it doesn't fool me for a moment!"

The student catches the arms of the patient, who is lunging at her; another nurse comes to help her. Together they lead the new patient over to a chair and assist her into it.

The student nurse introduces herself to the new patient, who continues to glare at her and mutter obscenities.

The student joins the rest of the staff for the morning report and then reads the new patient's chart. Anna Clark is fifty-two years old, believes her husband is trying to poison her, and charges him with having an affair with a redheaded woman down the street. She tells her doctor that her husband has hired someone to spy on her and that voices coming out of the walls keep her informed of his plans to do away with her. Both her doctor and husband had brought her to the hospital the previous evening after informing her that she was to undergo some special tests. When she found herself in the psychiatric ward, she became violently angry and had cursed and screamed obscenities until she was sedated.

Her history informed the student that the woman was a college graduate, mother of four grown sons and one daughter, that the present paranoid ideas began to be manifested about six weeks ago, and that her suspiciousness had increased steadily and her behavior worsened daily. She had a fine home, a steady, reserved husband who was a community leader, and had had an apparently happy married life up to this time.

THE QUESTIONS:

1. What pattern, or patterns, of behavior is Mrs. Clark manifesting?
2. What specific defense mechanisms is she using?

3. Can you give a reason, or reasons, why she is using these particular mechanisms?
4. What three delusions appear in the patient's history?
5. What delusion is seen in her initial contact with the student nurse?
6. Does she give any evidence of hallucinating?
7. Where would her behavior probably classify her—as psychoneurotic or psychotic?
8. Do you feel Mrs. Clark's civil liberties were denied her by bringing her to the hospital under a ruse and forcibly depriving her of her freedom without her consent or a court order?
9. Would partial hospitalization be an appropriate treatment modality to try first with high doses of psychotropic medication?

Patients with Personality Disorders, Sexual Disorders, Alcoholism, Drug Dependence

Personality Disorders

Behavioral Objectives

The student successfully attaining the goals of this chapter will be able to:

- Explain the difference between people who have a mental illness and those who have a personality disorder.
- List the 10 personality disorders discussed and identify the unhealthy characteristics of each.
- Compare and contrast the antisocial and dyssocial personality.

We discussed many of man's needs in Unit I; such psychological needs as tenderness in infancy, participation with others in the activities of childhood, sharing of experiences with peers in the juvenile period, and a close relationship with a member of the opposite sex in adolescence. In Unit II we discussed the nature and number of the defenses man constructs against aggressive tendencies, sexual tendencies, and some of the socially unacceptable feeling-attitudes he experiences for the important persons in his life, particularly during childhood. We have seen that one must have a normal ability to build up sufficient defenses and be able to channel excessive anxiety if he is going to be able to balance his needs and have a healthy personality.

If too many such defenses are built up to reduce tension and anxiety, the personality will become rigid, narrow, and non-spontaneous. If these defenses become pathologically exaggerated or disorganized, they will eventually result in neurosis or psychosis.

We have learned that everyone's basic personality forms in his early years, depending largely upon the way he learns to adjust to situations, and that his basic personality tends to remain identifiable in health and in disease (i.e., the personality traits are the same before, during, and after a psychotic episode, even though behavior tends to be more bizarre during the period of mental illness).

We have also learned that the kind, or type, of neurosis and psychosis one tends to develop when coping mechanisms fail depends largely upon the basic personality structure he has built up in childhood.

Up to this point, we have discussed mental health and mental illness in considerable detail. Let us now look at that vast number of people who seem to fit in between those whom we classify as mentally healthy or mentally ill. These are the persons whose adjustments to life are clearly not healthy ones because certain features of their behavior indicate serious inner problems, yet, their ego functioning and reality testing remain intact and allow most of them to adapt socially. We say these persons have **personality** (or character) **disorders.** In these disorders, the person does not, or at least need not, experience specific symptoms (in the ordinary medical sense of that term).

The *Diagnostic and Statistical Manual* of the American Psychiatric Association (See Chapter 15) lists 10 subdivisions under the category "Personality Disorders," 9 subdivisions under "Sexual Disorders," 4 subdivisions under "Alcoholism," 9 under "Drug Dependence," and 10 under "Psychophysiologic Disorders." This represents a marked change in nomenclature from that followed prior to 1974.

Paranoid Personality

Persons with this personality type tend to be hypersensitive, rigid, suspicious, jealous, and envious. They may have an exaggerated sense of their own importance, and generally tend to blame others and ascribe evil motives to them. These characteristics quite often interfere with the person's ability to maintain satisfactory interpersonal relationships.

Cyclothymic Personality

A person with this personality type tends to swing between moods of exhilaration and depression, but *not* to pathological extremes. However, it is this personality type that may develop manic-depressive psychosis in stressful life situations or, at times, for no apparent reason. (Changes in brain chemistry have been postulated.) Two subforms are often seen in which the person shows one of the moods much more than the other. If he shows exhilaration much of the time, he is classified as a **hypomanic** person. He is usually outgoing, cheerful, and thoroughly enjoys life. He is vivacious, buoyant, confident, aggressive, and optimistic. His energy level is high and he is gregarious. He has few inhibitions. Sometimes he is too easily swayed by new impressions. He usually makes an excellent salesman. A few of this type are blustering, argumentative and hypercritical. They all seem to have a ready excuse for their failures, and can usually talk themselves out of their difficulties. When these people become psychotic, they tend to become manic.

If a patient shows a depressed pattern, he is classified as a **melancholic** person. He is at the opposite pole of the cyclothymic personality from the hypomanic. He tends to be easily depressed, though he is often kindly, quiet, sympathetic, and even-tempered. He is seldom eccentric. In his moody periods, he is a lonely person, solemn, submissive, gloomy and self-deprecating. He often has feelings of inadequacy and hopelessness; he becomes discouraged easily, suffers in silence, and weeps easily, though not in the presence of others. He tends to be overly meticulous, conscientious, and preoccupied with his work. He is fearful of disapproval and feels responsibility keenly. It is hard for him to make up his mind, and his indecision and caution indicate his feeling of insecurity. Under stress he tends to become a neurotic-depressive or to develop a psychotic depression of the manic-depressive type. If his age places him at the "change of life" period, he may develop involutional melancholia.

Schizoid Personality

This behavior pattern manifests emotional coldness, sensitiveness, fearfulness, inability to socialize well with others, and a tendency to daydream and withdraw from reality.

Since there is such a wide range of behavior in the schizoid group, let us examine several of the behavioral patterns so as to understand that, basically, they all do fall into one category. Most persons with a schizoid type of personality are very sensitive people who feel lonely, imperfectly understood, and isolated. Many of them are timid, shy, self-conscious, and dissatisfied with themselves; others are more secretive and suspicious, and sometimes stubborn. Their feelings are very easily hurt. In childhood, this type of person is often teased by his playmates who look upon him as "strange" or a "sissy." He is shy, cries easily, seldom participates in rough play, talks little, and makes no close friendships. If the going gets too rough, he will retreat into fantasy and may become autistic.

In adolescence, many of these youngsters show a pattern of willfulness, disobedience, moodiness, passive stubbornness, and resentfulness. They resent advice, supervision, or correction. Such youngsters are often "loners" who prefer to get along without strong ties to other people. Yet, even though they may be disobedient and moody, they tend to do superior work in school.

In the upper grades and in college, they usually do very well, but tend to be quiet and unsociable. Their love of books is often a substitute for human companionship. They are often imaginative and idealistic and frequently are interested in plans for bettering humanity. They choose courses of an abstract or philosophical nature in preference to those of a concrete or objective type. Many of these persons become artists, poets, or musicians.

Others, while retaining an imaginative attitude toward life and its experiences, lack the fine sensitivity of the above group. These persons, while kindly and honest, are unsociable, dull, and taciturn; their personalities lack color and sparkle.

We have all known, or known of, persons who have a schizoid personality—the overly sensitive person, the extremely shy person, the recluse, the esthetic dreamer whom we could never really "reach." Often, to our surprise, we have found a sensitive and tender nature hidden beneath a cold and unresponsive exterior, or a deeply kind person hiding behind a gruff, apparently hostile facade. These types, fearful of hurt and intrusion into their inner world, camouflage their innate tenderness and kindness by erecting forbidding barriers.

Explosive Personality (Epileptoid Personality Disorder)

Persons with this personality disorder show gross outbursts of rage or of verbal or physical aggressiveness which are strikingly different from their usual behavior and for which they may be regretful and repentant. These people are generally considered to be excitable, aggressive, and over-responsive to environmental pressures. It is the intensity of the outbursts and the individual's inability to control them which distinguishes this group.

Obsessive-Compulsive Personality

These people tend to be punctilious, rigid, fastidious, formal, overinhibited, and overly conscientious. If a person of this type becomes too anxious, he feels compelled to perform some repetitive action or act of behavior in order to get relief from a rising sense of panic, and when this behavior evidences itself, we then classify him as having an obsessive-compulsive neurosis. But many of these basically compulsive people are able to control anxiety so that it does not go into the panic state; they remain socially adequate but are driven by their superego.

Hysterical Personality (Histrionic Personality Disorder)

This type of personality is characterized by traits of vanity, self-indulgence, and a flair for dramatization or exhibitionism. These persons are capricious, immature, self-centered, often vain and prone to emotional outbursts. Sexual behavior is provocative, seductive, and erotic. Actually, most of these people are fearful of sex. Their provocative, attention-getting behavior appears to overlie a driving dependency need which is demanding in quality. There is reason to suspect that many of these persons have been spoiled and overprotected in early years. Though they are usually actively engaged in the social world, they respond badly to the frustrations of reality.

Although this disorder is more common in women, the "Don Juan" character represents this personality type in men. The drive for sexual conquest and exhibitionism often rests upon a hidden feeling of masculine inadequacy. His repeated conquests prove his lack of satisfaction in each successive affair.

Asthenic Personality

Persons with this personality disorder show fatigability, low energy, a lack of enthusiasm and a markedly diminished capacity for enjoyment. They are oversensitive to physical and emotional stress. When neurotic symptoms develop, these patients are classified as having neurasthenic neurosis.

Antisocial Personality

Persons with this disorder are unable to form any significant attachment, or loyalty, to other persons, to groups, or to society. They are controlled by their ids and are given to immediate pleasures. They appear devoid of a sense of responsibility, and, in spite of punishment and repeated humiliations, they fail to learn to modify their behavior (i.e., they fail to learn by experience). They are lacking in social judgment and tend to turn their frustrations upon society. They are always able to rationalize their antisocial actions and consider them warranted, reasonable, and justified. The term **character neurosis** is often used to designate this group, because their character traits seem to be fixed expressions of neurotic conflict, and there is a certain compulsiveness to their antisocial acts.

The essential defect in their character structure is their failure to develop a socialized superego and ego ideals. If these do exist, they are directed toward personal acquisition of money and material goods and the control of others for immediate pleasures and satisfactions.

We are not sure of the factor, or perhaps factors, that produce such an individual, and as for helping him *change* his pattern of behavior, so far, society has failed rather badly. As one author puts it, "What causes him we do not know, and how to improve him we do not know."

As a group, these patients probably cause the most problems in society. They have frequently been in difficulty with the law, and might first be seen in psychiatric consultation on the recommendation of the court or probation office. They are unable to tolerate frustration, are easily enraged and can act out violently without feeling remorseful. They will sometimes describe themselves as "cold-blooded," and are often described by others as such. They can be ruthless and vindictive and tend to blame others for their behavior.

Someone with an antisocial personality demands much and gives little. He is typically affectionless, selfish, ungrateful, narcissistic, and may be exhibitionistic. He is unable to judge his behavior from another's standpoint, and so, even though he is inadequate and hostile from a social standpoint, he is quite satisfied with his behavior. To him, routine is intolerable. He shows few feelings of anxiety, guilt, or remorse. He demands immediate and instant gratification of his desires, with no concern for the feelings or interests of others. Some of these people use alcohol or drugs. They may react to alcohol poorly and, when under its influence, become noisy, quarrelsome, and destructive. Their behavior prevents psychosocial adjustment. The personality defect may be limited to a single form of misbehavior, such as stealing, running away, or promiscuity.

Psychologists have found that in many cases of psychopathic personality, the interpersonal relationships in the parental home have been very poor. The child is deprived of proper guidance and, if he is illegitimate or the product of a broken home or has been passed from foster home to foster home or institution, he may lack a parental figure, or have a poor parental figure, to identify with. To what extent these factors play a role in the development of antisocial personality is not known. However, a person may develop an antisocial personality in a good, stable family, with the other siblings all developing into mature and well-developed people. Therefore, while agreeing that cultural background, improper identification, and the social norms and behavior of other family members do certainly all contribute to the child's character formation, many researchers do not feel that the etiology of this type of personality is due solely to environment.

Our jails, prisons, and correctional institutions are filled with these antisocial people, but a mere history of repeated legal or social offenses is not sufficient to justify this diagnosis. **Dyssocial behavior** is no longer classified as a psychiatric disorder. It is a category for individuals who do not have antisocial personalities, but who are predatory and follow more or less criminal pursuits. This includes many racketeers, illegal gamblers, prostitutes, and dope peddlers. Unlike the antisocial person, the child who becomes dyssocial has an essentially normal personality growth pattern. His id, ego, and superego are all likely to be reasonably normal in their development. What is distinctive about this person is that he has identified in childhood with figures whose standards of values differ from those accepted by the society in which he may find himself when he is older. If, for instance, he has been raised in a family and in a neighborhood where all respect for government is absent and where he sees all the people about him breaking the laws, and he identifies with this pattern of behavior, he will tend, on moving into a different community, to treat all authority figures such as policemen, truant officers, and public health nurses, with suspicion, and his sympathies will naturally extend to the lawless elements of his new community. The dyssocial people differ from the antisocial group chiefly in their ability to form warm and strong loyalties to others, especially to others in their same group or gang. They have subjugated their values to a delinquent or criminal subculture and exhibit behavior acceptable to that group.

Sometimes the older terms "psychopath" or "sociopath" are used to mean antisocial personality. However, the student should use the current terminology.

Passive-Aggressive Personality

Persons with this behavior pattern show both passivity and aggressiveness. The aggression may take the passive forms of sullenness, procrastination, inefficiency, and obstructionism. Often in the background of such a person we find a history of hostility to a father who has been dominant, rigid, unapproachable, demanding, and difficult to please.

On the other hand, aggression may be seen in immature attitudes such as irritability, temper tantrums, and even destructive behavior. Many persons of this type show open, active hostility. They are hostile, provocative, antagonistic, competitive, and ambitious. They manifest a "chip-on-the-shoulder" attitude. Their speech is often sharp, biting, and argumentative. They demand special attention and assume unwarranted authority. These persons have usually shown open hostility to their fathers. But, in spite of their superficial air of aggression, beneath the surface lies a deep dependency. This type of aggression is referred to as a reaction formation.

Inadequate Personality

The people falling into this category usually have a normal or average intellectual endowment, but are so inadequate in personality resources that, in spite of often good educational opportunities, they fail in social, emotional, occupational, and economic adjustments. Some of them are easy-going and good natured, but are ineffectual, inept, and unconcerned about reaching any set goals. They seem to lack a sense of responsibility to themselves and to others. They lack physical and emotional stamina, perseverance, initiative and ambition, and their judgment is defective. On mental and physical examination, they seem normal enough, but psychological testing shows many of the above characteristics and attitudes. Many "drifters" belong to this category.

Other Personality Disorders

Immature personality and passive-dependent personality are classified here. The **passive-dependent** person is one in whom we see an absence of mature self-confidence and self-reliance. This individual is overwhelmed by feelings of helplessness, fear and indecision. He is irresponsible and childish and may cling to others as a dependent child clings to a supporting parent. He constantly requires approval and assurance. If married, the person depends on the spouse for all major decisions. Beneath his passive, fearful, timid exterior, he is unconsciously hostile. This persons has often been overprotected as a child.

References

Kolb, L. C.: Modern Clinical Psychiatry, ed. 8. Philadelphia, W. B. Saunders, 1973.

Kyes, J. and Hofling, C. K.: Basic Psychiatric Concepts in Nursing. ed. 3. Philadelphia, J. B. Lippincott, 1974

Sexual Disorders

Behavioral Objectives

The student successfully attaining the goals of this chapter will be able to:

- Explain the relationship between a persisting Oedipus complex and male homosexuality and give examples of circumstances in a boy's upbringing that can underlie this sexual disorder.
- Define the term lesbian and identify the major psychological basis for this sexual disorder.
- Identify the following sexual behaviors and explain the psychological reasons behind the actions involved: fetishism, transvestism, pedophilia, exhibitionism, voyeurism, and transsexualism.
- Describe the difference between a transvestite and a transsexual.

Before studying sexual disorders it would be good for us to review the stages of normal sexual development. (See Chapters 7, 8, 9.)

Normal children become aware of male and female sexual organ differences in the four- to seven-year-old stage. During this period, a child becomes frankly interested in his own genitalia and enjoys the pleasurable sensation that can be aroused when he rubs or handles them. According to psychoanalytic theory the four- to seven-year-old child passes through the Oedipus or Electra complex during this period. This belief system holds that the boy develops a deep emotional attraction for his mother and is resentful of any emotional exchange between his mother and father; the little girl becomes fiercely possessive of her father's love and is very jealous of the affection he shows toward her mother. In time, this sex-based attachment resolves itself with the child again identifying with the parent of the same sex and sharing his affection with both parents. The child then passes into the latency period and becomes less concerned with maleness and femaleness. The child prefers the company of his own sex. (This is an early, natural form of homosexuality.) This period extends from the seventh to about the eleventh or twelfth year.

With puberty and early adolescence, interest in sex again asserts itself. The sexually maturing body, with its new drives and urges, its hormonal thrust, its changed physiology, produces quite an upheaval in most boys and girls. Added to this is the confusing problem of dependency and the need to become independent. The desire to be considered "grown up" coexists with childish behavior.

But, if the adolescent's basic personality has developed up to this point in a balanced way, he should slowly but surely come to accept his sexuality and develop the necessary attitudes toward his role in life. He should be able to relate to members of both sexes and to enjoy their company. He should eventually be able to assume the responsibilities of marriage and the establishing and rearing of a family, if he so desires.

Let us examine a few of the common sexual disorders and the patterns of behavior evidenced by people with such disorders. Psychologists believe that some of the blocking, fixation, or deviation of these behavioral patterns arises from the family environment, some from the social environment, some from a combination of both, and that no real cause, or causes, have been determined to date for most of these disorders.

Homosexuality is a personality variant in which the predominant mode of sexual expression is with a member of the same sex. The Kinsey studies indicate that there is a wide range of homosexual behavior in both men and women. Some live lives exclusively homosexual and receive all adult sexual gratification from a partner of the same sex. There are others who are predominantly, but not exclusively, satisfied in this way. Then, there are those whose major sexual expression is heterosexual but who have occasional homosexual contacts, such as prisoners, men in isolated work camps, those who are in service (i.e., on Navy maneuvers for many weeks). Then there are those who practice homosexuality because they fear they lack true masculinity and fear failure in trying to express their heterosexual drives. There are those who will express themselves homosexually only when they are drinking heavily, or when they find themselves in situations of homosexual license. *Current thinking holds that homosexuality per se does not constitute a psychiatric disorder.*

According to classical psychoanalytic theory, the future homosexual male has a strong attachment to his mother. His Oedipus complex persists and does not resolve itself. Thus he develops a defect in his psychosocial maturation. If the mother, perhaps hating the father, encourages the child to identify with her and dislike his father, the boy will build her feminine attitudes into his personality. This may happen also because of a father's indifference to his son, or when the father is very punishing of the boy and the boy learns to hate his father.

Then there are situations in which the father dies, deserts his family, or secures a divorce; there are situations in which the father must be away for long periods of time due to working conditions, or in the service. All of these situations can account for a small boy attaching himself to his mother and identifying strongly with her. The student should realize that there are many normal homosexual males whose life history contains none of these scenarios.

These are the homosexuals whose personality development and ego function-ing appear intact and who conduct themselves both effectively and construc-tively in society.

A female homosexual is known as a **lesbian**. Here, as in the male, accord-ing to psychoanalytic theory, we find a girl child identifying with her father and building into her personality many of his masculine values and attitudes. She develops a fear of her feelings for her father and extends this fear of a sexual attachment to all men. She turns to another woman for sexual grati-fication in adulthood.

As with male homosexuals, there are many normal homosexual women with far different life histories than those mentioned here.

In many municipalities homosexuality is considered a crime. Indeed, there are cities where oral-genital and genital-anal contact between any two people (regardless of their sex or marital status) is against the law. These "victimless crimes" which constitute normal behavior between consenting adults are the result of archaic laws which prove vexing to all concerned.

Fetishism is a sexual disorder that is more common in men than women. The fetishist becomes attached to some object or body part. Perhaps this can be compared with the fetishistic attachment of small children to a toy or blanket or other object that will satisfy their love instincts in the absence of their mothers. Some psychoanalysts consider the fetishistic attachment as an effort to gain ego identification with a substitutive object. This object attains a highly exaggerated value, becomes the main source of erotic gratifi-cation, and relieves both psychic and sexual tension as contact with it leads to orgasm.

Transvestism is a sexual disorder in which the person has a strong desire to dress in the clothing of the opposite sex. It occurs somewhat more fre-quently in men than in women. There are many theories regarding the desire to cross-dress but the cause of this practice is really unknown and each person must be understood individually.

Pedophilia is a disorder in which sexual strivings are directed toward children. This is almost exclusively a male disorder. It occurs largely in im-potent and weak men. The pedophile seems to be functioning on an imma-ture psychosexual level and psychologists sometimes ascribe his actions to fear and doubt concerning his own maleness. Because he expects rejection and failure in adult sexual advances, he expresses himself to children. He may actually rape children, but much more often he may just fondle their sexual organs or expose his own to them with a request that they fondle his. **Child molestation** is very rarely homosexual. The usual case history is of an adult, adolescent, or mentally retarded male with a prepubescent female. It should be noted by the student that children are often sexually seductive. It is a generally accepted societal taboo for the adult to respond.

Exhibitionism is sometimes combined with pedophilia, but ordinarily the exhibitionist (often male) prefers to expose his genitals to more mature girls or women. This is a very common sexual disorder. These men rarely rape. They take their sexual enjoyment from exhibiting themselves sexually and may achieve orgasm at the height of this pleasure. Psychiatric theory holds that at the basis of the exhibitionist's behavior there is incestuous desire for the mother and that the taboo against incest is strong enough so that the boy will turn his insistent incestual wishes into exhibitionism so as to reassure himself against castration because of his immoral desire.

Voyeurism is another common sexual disorder. These boys and men are "peeping Toms," who find sexual pleasure in "looking in" on others undressing or engaging in sexual activity. The pleasure of watching is ubiquitous for both sexes, as is the pleasure of "showing off." When these pursuits cause the person discomfort or become an exclusive sexual outlet they are called "disorders."

Sadism and **masochism** are, respectively, the desire to inflict upon and the desire to receive from the sexual partner, physical and/or mental pain. In milder forms these desires are entirely compatable with normal sexual foreplay. In extreme forms they can substitute for normal sex and are considered "disorders."

Other Sexual Disorders is a category of DSM II for disorders not specifically listed above. Included here is **transsexualism.** There are male transsexuals and female transsexuals, but men who consider themselves women are about four times as common as women who believe themselves to be men. How many of these unhappy people there are, no one knows, but they may number in the tens of thousands. Transsexuals are physically normal men and women who cannot accept their sexual make-up. Thousands have changed sex by surgery; thousands more want to. They pose a unique medical and social problem. They differ from homosexuals and transvestites, with whom they are still commonly confused. Homosexuals, as we have said, are attracted to members of their own sex; transvestites get their sexual enjoyment by dressing in the clothes of the other gender. But clothes alone do not satisfy the transsexuals; they want to be physically changed to the opposite sex, and they disdain homosexuality. A transsexual man loves another man, emotionally *and* physically as a woman does.

Today, many psychiatrists are no longer certain that the sole criterion of sex is physical, but that what you *think* you are may be more important than what your genitals say you are. Sex used to be determined by the kind of equipment you were born with. But just where is the center that determines femininity or masculinity? Is it in the sexual organs, or is it in the brain?

At any rate, transsexuals are flocking to the few medical sex centers that have been established to date to have their sex changed surgically and to be given hormones that will develop the desired secondary sex characteristics.

They are deeply troubled people who are seeking help in their sex identification.

References

Kolb, L. C.: Modern Clinical Psychiatry. ed. 8. Philadelphia, W. B. Saunders, 1974.

Kyes, J and Hofling, C. K., et al.: Basic Psychiatric Concepts in Nursing. ed. 3. Philadelphia, J. B. Lippincott, 1974.

Morgan, A. J. and Moreno, J. W.: The Practice of Mental Health Nursing: A Community Approach. Philadelphia, J. B. Lippincott, 1973.

Sutterley, D. and Donnelly, G. Perspectives in Human Development: Nursing Throughout the Life Cycle. Philadelphia, J. B. Lippincott, 1973.

Alcoholism

Behavioral Objectives

The student successfully attaining the goals of this chapter should be able to:

- State the 2 factors either of which, when present, justifies a diagnosis of alcoholism.
- Compare and contrast the 3 types of alcoholism recognized by the American Psychiatric Association.
- Cite 3 statistics that indicate why alcoholism can be considered a major problem in the United States.
- Give 3 psychoanalytical theories and 3 physiological theories on the causes of alcoholism.
- Explain the role of disulfiram as a form of adversion therapy for alcoholism.
- List the types of psychotherapy which may be used in the treatment of alcoholism.
- Describe the type of psychological support which A.A. provides for alcoholics in their struggle to stop drinking.

Patients are given the diagnosis "alcoholism" when "alcohol intake is great enough to damage their physical health or their personal or social functioning, or when it has become a prerequisite to normal functioning."*

The following types of alcoholism are recognized.

Episodic Excessive Drinking

When alcoholism is present (see first paragraph of this Chapter) and the patient becomes intoxicated four times a year or more, the diagnosis of "episodic excessive drinking" can be made. **Intoxication** exists when "the individual's coordination or speech is definitely impaired or his behavior is clearly altered."*

Habitual Excessive Drinking

When alcoholism is present and the patient becomes intoxicated more than 12 times a year or is recognizably under the influence of alcohol more than

* *Diagnostic and Statistical Manual of Mental Disorders*, ed. 2 (DSM-II), American Psychiatric Association, Washington, D.C., 7th printing, 1974.

once a week, even though not intoxicated, the diagnosis of "habitual excessive drinking" applies.

Alcohol Addiction

This diagnosis is made "when there is direct or strong presumptive evidence that the patient is dependent on alcohol."* The best direct evidence is the appearance of withdrawal symptoms. Presumptive evidence includes the inability of the patient to go one day without drinking, or when heavy drinking continues for three months or more.

Simple drunkenness is classified as "nonpsychotic organic brain syndrome with alcohol."

Alcoholic psychoses, psychoses caused by poisoning with alcohol, and their subdivisions (delirium tremens, Korsakoff's psychosis, etc.) are discussed in detail later in this Chapter.

Incidence of Alcoholism

There are an estimated 9 million alcoholic persons in the United States. Three to 5 percent of alcoholics are "skid row" types. Most alcoholics live with their families and are able to work and function. Of the country's work force, 5 percent are alcoholic and another 5 percent are serious abusers of alcohol.

Costs. Alcoholism in America costs about 15 billion dollars each year— 10 billion dollars from lost work time, 2 billion dollars for health and welfare services, and 3 billion dollars in property damage and other "overhead" costs.

Arrests. Forty to 49 percent of all arrests each year are alcohol related (including drunken driving, disorderly conduct, vagrancy, etc.). Over 30 percent of all arrests each year (included in the 40 to 49 percent) are for public intoxication.

Sex. Male to female ratio of known alcoholics is 5½ to 1. However, more female alcoholics are being discovered each year, as they seek treatment and join the work force. Traditionally a woman was protected in her home and escaped social or even family detection. It is becoming less and less possible (i.e., less socially acceptable) for women to be secret alcoholic housewives. Some researchers believe that the true prevalence (actual number of cases) of alcoholism is essentially the same for women as it is for men in a given population.

Culture. Alcoholism among American Indians is estimated to be at least twice the national average. On some Indian reservations the rate of alcoholism is as high as 50 percent of the total population. Jews have the lowest incidence of alcoholism in America.

* DSM-II.

Personality Factors in Alcoholism

There is no known personality type that is found in, or that is predisposed to develop, alcoholism. However, various "types" of alcoholics have been identified according to personality considerations.

Reactive Alcoholic Persons. Some persons drink after some overwhelming external stress has depressed them. The alcohol deepens the depression. Physical dependence fixes the pattern. Some reactive alcoholics appear to use alcohol to blur the anxiety associated with homosexual feelings or the fear of appearing in public. These persons are relatively normal before their encounter with alcohol.

Addictive Alcoholic Persons. These persons have a marked self-destructive component in their pre-alcoholic personality along with marked evidence of inadequate and unsatisfactory interpersonal relations.

Interpersonal Relationship Factors. In alcoholics, relationships are often rigid and sterotyped and unrewarding. Uncomfortable feelings are denied. The alcoholic tends to feel aloof, omnipotent, invulnerable, depressed, with a great deal of hostility, and to have an unsatisfactory sex life.

Causes of Alcoholism

Psychoanalytic Theories

Freud: Strong oral influences in childhood, regression, escape from reality.

Menninger: Intense rage against parents becomes a self-destructive impulse. Alcoholism is a form of chronic suicide.

Knight: Oral over-gratification by over-protective mother. The child lacks self-control and reacts to frustration with rage, impulsivity, and guilt.

Adler: A perpetual state of insecurity and desire to escape responsibility resulting from over-indulgence and excessive coddling.

Schilder: Ridicule and passivity create insecurity in the child.

Other writers discuss inconsistent satisfaction of dependency needs, confusion in self-image, the collapse of a false self-image, and the emergence of repressed dependent traits.

Learning Theories

Alcohol temporarily reduces fear and conflict. The alcoholic learns to count on this reduction of fear and conflict. Upon withdrawal of the alcohol he finds himself in a state of misery. He turns again to alcohol and the addictive cycle continues. Relief from anxiety is rapid with alcohol, bringing into play reinforcement principles.

Physiological Theories

The theories cited in current literature include: (1) nutritional deficiencies, especially vitamin B, (2) genetically determined and enzymatic defects which impair carbohydrate metabolism and for which alcohol acts as a replacement, (3) structural physiological aberrations in some persons causing them to function more effectively with alcohol, and (4) other theories which cite thyroid deficiencies, "masked allergy" to alcohol, and development of toxic products of alcohol metabolism.

Sociological Theories

There appears to be antialcoholic potential in certain group attitudes and practices. In studies of American Jews and Chinese, two groups having a very low incidence of alcoholism, certain attitudes appeared to act as a deterrent to abuse of alcohol. These included the ritualization of alcohol use in traditional and social customs, the abhorrence of intoxication, and the minority status of the two groups studied, which encouraged the maintenance of control to avoid scandal.

Treatment of Alcoholism

There is no treatment for alcoholism per se. The alcoholic who wants to stop drinking or to control his drinking will find a way to do so. The treatments that are available are for the problems that are associated with drinking, such as toxic states, dehydration, convulsions, tuberculosis, atypical pneumonia, subarachnoid hemorrhage, pancreatitis, and liver disease. Family therapy, vocational rehabilitation, aids to developing interpersonal skills, and psychotherapy and/or chemotherapy for any underlying psychopathology may help, once drinking is under control.

Aversion Therapy

Emetine and apomorphine are medications which cause vomiting when combined with alcohol. They are used in an effort to create an association between alcohol and feeling ill. Disulfiram therapy is used more frequently and will be discussed at greater length.

DISULFIRAM THERAPY (ANTABUSE)

Patients taking 0.5 grams of disulfiram daily have an abnormal reaction to alcohol beginning 5 to 10 minutes after ingestion of alcohol, with peak intensity 30 minutes after alcohol ingestion. The patient feels uneasy and apprehensive, vomits, and is hypotensive. Patients should be cautioned about obscure sources of alcohol such as wine sauces in food or the breathing in of alcohol-containing aftershave lotions or perfumes.

Some patients, desiring to drink, will stop the Antabuse for five days first, then drink. Others will simply drink and put up with the discomfort.

Psychotherapy

Group and individual psychotherapy, psychoanalysis, milieu therapy, family therapy, and behaviorally oriented psychotherapy have all been used to treat the alcoholic, with no consistent outcome. As with other disorders, the personality of the therapist rather than his school of thought seems to be the therapeutic agent.

Alcoholics Anonymous

This voluntary group has as its goal sobriety and appears to gratify dependency needs through group identification or by caring for new intoxicated members. Switching from alcohol to A.A. seems to offer a less destructive social outlet for addictive needs.

A.A. evolved in 1935 from the experience of two men, Bill W., a former New York stockbroker, and Dr. Bob S., an Akron, Ohio, surgeon. Bill, whose compulsive drinking had caused him to be declared a hopeless drunkard, achieved sobriety in December, 1934, following an unusual spiritual experience. The following spring he was able to help free Dr. Bob from his alcoholic compulsion. The two men noted that their own desire to drink disappeared when they tried to share their recovery experience with other alcoholics. The chain reaction resulting from this discovery has been responsible for the consistent growth of the movement. Dr. Bob died in 1950. Bill W. continued to be active in the movement as a writer and adviser until his death, early in 1971.

AA. is completely self-supporting and does not seek or accept funds from outside sources. There are no dues or fees for membership. Local group expenses (rental of meeting places, refreshments, and literature) are defrayed by "passing the hat."

A.A. does not recruit members. Unless the problem drinker wants help for himself, and unless he approaches a member for assistance, or comes to an open meeting of his own accord, no effect is made to enroll him.

The only requirement for A.A. membership is a desire to stop drinking.

Though the need for religious help runs through the A.A. program, A.A. is not affiliated with any particular faith or sect. Many of the principles of the A.A. recovery program are based on the concept of man as a spiritual being.

Each A.A. group has one primary purpose—to carry its message to the alcoholic who still suffers. A.A. meetings are generally of two types: Open meetings, at which, in most areas, anyone interested in the problems of recovery from alcoholism is most welcome; and closed meetings, for alcoholics only.

A.A. members achieve and maintain sobriety primarily by sharing their experiences, strength, and hope as recovered alcoholics with others and by a philosophy embodied in "Twelve Suggested Steps." These steps define the experience of the first members who achieved stable sobriety in A.A. They are:

1. Admitted they were powerless over alcohol—that their lives had become unmanageable.
2. Came to believe that a Power greater than themselves could restore them to sobriety.
3. Made a decision to turn their wills and lives over to the care of God as they understood Him.
4. Made a searching and fearless moral inventory of themselves.
5. Admitted to God, to themselves, and to other human beings the exact nature of their wrongs.
6. Were entirely ready to have God remove all these defects of character.
7. Humbly asked Him to remove their shortcomings.
8. Made a list of all persons they had harmed, and became willing to make amends to them.
9. Made direct amends to such people wherever possible, except when to do so would injure them or others.
10. Continued to take personal inventory and when they were wrong promptly admitted it.
11. Sought through prayer and meditation to improve their conscious contact with God as they understood Him, praying only for knowledge of His will for them and the power to carry that out.
12. Having had a spiritual awakening as a result of these steps, they try to carry this message to alcoholics and to practice these principles in all their affairs.

Alcoholics Anonymous, then, is a form of group therapy. When a person really wants to achieve sobriety, the members of A.A. offer him help and tremendous reinforcement. If he is tempted to drink, or if he succumbs to that temptation and falls off the wagon, members will come to him and help him wrestle with his problem. He is urged to live one day at a time, to commit himself to sobriety for twenty-four hours at a time. He is asked to start that day with a prayer to God to help him remain sober, and to conclude the day with a prayer of thanksgiving for that strength. And the fact that his brothers in A.A. accept him as a person of real worth helps instill in him a sense of self pride. Above all, the knowledge that his brothers in A.A. are also unable to handle liquor; that they, too, must fight the same battle day by day, and that many of them have achieved sobriety for many, many years, is powerful proof that with sufficient motivation, effort, and help, he can likewise become a sober and responsible person. The opportunity to discuss his problems with the group and to listen to their problems is an excellent way of ventilating his anxieties and fears and of receiving inspiration to continue on the path of sobriety.

References

Detre, T. P. and Jarecki, H. G.: Modern Psychiatric Treatment. Philadelphia, J. B. Lippincott, 1971.

De Ropp, R. S.: Drugs and the Mind. New York, Grove Press, 1960.

Kolb, L. C.: Modern Clinical Psychiatry. ed. 8. Philadelphia, W. B. Saunders, 1974.

Morgan, A. J. and Moreno, J. W.: The Practice of Mental Health Nursing: A Community Approach. Philadelphia, J. B. Lippincott, 1973.

Drug Dependence

Behavioral Objectives

The student successfully attaining the goals of this chapter will be able to:

- Explain why some personality types abuse drugs and become dependent upon them.
- Draw up an outline using the following drug or drug categories: (1) morphine (opium, heroin), (2) barbiturates, (3) tranquilizers, (4) marihuana, and (5) amphetamines, and under each of these major drug headings list information according to the following subheadings:
    (1) name of most commonly used forms of the drug
    (2) the basic physical effects of each
    (3) the legitimate medical use (past and present) of the drug
    (4) the effects which result when the drug is abused
    (5) the withdrawal symptoms
    (6) the treatment for withdrawing the patient from the drug
- Give the full name of LSD, identify the drug category to which it belongs, and describe the effects it has.

The diagnosis "drug dependence" is now used in place of the term "drug addiction." It is used for patients who are either addicted to or dependent on drugs other than alcohol, tobacco, and ordinary caffeine-containing beverages. Excluded is dependence on medically prescribed drugs taken as medically indicated. Withdrawal symptoms are not the only evidence of dependence. They are always present when opium derivatives are withdrawn, and may be entirely absent when cocaine or marihuana are withdrawn.

Opium, Opium Alkaloids and Their Derivatives

Opium smoking goes back into Oriental history so far that we do not know the date of its first use as a producer of pleasant dreams. It is still smoked in some areas in Asiatic countries, but in western countries, the alkaloids of opium are preferred. Morphine is one of the main alkaloids of opium, and heroin is a derivative of morphine. **Heroin** appears to be the narcotic most widely used by addicts today. Because of its strong addictive power, it has been outlawed in our country and cannot be made, imported, or sold legally.

When a person becomes dependent on heroin his body craves repeated and larger doses of the drug. Once the habit starts, larger and larger doses are required to get the same effects. This happens because the body develops a tolerance for the drug.

One of the signs of heroin addiction is **withdrawal sickness.** When the user stops the drug, he sweats, shakes, gets chills and diarrhea, vomits, and suffers sharp stomach pain. In addition to physical dependence on narcotics, there is also a strong psychological dependence.

Typically, the first emotional reaction to heroin is an erasing of fears and a relief from worry. This is usually followed by a state of inactivity bordering on stupor. Heroin, which is a fine white powder, is usually mixed into a liquid solution and injected into a vein. It tends to dull the edges of reality. Addicts have reported that heroin "makes my troubles roll off my mind," and "it makes me feel more sure of myself." This drug also reduces feelings of pain.

The drug depresses certain areas of the brain and reduces hunger, thirst, and the sex drive. Because addicts do not usually feel hungry, one part of their treatment in the hospital is for malnutrition.

Synthetic Analgesics With Morphine-like Effects

The synthetic analgesics include demerol and methadone. The effects are essentially the same as with the opiate category above.

Barbiturates

The **barbiturates** belong to a large family of drugs manufactured for the purpose of relaxing (depressing) the C.N.S. They are synthetic drugs made from barbituric acid (a coal-tar product). Doctors prescribe these drugs widely to treat insomnia, high blood pressure, and epilepsy. They are frequently used in the treatment of mental illness and to sedate patients before and during surgery. They are often used in combination with other drugs to treat many other types of illness and medical conditions.

Taken in normal, medically supervised doses, the barbiturates mildly depress the action of the nerves, skeletal muscles, and the heart muscle. They slow down the heart rate and breathing and lower the blood pressure.

In higher doses, however, the effects resemble alcoholic drunkenness, with confusion, slurred speech, and staggering. The ability to think, to concentrate, and to work is difficult, and emotional control is weakened. Users may become irritable, angry, and want to fight someone. Sometimes, they fall into a deep sleep from which it is difficult to arouse them.

Often barbiturates are obtained illegally. Because doctors prescribe these drugs so frequently, many people consider them safe to use freely, and as they choose. They are not safe drugs. Overdoses can cause death. They are a leading cause of accidental poison deaths in the U.S. These drugs distort how people see things and slow down their reactions and responses. They are an important cause of automobile accidents; especially when taken with alcohol, they tend to potentiate (enhance) the effects of the alcohol.

Because they are so easily obtained, and produce sleep readily, barbiturates are frequently used in suicide attempts.

Barbiturates range from the short-acting but fast-starting pentobarbital sodium (Nembutal) and secobarbital (Seconal) to the long-acting but slow-starting phenobarbital (Luminal), amobarbital (Amytal), and butabarbital (Butisol). The short-acting preparations are the ones most commonly abused. In the doses ordinarily taken by the drug abuser, barbiturates produce mood shifts, restlessness, euphoria, excitement, and, in some individuals, hallucinations. The users become confused and may be unable to walk or perform tasks requiring muscular activity.

The barbiturates are physically addictive. The body needs increasingly higher doses to feel the effects. But true addiction requires the taking of a large dose of the drug for quite a long time. The dosage prescribed by the physician seldom leads to addiction.

Sudden withdrawal of barbiturates from someone dependent on them is extremely dangerous because it may result in death. A physician will hospitalize the addict and withdraw the drug very slowly so as to lessen the cramps, nausea, delirium, and convulsions that attend withdrawal. Some experts consider barbiturate addiction more difficult to cure than a narcotic dependency. It takes several months for a barbiturate user's body chemistry to return to normal.

Other Hypnotics and Sedatives or "Tranquilizers"

Methaqualone

A nonbarbituate sedative-hypnotic, methaqualone (Quaalude) was first introduced in America in 1966. Marketed as having little potential for abuse and as having no effect on dreamstage sleep, it rapidly became used as a recreation chemical. It was found, however, to suppress REM sleep (rapid-eye-movement associated with dreaming) and upon withdrawal, REM rebound occurs with symptoms described below. Tolerance to the drug may develop. It is capable of producing both considerable psychological and physical dependence.

A withdrawal syndrome has been observed in people using over 600 mg. per day for prolonged periods of time. The withdrawal syndrome begins within 24 hours of cessation of use of the drug, persists for 2 to 3 days, and consists of insomnia, headache, abdominal cramps, anorexia, nausea, irritability, and anxiety. Hallucinations and nightmares have also been reported.

Withdrawal may be interrupted by giving the patient methaqualone and tapering the dose gradually.

Meprobamate

Introduced as an antianxiety drug in 1954, meprobamate's therapeutic usefulness is in considerable doubt, but it is still widely prescribed and popular. Tolerance develops and withdrawal symptoms can occur. Abrupt withdrawal causes tremors, ataxia, headache, insomnia, and gastrointestinal disturbances for several days. Occasionally convulsions occur (usually upon withdrawal from 3 gm. or more daily). A delirium tremens-like state may occur in 36 to 48 hours.

Diphenylhydantoin sodium I.V. is useful in controlling convulsions. Withdrawal should occur gradually with either meprobamate or a barbiturate.

Benzodiazepines

Chlordiazepoxide (Librium) and diazepam (Valium) are widely used as "minor tranquilizers" for the control of anxiety. They produce less euphoria than the preceding two hypnotics but a withdrawal syndrome may occur when large doses (several hundred milligrams per day) are abruptly stopped. Convulsions may be delayed by several weeks and are managed as with meprobamate withdrawal.

Cocaine

Cocaine is an alkoloid derived from the leaf of the plant *Erythoxylon coca,* a shrub indiginous to Bolivia and Peru. Its leaves have been chewed by natives of these countries for many years, producing central nervous system stimulation. The "high" is similar to that achieved by amphetamines (i.e., euphoria, exhilaration), and a powerful sense of well-being and confidence.

Tolerance develops as well as physical dependency. Acute toxic effects may be treated with a short-acting barbiturate administered intravenously. A toxic psychosis with visual, auditory, and tactile hallucinations and a paranoid delusional system may develop as with amphetamines.

When psychosis develops it is classified as an organic brain syndrome (secondary to drug or poison intoxication) as are other drug-induced psychoses.

Cannabis Sativa (Hashish, Marihuana)

Marihuana has been a subject of controversy since 500 B.C. in China. In modern times, during the 19th century, cannabis was widely prescribed for a variety of ailments and discomforts (coughing, fatigue, migraine, asthma, delirium tremens, etc.). It remained in the *U.S. Pharmacopoeia* until 1941.

Its ability to cause euphoria has been of principal interest throughout history. The effects from smoking marihuana last 2 to 4 hours, and, from ingestion of the drug, 5 to 12 hours. Marihuana is commonly referred to as a hallucinogen, and it has a tendency to produce sedation. There is no substantial evidence in the world literature, however, that cannabis induces either mental or physical deterioration, at least not in well-integrated stable persons.

Adverse reactions to cannabis appear to be dose related and dependent on the set and setting in which the drug is used. Although rare, anxiety states, with or without paranoid thinking, panic states, and toxic psychosis have been reported.

An amotivational syndrome has been discussed in association with cannibis use but careful studies fail to prove that this syndrome does in fact follow the use of the drug. It may be a sociocultural phenomenon that happens to coincide with the regular use of marihuana.

On balance, cannabis use appears far less dangerous than alcohol use, and this realization has resulted in a reduction of the legal strictures on its possession in many states.

Other Psycho-Stimulants

Amphetamines are one of the most common psycho-stimulants. In spite of a vast medical literature that describes the amphetamines (Dexedrine, methedrine, dextro-amphetamine, benzedrine, etc.) as nonaddicting, and in spite of their widespread use in obesity, by students to stay alert and study, by truck drivers to stay awake, and by soldiers to decrease fatigue and increase aggression, the preponderance of evidence today compels the belief that they *are* addicting, tolerance *does* develop to their use, they produce both dependency and withdrawal states, and that they are clearly among the most dangerous drugs presently available. They are able to produce a toxic psychosis in the most mentally stable person which is clinically indistinguishable from paranoid schizophrenia, for all practical purposes. Death from overdosage is usually associated with hyperpyrexia, convulsions, and cardiovascular shock. The intravenous use of these drugs since the 1960s has resulted fairly often in cases of severe serum hepatitis, lung abscess, and endocarditis. In 1970 necrotizing angiitis was first reported.

In most cases, amphetamine psychosis clears in a matter of days or weeks following withdrawal of the drug, differentiating it from paranoid schizophrenia. Antipsychotic agents (phenothiazines or haloperidol) often help. The withdrawal depression, which may reach suicidal proportions, may be treated with tricyclic antidepressants.

The amphetamine psychotic may be assaultive and should be hospitalized.

Because the amphetamines are far more dangerous than heroin, both physically and mentally, there is a slowly growing belief that they should never be used. Street wisdom which states that "speed kills," appears in this case to be closer to the truth than traditional medical mythology.

Hallucinogens

The best known hallucinogens are LSD, peyote, mescaline, psilocybin. More recent synthetic products are less well known and include DOM (also called STP), DMT, DET, DPT, MDA, and the animal tranquilizer PCP. Also used are nutmeg, morning glory seeds, and dried sea horses.

These drugs produce a host of contradictory effects which appear to be related to the underlying personality structure of the user as well as to the set and setting. Persons who are comfortable and open to the experience report profound insights, mystical union, and an increase in creativity.

These drugs may have some slight capacity for psychological dependence but none for physical dependence. Tolerance develops rapidly. If they are used continually for 3 or 4 days, there is little psychodelic effect from them.

The most important treatment approach to the person having a "bad trip" is the giving of reassurance, comfort, and support, preferably by someone experienced in the use of hallucinogens.

The impact on society of the widespread use of these drugs may well rival that of the industrial revolution when viewed by future historians.

Other Drug Dependence

Glue sniffing in the 1970s has been a fairly common practice among the very young (age six to sixteen). Tolerance develops over weeks or months and the user may require up to seven tubes of glue to achieve the desired C.N.S. depressant effect which is inebriation accompanied by a breakdown of inhibitions. As in an alcohol "drunk," amnesia for the acute intoxication may occur.

A severe psychological dependence may develop. Irreversible tissue damage to the bone marrow, brain, liver, and kidneys may occur. The solvent toluene is the usual active agent.

References

Bomberg, W.: The marijuana hassle: Away out. Med. Insight, 4:24 (September) 1972.

Brill, H.: Young people and the drug scene—who is to blame? Family Health, 3:46 (May) 1971.

Brink, P.: Behavioral characteristics of heroin addicts on a short-term detoxification program. Nurs. Research, 21:38 (January-February) 1972.

Detre, T. P. and Jarecki, H. G.: Modern Psychiatric Treatment. Philadelphia, J. B. Lippincott, 1971.
Morgan, A. J. and Moreno, J. W.: The Practice of Mental Health Nursing: A Community Approach. Philadelphia, J. B. Lippincott, 1973.
Zwick, D., et al.: Workshop on drug abuse. Nurs. Outlook, 19:476 (July) 1971.

Discussion Questions

THE SITUATION:

In the psychiatric division at University Hospital, a new patient is admitted. He is twenty-three years of age, a native of India, who has just started his third year of university work. His history records that he has roomed with three American students and that until just recently they had found him to be highly intelligent, very studious, gentle and mild in his manners, and deeply appreciative of their friendship and help in learning American manners and idioms. While they had gone to their various homes during the past summer vacation, Jim, as they called him, had stayed on in the apartment, taking some summer classes.

When they returned, they noticed that Jim seemed more quiet than usual. At times, he seemed lost in reflection, and he did not join in their fun. He seemed to find it increasingly difficult to socialize with them. They wondered if he had been studying too hard, or if he were ill. They urged him to go over to the Student Health Center for a checkup. His appetite was very poor and he did not seem to be resting well at night, often getting up and walking around. They wondered if he were worried about something. His withdrawal became more pronounced.

Then Jim started cutting classes. He kept insisting he was all right, refusing to go to the clinic. His friends found out that he had not been in classes all week. When they pressed him for a reason, he startled them by telling them that an enemy had planted a woman's uterus in his abdomen and that it was upsetting him all over. He said he would not go to a doctor unless the doctor would believe in his problem, that he had to have this uterus removed surgically or it would kill him!

Two of his roommates went over to the clinic and discussed the situation with one of the staff doctors, who sent them to the hospital to talk to a psychiatrist on the staff there. It was decided that Jim must be admitted at once to the psychiatric ward, willingly or unwillingly.

The three friends tried to talk Jim into going over to the hospital with them but he refused. They finally forced him downstairs and into their car and drove him to the hospital. He was most angry with them all, accusing them of siding with the enemy.

Arriving on the ward, he wandered back and forth in the day room, moaning in his anguish. He stopped every nurse and every doctor who came and went on the ward, to tell them of the distress this uterus was causing him, and pleading for immediate surgery to remove the organ.

A student nurse, deeply compassionate, listened to his story repeatedly and tried to comfort him.

QUESTIONS:
1. Is this patient suffering with a neurosis or with a psychosis?
2. Is he delusional or hallucinative?
3. What environmental factors might have contributed to his disturbance?
4. What should the student nurse do in the face of his insistence as to his having a uterus?
5. What are some of the things she could say to him that would ease some of his anxiety and comfort him, at least temporarily?
6. From his personality traits and symptoms, what might be the diagnosis of his type of mental disturbance?
7. What do you think of the decision to hospitalize Jim "willingly or unwillingly"?
8. In what ways were Jim's civil liberties safeguarded?
9. If Jim's thinking clears in 48 hours would you consider the diagnosis of amphetamine psychosis? How would you prove this?

Developmental
Disabilities
and Epilepsy

The History and Scope of Mental Retardation

Behavioral Objectives

The student successfully attaining the goals of this chapter will be able to:

- Compare past attitudes toward the mentally retarded with the attitudes today and explain how care of the mentally retarded has changed over the years.
- Explain how the National Association for Retarded Children has helped and continues to help improve the care of the mentally retarded.
- Describe the advances which have been made in regards to the education of the mentally retarded.
- List the 3 categories of mental retardation and describe the ability level of each.

The most universally accepted definition of mental retardation in use today is that adopted by the American Association on Mental Deficiency in 1961: "Mental retardation refers to sub-average intellectual functioning which originates in the developmental period and is associated with impairment in adaptive behavior."

The terms "idiot," "imbecile," and "moron" are still in common use in Europe. "Feeblemindedness" was used in the past in America to refer to the mild forms of mental retardation and continues to be used in Great Britain. "Oligophrenia" is still commonly used in the U.S.S.R. and some other Western European countries. None of these terms are currently popular in the U.S.

Incidence

Approximately 3 percent (6 million) of the population of the United States is said to be mentally retarded, but precise data are not available.

The vast majority (87 percent) of the mentally retarded are classified as "borderline" or "mildly retarded," while the remainder (13 percent) are classified as "moderate," "severe," or "profound." Only about 60,000 to 90,000 of the mentally retarded population, those in the severe or profound categories, require lifetime custodial care. A disproportionately large number of the mildly retarded group of 5 million come from the lower socioeconomic levels of society.

History

The recorded history of man clearly indicates that among all races and in every civilization, there have been persons who have had subnormal minds. The overall attitude toward these helpless people has been one of ridicule, disparagement, and rejection. They have been considered unworthy of respect as individuals, less than human, without dignity, and of little value to society.

The parents of retarded children have invariably felt stigmatized. Feelings of guilt and disgrace have often overwhelmed them so that they have often kept such a child in seclusion, so that society would not know of its existence. The cry of "Why has this happened to us?" is heard over and over again. Even today, in spite of open discussion and publicized information about retardation, young parents of a retarded child still have great difficulty in accepting this verdict.

Although we were told many centuries ago that we were indeed our "brothers' keepers," it has taken society a very long while to put this concept into practice. First, we became interested in the welfare of the physically handicapped—the crippled, the blind, the deaf, the ill. Then we began to perceive that the mentally ill needed and deserved more than incarceration behind locked doors and barred windows. We slowly developed the concept that illness of the mind was akin to illness of the body, and that to become mentally ill was not a disgrace. With this changed attitude, we began to unlock the doors, remove the restraints, and to start treating the mentally ill like first-class citizens.

And now, at last, the plight of the retarded members of society is coming to the foreground. Attitudes toward the retarded are changing. New knowledge and understanding is motivating us to change our old negative attitudes for fresh, positive ones. In our institutions and homes for the retarded, a new sense of expectancy is in the air. The old custodial care is being replaced by therapeutic care. We are coming to realize that it is a rare person who cannot change in some way for the better. We are busy learning new ways to activate and motivate our patients. Hospital teams are searching for means to develop each and every patient up to his full potential, to help him grow to his maximum capacity mentally, emotionally, and physically.

Growing Interest in Retardation

What are some of the factors behind this sudden upsurge and interest in retardation? They are multiple. A few of the outstanding activators are: (1) The national, state, and local chapters of the Association for Retarded Children. This organization is composed chiefly of parents of retarded children who have pooled their strength and are highly motivated to lobby and legislate for research in the field of retardation, for its prevention, and for better care for their children. (2) The space given by our advertising media (papers, books, magazines, films, and television) to acquaint the public with the problem. (3) Increased research into the cause and prevention of retardation. (4) Federal assistance in the form of grants to states, foundations, and groups to aid them in the study of retardation. (5) President Kennedy's deep interest in the subject of retardation and the panel he set up in 1962 to study and combat it.

All of these factors are acting together as a ferment, and many new training programs and research projects are under way. On May 11, 1966, President Johnson established the President's Committee on Mental Retardation to supervise federal programs and to study and make bold new plans for the retarded.

Education for the Retarded

Too often, in the past, we have assumed that because a retarded person seemed to be functioning at a certain limited level, that that level was all he was capable of. Those who work with the retarded can assess the capacities and the abilities of their charges, evaluate their own attitudes on retardation, and try new means of stimulating, motivating, and teaching the retarded.

In a number of states, local school districts have set up special classes for the educable retarded in the public school systems. Instructors must take special training in the area of teaching the slow learner. With these special classes, fewer and fewer mildly retarded children need to be institutionalized. They live at home and pursue academic learning in classes geared to their level of accomplishment.

Some public schools now have classes for trainable retardates. As this trend grows, it is likely that many trainable children will be helped in the public school system, and very few will be institutionalized in the future.

In recent years a number of daytime activity centers have been started in towns and cities. Community mental health/mental retardation centers examine and diagnose retardates and counsel parents. The problem of retardation is being approached in many ways; tremendous progress has been made this past decade. A few years ago, parents of a retarded child had only three resources open to them: to keep their child at home without special care, place him in a state institution, or place him in a very expensive private residential school.

A variety of community services have been established to bridge the gap between these extremes. The child can have the love and care of his parents at home and still receive special training and education in local agencies.

The National Association for Retarded Children, with its state and local branches, is very active in lobbying for better legislation and more funds for the mentally retarded. This organization is also of great help to the parents of retarded persons, providing the understanding and emotional support they need.

The Levels of Retardation

The Mildly Retarded

The large majority of our retarded belong to the mildly retarded class. Most of them are capable of academic learning, though they learn more slowly than normal children of the same age. They need prolonged and repeated exposure to new areas of learning. They tend to retain learning once they have acquired it, and their thinking tends to be concrete; they have difficulty with abstract thinking. Mathematics, being an abstract subject, is difficult for many mildly retarded persons to grasp.

Most of this group live at home. They are seldom institutionalized unless they have behavior problems or are also the victims of frequent epileptic seizures. If they socialize well with others, they may earn their own living, marry, and raise families, and never be considered by society to be subnormal. These people form a large segment of the group of unskilled laborers. They are the cheerful, kindly, responsible workers who take pride in their jobs and make good neighbors, parents, and citizens. Few of them finish high school, most dropping out in the elementary grades because of inability to keep up with regular classes.

The Moderately Retarded

The moderately retarded group are more handicapped in adjusting to life and living. They may be trained to be fairly self-sufficient in the simple activities of daily living (feeding, toileting, dressing themselves, etc.) and trained to perform simple work tasks, but they need varying degrees of supervision in all these areas. Few of them learn to read and write. They are usually able to adjust to home or institutional routines but are not able to support themselves or supply their own needs.

The Severely Retarded

The severely and profoundly retarded almost all need total care. Their intellectual level is too low to enable them to meet any but the simplest needs. Some can finger feed themselves; a few can use spoons or forks; many cannot be toilet trained; many are nonverbal; those who are verbal usually communicate with single words or short phrases.

The lower the level of intelligence, the more dependent the person is on the services of others.

Table 23-1

Developmental Characteristics of the Mentally Retarded*

DEGREE OF MENTAL RETARDA-TION	PRESCHOOL AGE 0–5 MATURATION AND DEVELOPMENT	SCHOOL AGE 6–20 TRAINING AND EDUCATION	ADULT 21 AND OVER SOCIAL AND VOCA-TIONAL ADEQUACY
Profound I. Q. 0-20	Gross retardation; minimal capacity for functioning in sensorimotor areas; needs nursing care	Some motor development present; may respond to minimal or limited training in self-help	Some motor and speech development; may achieve very limited self-care; needs nursing care
Severe I. Q. 20-35	Poor motor development; minimal speech; generally unable to profit from training in self-help; little or no communication skills	Can talk or learn to communicate; can be trained in elemental health habits; profits from systematic habit training	May contribute partially to self-maintenance under complete supervision; can develop self-protection skills to a minimal useful level in controlled environment
Moderate I. Q. 36-51	Can talk or learn to communicate; poor social awareness; fair motor development; profits from training in self-help; can be managed with moderate supervision	Can profit from training in social and occupational skills; unlikely to progress beyond second grade level in academic subjects; may learn to travel alone in familiar places	May achieve self-maintenance in unskilled or semiskilled work under sheltered conditions; needs supervision and guidance when under mild social or economic stress
Mild I. Q. 52-67	Can develop social and communication skills; minimal retardation in sensorimotor areas; often not distinguished from normal until later age	Can learn academic skills up to approximately sixth grade level by late teens; can be guided toward social conformity	Can usually achieve social and vocational skills adequate to minimal self-support but may need guidance and assistance when under unusual social or economic stress

* Adapted from *Mental Retardation Activities of the U. S. Department of Health, Education, and Welfare*. United States Government Printing Office, Washington, D.C.

Multiple Afflictions

Mental illness can afflict people at all intelligence levels—the genius, the brilliant, the normal, and the subnormal individual. Thus, we may find overlays of mental illnesses in retardates.

Physical abnormalities often appear in retardates also, especially in the profoundly retarded group. Often the genetic defect responsible for defective intelligence also causes abnormal formation and functioning of the physical structure.

It is estimated that about 30 percent of all institutionalized retardates are also epileptic. The seizures may or may not be associated with the nervous system damage that produces the retardation.

Consider, then, the triply afflicted child, one who may be physically handicapped, mentally defective, and seizure prone. If he should also have an overlay of mental illness, it would seem that all the woes to which man is heir can meet here in one small, frail body.

References

Carter, C. H.: Handbook of Mental Retardation Syndromes. ed. 2. Springfield, Charles C Thomas, 1970.

Masterson, J.: Treatment of the adolescent with borderline syndrome, Bull. Menn. Clinic, 35:5, 1971.

Schwartz, L. and Schwartz, J.: The Psychodynamics of Patient Care. Englewood Cliffs, N.J., Prentice-Hall, 1972.

Tredgold, R. R., and Soddy, K.: Textbook of Mental Deficiency. ed. 11. Baltimore, Williams & Wilkins, 1970.

Causes and Criteria of Mental Retardation

Behavioral Objectives

The student successfully attaining the goals of this chapter should be able to:

- List 10 physical causes of mental retardation, occurring before the birth of a child, during birth, and in early childhood.
- Explain the concept of scholastic educability as a basis for judging mental ability and indicate why it is not a reliable basis of judgment.
- Write down the equation for determining I.Q. and explain the meaning of the various parts of the equation.
- Calculate the I.Q. of a 10-year-old child whose level of achievement is equivalent to a 12-year-old; then calculate the I.Q. of a 10-year-old whose level of achievement is equivalent to an 8-year-old.
- Identify the 8 classifications of mental ability, noting the I.Q. range of each, the age level reflected by this range, and the ability implied.
- Describe the responsibility which society has toward the mentally retarded.

Retardation may be present at birth or it may begin during childhood. Its causes are many and diverse and, in some cases, as yet unknown.

Some forms are familial or genetic (i.e, they are transmitted through parental genes from generation to generation or parental genes may become damaged or rearranged by accident or radiation).

Some forms are thought to be due to damage of the developing nervous system of the embryo in the mother's uterus. This damage may be due to a variety of things.

Some forms are blamed on the stress of birth. The baby's head molds and is subjected to great pressure as it advances in the birth canal, and considerable damage can occur to the delicate blood vessels in the brain.

Anoxia, or lack of sufficient oxygen to the brain, can cause retardation. This oxygen starvation can occur prenatally, paranatally, or postnatally.

Childhood diseases, with high fever and toxicicity, can result in brain damage, especially in the very young; glandular imbalances may prevent normal C.N.S. growth; chemical imbalances in the blood may result in brain damage; accidents and falls may seriously injure the brain.

By far the greatest cause of mental retardation can be ascribed to social, cultural, and economic factors. These are classed as environmental factors, and we are just becoming more and more aware of the importance of the environment on our learning processes. If a child is functioning at a lower level than normal, and this is due to cultural deprivation, it is thought quite possible for him to achieve normal intellectual growth, provided he receives early and adequate help. Other forms of retardation, however, appear to be self-limiting; it is possible for us to develop a mind up to its full potential, but we are not able to change its innate intelligence level.

How and where do we draw the line between normal and subnormal mental development, between so-called complete and incomplete development?

There are, today, three commonly accepted criteria by which we attempt to evaluate, or judge, the normal or complete mind. These are: the **educational** criterion, the criterion of the intelligence quotient (the **I.Q.**), and the **biological and social** criterion. Let us examine these three standards and see how well they perform their function.

The Educational Criterion

Scholastic educability or the ability to maintain a certain standard of scholastic efficiency was the earliest standard used to measure intelligence. It boils down simply to this: can a child learn certain academic subjects in school at the same rate of speed as his peers? If he can, he is labeled "normal." If he falls behind, if he cannot grasp new ideas or concepts as rapidly as his classmates, he is labeled "subnormal."

But this criterion, if used alone, may fail to determine true subnormality. There are very wide differences in individual responses to scholastic instruction and in ability to learn particular subjects. A child may be apt at mathematics and very poor in languages; he may do well in social studies and badly in mathematics; he may be a slow learner because of anemia, poor vision, poor hearing, emotional problems, lack of motivation, or lack of environmental stimulation.

Many children who have failed in school are, after leaving school, found to be quite capable of earning a living, of protecting their interests, and of fending for themselves. Therefore, it would seem that scholastic educability alone is not a scientific or justifiable criterion.

The Criterion of the Intelligence Quotient

At the turn of the century, two Frenchmen, Binet and Simon of Paris, compiled a series of tests for each year between three and sixteen which the average child of these years was able to pass. It was considered that ability to do so was dependent upon "natural intelligence." The response to these tests, expressed as a percentage, constitutes the intelligence quotient (I.Q.).

The formula for determining this is $I.Q. = \dfrac{M.A.}{C.A.} \times 100$.

M.A. stands for the mental age of the patient as established by a series of tests, and C.A. for his chronological age. His mental age is divided by his chronological age and this result is multiplied by 100 to put it into percentage.

Thus a child who has a chronological age of 8 (i.e., he is 8 years old), and who has a mental age of 8 (he successfully passed those tests pertaining to the 8-year-old level) would have an I.Q. of 100 (which is the mean average).

$$\frac{8 \text{ M.A.}}{8 \text{ C.A.}} \times 100 = 100$$

Should this 8-year-old successfully pass the tests applicable to the 12-year-old level, his I.Q. would be 150.

$$\frac{12 \text{ M.A.}}{8 \text{ C.A.}} \times 100 = 150$$

Should he be unable to pass the tests compatible with his chronological age and test at only the 6-year-old level, he would have an I.Q. of 75.

$$\frac{6 \text{ M.A.}}{8 \text{ C.A.}} \times 100 = 75$$

The original Simon-Binet tests have been changed and modified and many new intelligence tests are in use today. One, widely used, is a modification of the Binet test made at Stanford University in California, known as the Stanford-Binet Test.

At the present time, using a new classification decided upon within this past decade, the various intelligence levels are grouped thus:

Profoundly Retarded (0–20 I.Q.). These persons are functioning mentally at the approximate level of babies and small children. Their ability to think, reason, and express themselves will ordinarily not surpass the level of a normal three-year-old. They usually require total care. However, we must remember that a person with such a mental level may be forty years of age and have a normal, maturely developed body. He will have been subjected to many experiences and feelings that a normal three-year-old has not experienced. Therefore, we must realize that such a comparison cannot be a rigid or accurate one.

Severely Retarded (20-35 I.Q.). These persons have a mental competence comparable to that of a three-to-five-year-old child. Again, I must caution you that considerable modification can occur just because this person may have lived for many years more than the three-to-five-year-old child. Some of the patients at this level are trainable in the simpler activities of daily living, such as being able to finger-feed themselves, use a spoon, and drink from a cup or glass; some can be toilet trained. Most of those who are verbal tend to use single words or very short phrases. They can usually make their wants known. They need considerable help in dressing themselves and are very dependent on others.

Moderately Retarded (36-51 I.Q.). These persons have a mental competence comparable to that of the five- to seven-year-old child. They are much more independent than the severely retarded group in self care, but they still need considerable supervision. Many of these persons can be trained to sew, knit, iron, do housework, care for stock and animals on farms, and perform valuable services in institutions.

Mildly Retarded (52-67 I.Q.). These persons are functioning at the seven-to-ten-year-old level. Most of them are educable up to about the fourth or fifth grade; a few may go a little higher.

Borderline (68-83 I.Q.). These people are functioning at about the twelve-year-old level and are educable. Given sufficient time for a slower learning ability, many of them are capable of finishing all eight grades, and a few are able to go part way through high school. This group includes the largest group of retardates, most of whom live in their own homes, and many of whom will become self-supporting and raise families.

Normal (84-115 I.Q.). We consider 100 I.Q. as representing the *average normal* intelligence; thus, 88 would be a low normal; 112 would be a high normal.

Brilliant (115-140 I.Q.). In this range are found the highly intelligent persons who are capable of contributing much to society.

Genius (I.Q. from 140 . . .). Here we find the exceptionally gifted, and there *is* no upper limit.

While the I.Q. concept does measure the comparative ability to learn fairly well, it should not be accepted as the sole criterion for the diagnosis of mental retardation; there are some persons who are regarded by society as being mentally defective who have I.Q.'s higher than many who are considered of normal intelligence.

Today, much thought is being given to redesigning intelligence tests to insure that they make adequate allowance for cultural differences.

Consideration is being given to the development and standardization of tests of social competency—since this plays an equally important role in establishing the presence or absence of mental retardation.

All tests, of whatever type, should be administered with great care. They should preferably be conducted by a team of specialists in several disciplines, and should include psychological, social, and educational examinations.

The Biological and Social Criterion

Man's increased development of mind has given him a capacity for survival greater than that possessed by the animals. By means of conscious skill and strategy, cunning and inventiveness, intelligence and reason, he is not only enabled to escape his enemies, secure his food, and protect his body from extremes of heat and cold, but also to make provision against contingencies, and by these means he has not merely been enabled to survive, but has become the ruling species on earth. In short, in the case of man, the maintenance of existence has ceased to be entirely a matter of brute force, unconscious adaptation, and instinct; it has become a conscious process and an essential function of the mind.

The essential purpose of the mind is to enable the individual to adapt himself to his environment so as to maintain an independent existence, and it is for this reason that we regard as normal (both from the biological and social aspects) the one who can do this, while the one whose mental development does not permit this is regarded as mentally retarded.

In order to justify the above statements, we must presuppose a normal environment as an essential background. Because great differences in such factors as climate, food, enemies, or financial endowment, might make it possible for some retardates to survive without difficulty, and some with great intelligence to fail to preserve life, it becomes obvious that the most logical and scientific criterion we can use is the social criterion, and it is the only one which the community can justly impose.

If an individual can conform to accepted standards of behavior in the community of which he is a part, we consider him a normal individual; if he can react to others in a healthy and socially acceptable way, adjusting his personal likes and dislikes, his sense of values, to those held by the community, he is classed as normal.

But, even using social conformity as the final criterion, we discover limitations here, for if we consider a man's ability to conform to accepted standards of behavior as a sign of his normalcy, we must also accept the possibility that he may be conforming to the standards of a criminal group of which he is a part, and in this event, it would be a sign of health to be equally criminal!

However, good social conformity has proven a more satisfactory criterion than others and coupled with I.Q. forms a basis for our legal concept of mental deficiency.

The Importance to Society of Mental Retardation

Many mildly retarded persons who are capable of useful employment under supervision are incapable of independent social adaptation unless they have special training and care. We must not only protect the retardate and society from the harm which can result from uncontrollable behavior, but we must strive to promote the happiness of the retardate by helping him to acquire the skill and the opportunity to be of value to the community, to help him become an asset to society instead of a liability.

Society must accept the retardate as its responsibility; it must learn to assess the abilities of all people and do all in its power to develop these abilities to their highest potential. The retardate does not deserve to be a social outcast; he has the same need for acceptance, love, and respect as have all other human beings.

References

Bower, E. M.: Early Identification of Emotionally Handicapped Children in Schools. Springfield, Charles C Thomas, 1969.

Carter, C. H.: Handbook of Mental Retardation Syndromes. ed. 2. Springfield, Charles C Thomas, 1970.

Gardner, L. I., ed.: Endocrine and Genetic Diseases of Childhood. Philadelphia, W. B. Saunders, 1969.

Milton, O., and Wahler, R. G., eds.: Behavior Disorders: Perspectives and Trends. ed. 2. Philadelphia, J. B. Lippincott, 1969.

Ross, A. O.: Exceptional Child in the Family: Helping Parents of Exceptional Children. New York, Grune & Stratton, 1964.

Tredgold, R. R., and Soddy, K.: Textbook of Mental Deficiency. ed. 11. Baltimore, Williams & Wilkins, 1970.

Valentine, G. H.: Chromosome Disorders: An Introduction for Clinicians. ed. 2. Philadelphia, J. B. Lippincott, 1970.

Classification and Clinical Varieties of Mental Retardation

Behavioral Objectives

The student successfully attaining the goals of this chapter should be able to:

- List 3 types of prenatal conditions which can result in mental retardation and indicate the preventive measures which can be taken to offset or prevent the damaging effects of each.
- Summarize the types of retardation which may result from birth trauma.
- Explain the pathophysiological basis of phenylketonuria and goitrous cretinism, noting the effects each has on the central nervous system as a cause of retardation, and the preliminary measures which can be taken to counteract the effects of each.
- Identify 5 causes of mental retardation related to abnormal growth of the head or pathologic eye development.
- Explain the origin of each of the following terms as appropriate descriptions of the same condition: Down's syndrome, mongolism, and Trisomy 21.
- Identify the criteria used to classify mental retardation as cultural-familial in origin.

The classification system adopted by the American Psychiatric Association in DSM-II lists first the level of mental retardation and then the causative agent. The levels, as discussed previously, are as follows:

> Borderline mental retardation—I.Q. 68 to 83
> Mild mental retardation—I.Q. 52 to 67
> Moderate mental retardation—I.Q. 36 to 51
> Severe mental retardation—I.Q. 20 to 35
> Profound mental retardation—I.Q. under 20

There is also a category of mental retardation called "unspecified mental retardation." This is used when the patient is clearly subnormal but his level of intellectual functioning has not or cannot be evaluated precisely.

The subdivisions presently recognized as causative agents of mental retardation are as follows:

Following infection or intoxication
Following trauma or physical agent
With disorders of metabolism, growth, or nutrition
Associated with gross brain disease (postnatal)
Associated with diseases and conditions due to (unknown) prenatal
    influence
With chromosomal abnormality
Associated with prematurity
Following major psychiatric disorder
With psychosocial (environmental) deprivation
With other (and unspecified) condition

Most retardates, belonging as they do to the mildly retarded group, have no distinguishing physical characteristics. Their appearance does not differ particularly from the normal person's. But there are several special groups of retardates that do have physical characteristics that set them apart. They exhibit a **syndrome** that classifies them as having a particular variety of retardation. (A syndrome consists of a number of symptoms occurring together that identify a particular disease, disorder, or pathological condition.) We shall discuss just a few of these clinical varieties. Some of these are included because of their frequency of occurrence, some because of recent research which promises prevention, some because of symptoms which pose problems.

In discussing these syndromes we shall follow the classification system listed above.

Mental Retardation Following Infection and Intoxication

This category includes cases of mental retardation which result from cerebral damage due to infection, serums, drugs, or toxic agents. A few will be discussed here.

Rubella—Congenital

Rubella, or German measles, is one of the very few infective diseases which can be transmitted from a pregnant mother to her child in-utero. It has replaced syphilis as the major cause of congenital malformations and mental retardation due to maternal infection. If the disease strikes in the first trimester (three months) of pregnancy, the chances are very strong that the disease will damage the small developing fetus. Congenital anomalies of the ear, eye, and heart are usually seen. The baby is often born mentally defective.

Some doctors advocate that all girl children be deliberately exposed to rubella whenever an epidemic is around, so that they may build up an immunity to it and thus prevent the possibility of developing it when they are in the child-bearing age. In recent years a measles vaccine has been developed which offers the hope of eliminating birth defects due to rubella. If all children were immunized, rubella epidemics would be prevented.

Syphilis—Congenital

Syphilis may pass directly from an infected mother's bloodstream to the bloodstream of the fetus through the placental circulation.

There are two types of congenital syphilis, dependent upon whether gross lesions are, or are not, present in the brain. Where there are no gross lesions, the retardation is mild, most of the patients reaching a state upon the borderline of moderate and mild retardation. Many of these people may reach middle age without showing signs of further deterioration, and they may be capable of trade training and of partially supporting themselves. As they progress, however, neurological degeneration will occur and most of them will become demented and paralyzed.

In cases which present neurological signs pointing to gross brain lesions, the defect is much more severe and the mental level is usually that of profound or severe retardation. These people make little response to training: they gradually become demented and rarely survive to adult age. They are usually epileptic and often paralyzed. Post mortem examination of the brain will show gross pathological lesions such as gummas, localized atrophy, softening or sclerosis, and hydrocephalus.

In spite of the availability of adequate diagnostic and treatment techniques, the incidence of syphilis is increasing at an alarming rate.

Bilirubin Encephalopathy (Kernicterus)

There is an agglutinating factor in human blood which is also present in the Rhesus monkey. For this reason, it is called the Rh factor. In the United States, a study of the white population shows that 85 percent of the population have the factor (they are Rh+) and 15 percent do not have it (they are Rh—).

If an Rh— person receives a blood transfusion from an Rh+ person, the recipient will develop an anti-Rh agglutinin which may cause a hemolytic reaction (the destruction of red blood cells with resultant escape of hemoglobin).

If an Rh+ person receives a blood transfusion from an Rh— person, there is no problem, as the absence of the factor does not cause a reaction.

If a mother is Rh— and the father is also Rh—, all children will be Rh— and there are no complications.

If both parents are Rh+, most of the children will receive the factor from both parents and should be Rh+. (The exception is where *both* parents have one gene for the agglutinating factor (+) and one for its absence (−). In this event, ¼ of the children will be Rh—.)

If the mother is Rh+ and the father is Rh—, there should be no problem, for the child will receive the dominant Rh+ factor from its mother, and baby's and mother's blood will be compatible.

But, if the mother is Rh— and the father is Rh+, there is a good possibility of trouble ahead. The child will usually take the dominant Rh+ factor from its father. If, during birth, some of the child's blood is forced by uterine contractions through the placental wall into the mother's blood (and this happens frequently), the blood, containing a substance foreign to the mother's blood, will set up a chain reaction which will result in the mother's blood building up anti-Rh agglutinins. Then, when she becomes pregnant again, these antibodies will pass through the placental wall into the blood of this child, where they will destroy his red blood cells. His R.B.C.'s will clump together (agglutinate). His body will try to replace these cells by rushing bilirubin (which is an incomplete form of hemoglobin) into the bloodstream. This results in icterus (jaundice) and a toxic reaction in certain body tissues, including the brain.

Jaundice of a mild type affects 50 percent of all newborn infants between the second and fifth day after birth, and disappears after a few days, leaving no ill effects. This is called *physiological jaundice*. But, when severe jaundice is present at birth or appears within 12-24 hours after birth, and when it affects all or most of the siblings (it is specifically called **hemolytic anemia of the newborn**), we say it is a **familial type**. It is due to one of two things; either it is due to blood hemolysis (**erythroblastosis fetalis**) as a result of RH incompatibility, or, less often, to an incompatibility of blood type between parent and child (an **A-B-O combination**).

Death may occur from hemorrhage. If not, there may be mental defect, athetosis, and rigidity. The degree of defect will vary from mild to profound retardation.

For the past several years, many babies have been saved from death or from retardation by fractional blood transfusions from the father or from a donor with the same type of blood containing the Rh factor.

Today, obstetricians check each new prospective mother for the Rh factor. If she has it, the doctor feels safe. If she is Rh—, the doctor will call the father in to check him. If he, too, is Rh— there should be no problem. But, if he is Rh+, the doctor will explain the odds and make arrangements for a blood donor to be available if needed. The first child of such a marriage is rarely jaundiced; it takes time for a strong supply of anti-Rh agglutinins to build up. But, with each succeeding pregnancy, this supply tends to increase and the odds go up against a normal birth. Doctors have been experimenting with fractional blood transfusions with the fetus still in-utero.

Now a new immunization substance, called **Rho-gam,** is being given to

Rh— mothers immediately after they have given birth to their first Rh+ infant. It contains, in addition to gamma globulin, a fraction of serum taken from Rh— women who have developed strong antibodies through previous births. This serum is supposed to destroy any of the infant's cells that may be present in the mother's bloodstream before she can build up her own antibodies to the agglutinin. However, since this substance is foreign to her own blood chemistry, it is slowly disposed of by the blood thus necessitating a new injection with the birth of each successive child.

Other maternal conditions and infections that can cause mental retardation in the child are cytomegalic inclusion body disease, toxoplasmosis, toxemia of pregnancy (particularly eclampsia), meningitis, influenza, immunizations (tetanus, small pox, rabies and typhoid), and toxins (lead, carbon monoxide, and botulism).

Mental Retardation Following Trauma or Physical Agent

Subdivisions recognized in this category are encephalopathy due to prenatal injury (including prenatal irradiation and asphyxia), encephalopathy due to mechanical injury at birth, encephalopathy due to asphyxia at birth (such as due to premature separation of the placenta, placenta praevia, and cord difficulties), encephlopathy due to postnatal injury (including postnatal asphyxia, infarction, thrombosis, laceration, and contusion of the brain).

Formerly, these disorders were not subdivided as above, but were called "Little's Disease." In 1862, Dr. John Little, an English obstetrician, drew attention to the importance of birth injuries to the brain. Because of his research on brain damage caused by difficult deliveries, the forms of retardation due to birth trauma were named after him.

Natal damage to the brain may be of several different kinds and produced in different ways; but it is commoner in first-born children and in difficult labors, although it may occur in premature and in precipitate births, also.

Intracranial hemorrhage, to some extent or other, is fairly common during birth. If the blood is not great in amount, it may be absorbed without producing any marked clinical sign or any subsequent ill effects.

On the other hand, severe hemorrhage can be quickly fatal and a considerable proportion of the deaths which occur within the first few days or weeks of life are due to this cause. Between these two extremes, there is a large intermediate group in which, although death does not occur, permanent brain damage results.

Occasionally, there may be a fracture of the skull with contusion or actual laceration of the brain and intracranial hemorrhage, but such cases are rare. The hemorrhage is practically always venous, and its site, in order of frequency, is subdural, subarachnoid, intracerebral, and intraventricular.

A child whose brain has been injured during delivery may be stillborn;

another may be cyanosed or markedly pale and be revived with great difficulty. He may then be restless and fretful for a time; but he usually will gradually pass into a state of stupor and remain this way for several days with feeble pulse and respiration. His pupils will be contracted and his anterior fontanel will bulge. He does not cry, and it is difficult to rouse him to take food. His sucking reflex may be absent or defective. His muscles are rigid and there are often frequent muscular twitchings or even convulsions.

Although newborns who present signs as grave as these do sometimes recover without subsequent physical or mental impairment, many of them die within a few days, and a large proportion of those who escape death show indications of permanent cerebral damage. Some form of spastic paralysis is often the first sign to appear. Then it is noticed that the child's mental development is retarded. He is lacking in interest and initiative, is late in sitting up, in understanding what is said to him, in saying his first words, and in acquiring sphincter controls. As time goes on, he lags further and further behind the normal child, and it becomes clear that his intelligence is impaired. In some cases, the child is severely retarded from the beginning and remains so throughout life. In others, the initial signs pass. The child may appear to be developing normally, but, then, when he starts to school, he is found to be incapable of sustained mental effort and of acquiring knowledge at the rate of his peers.

Some children who have a definite history of birth trauma do not show signs of motor disability, but they will show signs of intellectual impairment. This impairment is often associated with poor emotional control and abnormal behavior.

From these variations, it can be seen that sufferers from birth trauma can differ greatly in their physical condition and degree of mental defect. Some of the profoundly and severely retarded are badly crippled, or dwarfed. Others are well developed, and free from any paralysis. If paralysis develops, it is usually of the spastic type, with greatly exaggerated reflexes. The degree of involvement can vary from a slight monoplegia (paralysis of a single group of muscles or of a single limb), to a severe hemiplegia (paralysis of one side of the body), paraplegia (paralysis of both legs), or quadriplegia (paralysis of both arms and both legs). These paralyses are often followed by contractures and deformities.

In other cases, there is no definite paralysis, but a marked degree of **athetosis,** consisting of irregular, incoordinated squirming movements somewhat resembling chorea (St. Vitus' Dance), which are increased by emotion or voluntary effort. Athetosis often seriously interferes with articulation and swallowing.

Occasionally, both spastic paralysis and athetosis are found together in a patient. Convulsive attacks are frequently found in this type of patient, also.

To review the scope of mental retardation following trauma, sufferers may need complete care, be severely retarded, or physically deformed, or merely be mildly retarded persons who have well formed and perfectly functioning bodies. Some patients are stable, contented, affectionate, and well behaved. Others display marked loss of emotional control, impulsiveness, and irritability. This latter group are often highly suspicious, unduly sensitive, take affront easily, are intolerant of discipline and authority, act perversely, and are prone to serious acts of misconduct.

Mental Retardation with Disorders of Metabolism, Growth, or Nutrition

Included here are all conditions of mental retardation directly due to metabolic, nutritional, or growth dysfunction. They include the disorders of lipid metabolism (infantile type—Tay-Sach's disease; late infantile type—Bielschowsky's disease; juvenile type—Spielmeyer-Vogt disease; late juvenile type—Kuf's disease; kerasin type—Gaucher's disease; phosphatide type—Neimann-Pick's disease); phenylketonuria; hepatolenticular degeneration (Wilson's disease); porphyria; galactosemia; glucogenosis (Von Gierke's disease); and hypoglycemosis.

Phenylketonuria

Phenylketonuria is the result of an inborn metabolic defect. Each year, a small but significant number of infants are born with phenylketonuria (P.K.U.). One out of a hundred institutionalized children is retarded from this cause.

Clinical experience to date indicates that dietary control in infancy and childhood has a good chance of decreasing the occurrence of mental retardation. Therefore, in recent years, a great amount of work has been done toward determining at the earliest possible date those infants who have this inborn error of metabolism. A number of states have made it mandatory that each newborn infant be checked for phenylketonuria immediately after delivery. Thus, when a case is found, dietary control can be instituted at once and the child can be given every chance of mental normalcy.

Phenylketonuria is transmitted by the inheritance of an autosomal recessive gene. One person in 50 harbors this recessive gene. These individuals can produce an offspring who is homozygous for the phenylalanine hydroxylase defect and will suffer from the disease phenylketonuria.

Phenylketonuria is indicated by the presence of phenylpyruvic acid in the urine. Normal urine should never show this acid. When it is found there, it means that the amino acid phenylalanine is not being broken down into tyrosine by a special enzyme normally produced by the liver.

In babies with P.K.U., this enzyme, called phenylalanine hydroxylase, is missing. The liver simply does not produce it.

Protein foods—especially animal proteins—are very necessary to our well-being. Their end products, the amino acids, are essential for the building and repairing of tissue. One of these amino acids, phenylalanine (which results from the chemical breakdown of meats, milk products, fish and eggs), must be finally changed into tyrosine before it can be taken into the tissue cells. The liver normally secretes the enzyme phenylalanine hydroxylase, which splits the phenylalanine into tyrosine. When the liver fails to secrete this enzyme, the phenylalanine accumulates in the bloodstream and this excess is injurious to the nervous system, apparently preventing the formation of the myelin sheaths on the axons of the neurons. At six months of age, many affected infants have nonreversible brain damage and are obviously retarded.

The inability to metabolize phenylalanine also results in a decrease in melanin formation (a brownish pigment produced by the spleen); hence the fair-skinned, blond, and blue-eyed characteristics of these unfortunate children.

Phenylketonuria can be diagnosed by a urine test and by a blood test. Many state laws insist on both. The urine test is very simple and can be performed by anyone. However, it is not as accurate as the blood test, for some babies afflicted with this disorder do not show phenylpyruvic acid in the urine. On the other hand, an accurate blood test will show any abnormal amount of phenylalanine in the bloodstream. The blood test is called the Guthrie test. It must be done on a blood sample in the laboratory. The urine test can be performed in the ward. The easiest variety is the diaper test. You simply drop a drop of 5 to 10 percent ferric chloride (iron chloride— a clear, colorless liquid) on a freshly wet diaper. If the urine contains phenyl-pyruvic acid, a bright green spot will form where the ferric chloride was dropped.

When the condition is diagnosed, the infant is placed on milk with the phenylalanine removed by charcoal filtration. As he grows, his diet must contain no animal or vegetable protein. It is a very limited, monotonous diet for him, but by the time he is about seven years of age and his nervous system is normal and well developed, it is thought that the gradual addition of meat, fish, eggs, regular milk, and cheese to his diet will not be injurious to his neurons.

Goitrous Cretinism

This is a condition caused by severe thyroid deficiency. The infant either does not possess a thyroid gland or, if it does, the gland is so infantile as to be practically nonfunctioning. If there are other cretins in the family, the cause is probably genetic, but most cretins are not of the familial type; the causes of thyroid deficiency are multiple.

At birth, the newborn infant does not show the symptoms of severe thyroid deprivation. It is usually a normal, beautiful, healthy-looking infant. This is due to the fact that, during prenatal life, the mother's blood is supplying sufficient thyroxin for all its needs.

With the cutting of the umbilical cord, this supply of hormone is cut off and the baby is unable to supply its own. Between the sixth and twelfth weeks of postnatal life, the signs of severe deprivation of thyroxin become increasingly apparent. By the time the child is six months old, his condition is attracting attention and some irreversible damage has occurred in his brain.

The earlier the condition is diagnosed, the better the prognosis will be for the child. As soon as his condition is recognized, he can be placed on thyroid medication, and, if this is done in early infancy, his mental and physical development may suffer very little. Like the diabetic, who must take insulin daily, the cretin must take thyroid medication daily throughout his lifetime. The newer thyrotropic drugs are proving much more satisfactory than the old, crude thyroid preparations.

These are the symptoms that commonly have appeared, or have started to appear, by the sixth month, giving the cretin his unusual appearance:

The child's growth is defective as compared with a normal child of corresponding age. He is apathetic and slow in all his movements, does not readily laugh or smile, and may be so lethargic as to refuse to suck.

His tongue is abnormally large and protrudes from his mouth, which is carried partly open.

The child has a peculiar cry—a dry, "muffled" cry which is the result of submucous infiltration. His breathing is similar to that resulting from a head cold. It is snorting and snoring in character. His temperature is subnormal. His skin is often yellowish in color, loose and wrinkled, especially over the forehead, and there is usually a puffiness of the features with thickening of the eyelids, nostrils, and lips, and also of the hands, feet, and back of the neck, due to myxoedematous swelling. Prominence of the abdomen with umbilical hernia is very common.

The hair on his scalp and the eyebrows is often very scanty. The child is slow in attempting to sit up, stand, or walk. In fact, he may not attempt to walk until the fifth year or later if he is untreated. The anterior fontanel is late in closing and has been observed open in adults. Speech is always delayed and may not appear until the seventh or eighth year.

But, with all this delayed structure and function, there is no delay in the eruption of the primary teeth and, unlike the mongoloid child, the cretin's teeth are usually strong, well spaced, and even.

By the time the untreated child is a few years old, he has acquired an unmistakable cretinous appearance. His body is greatly dwarfed and he may not measure more than three feet in height by the time he is sixteen. His head is large and the skull is abnormally heavy; his neck is short and thick. His nose is broad, flattened, and pug-shaped; his eyes are widely separated and the eyelids puffy; his forehead is wrinkled and his hair is coarse and scanty. He holds his mouths open and his large, coarse tongue protrudes. His skin is exceedingly dry and rough, deeply wrinkled and sallow. His belly is protuberant, and his legs and arms are very short. Puberty is usually late in appearing and the external genitals may appear infantile at a mature age. Many of these patients are sterile.

The pulse and respiration are slow, and the body temperature is two to three degrees below normal.

Though cretins are often voracious eaters, and often fat, there is general muscular weakness and this, plus their short limbs and mental slowness, causes the body balance to be unsteady, the gait slow and waddling, and all movements to be performed with a labored clumsiness. There is general slothfulness, apathy, and lack of expression.

Mentally, cretins are characterized by a general impairment of all the faculties. While many of them fall into the severely retarded group, many are also found in the moderately retarded class and, of these, the brighter ones can be taught to read and write simple words, to count and do addition and subtraction, and to perform small tasks.

Most of them can be taught to be methodical and clean in their habits. As a group, they are placid, harmless, good-tempered and affectionate, and, although they show little trace of emotion, they are, nevertheless, capable of being pleased and amused in a dull, heavy sort of way. They are among the least troublesome of the retarded.

It must be remembered that illness in early, or in adult, years may produce a thyroid deficiency with symptoms similar to cretinism, but this is to be regarded as a case of acquired myxedema.

Mental Retardation Associated with Gross Brain Disease (Postnatal)

This category includes neoplasms and structural reactions (which may be degenerative, infiltrative, inflammatory, proliferative, sclerotic or reparative) where the etiology is unknown or uncertain but presumed to be hereditary or familial. A few of the more familiar will be mentioned.

Neurofibromatosis (von Recklinghausen's disease)

This disease is transmitted by a dominant autosomal gene and is characterized by cutaneous pigmentation ("cafe au lait" patches) and neurofibromas of nerve, skin, and the central nervous system. The intellectual capacity of the patient may vary from normal to severely retarded.

Spinal Sclerosis (Friedreich's Ataxia)

This is a disease of early onset followed by dementia and characterized by cerebellar degeneration.

Mental Retardation Associated with Diseases and Conditions Due to Unknown Prenatal Influence

This group includes the primary cranial anomalies and congenital defects of undetermined origin, known to have existed at the time of, or prior to, birth.

Microcephaly—Primary

Microcephaly means "small head." It is a genetic or hereditary form of mental deficiency characterized by a peculiarly shaped, small, conical head. The bone structure is thick, the fontanels close early, there is a marked recession of the frontal bone and a flattening of the occipital bone so that the cranium shelves away in a curiously cone-like manner. This shape of skull is always present in microcephaly, and, in conjunction with a large aquiline nose and a receding chin, gives a characteristic bird-like appearance to these patients that is accentuated by bright, restless eyes. The circumference of the average normal adult skull is about 22 inches; that of the average microcephalic skull is about 14 inches, a difference of 8 inches.

The scalp is extraordinarily thick and may have a series of antero-posterior furrows in it. The hair is rough and thick.

Their bodies are usually normal in size and fully developed.

The intellectual capacity of these persons varies considerably. They are found in each of the degrees of deficiency. The majority belong to the moderately retarded class; a few are found in the upper mildly retarded group, and a considerable number are found in the profoundly and severely retarded groups, unable to do anything for themselves, unable to understand more than a few words, and incapable of speech.

Those belonging to the moderately retarded group tend to be vivacious, restless, have extremely quick powers of observation, good sensory powers, and muscular activity. They have a considerable capacity for imitation and their power of mimicry is excellent. They are the droll entertainers of the ward.

In disposition, the majority are affectionate and well behaved, and they become quite amenable to institutional discipline. Many are subject to epileptic seizures.

There is another form of microcephaly that is not genetic in origin. It does not occur through the transmission of hereditary factors; it is thought to result from irradiation (such as might damage the foetus if the mother is x-rayed repeatedly during early pregnancy), toxoplasmosis, and other prenatal infections. The appearance of this acquired type is the same as for the genetic. In addition, there is spastic paralysis of the limbs. This form would be classified under the appropriate causative agent, if known.

Craniostenosis

One of the most common conditions included in this category is oxycephaly (also called acrocephaly). It is characterized by an upward distention of the cranium. The head is abnormally high in the frontal region, rising to a blunted apex. Its shape gives rise to two common descriptive words: "tower skull" and "sugarloaf head." The oddly shaped cranium of these patients is caused by a pathological closure of the lateral sutures of the skull during intrauterine life. Thus, as the brain grows, the skull, unable to enlarge at the lateral sutures, grows upward. While the skull is abnormally high, it is, at the same time, abnormally thin, and presents a marked bulge in the temporal regions, causing the ears to look deformed or misplaced.

Another strange feature accompanies the "tower skull" in the form of abnormally shallow eye sockets, which cause the eyeballs to protrude markedly. At times, this condition is so great as to cause the eyeballs to be dislocated outside the lids on slight exertion. Vision is usually markedly impaired, and divergent strabismus is quite common. Severe headache is usually present, and in some cases smell is entirely lost. Craniotomy has, in several instances, been successful in relieving the headache and improving the vision.

While occasionally persons with this type of skull have been found to have normal intellects, most of them presenting this skull conformity are mildly subnormal. These patients usually have normal, well developed bodies. Oxycephaly is thought to be genetic in origin.

Hypertelorism (Greig's Disease)

This is a comparatively rare form of mental deficiency. The essential feature is the great breadth between the eyes, which is attributed to an abnormality in the development of the sphenoid bone (the cause is not positively known).

The skull is wide laterally, but very short from front to back: the frontal eminences are prominent, with a median furrow in the frontal bone; the occipital bone is very flat. The nose is usually small, broad, turned up and with a flattened bridge; the palate is narrow and high, the chin small and pointed; the upper teeth protrude in front (buck teeth), the mouth is carried slightly open, and the ears are large and outstanding.

The body is small, frail, and underdeveloped. These people are prone to heart defects and visual defects.

The majority of them fall into the borderline or mildly retarded group. They are usually able to read and write, handle money well, and give valuable services wherever they are, as they tend to perform well at given tasks—too well at times, for their frail physiques are not up to the driving power of their desire to succeed. Their slight retardation is reflected chiefly on the emotional level. Hypertelorism is considered to be familial or genetic in origin. Widely spaced eyes are found in many other forms of retardation, combined with other symptoms that identify them as belonging to other syndromes. Then we simply say the eyes are hyperteloric; the patient does not display the syndrome of hypertelorism.

Laurence-Moon-Biedl Syndrome

This is a condition in which a pigmentary degeneration of the retina of the eye is associated with a mental defect. The complete syndrome is as follows:

1. Pigmentary degeneration of the retina with a marked defect in vision (gun barrel vision), with progressive optic atrophy and nystagmus (an oscillatory movement of the eyeballs).
2. Mental defect. Backwardness is usually noticed in infancy. This becomes well advanced before school age. The majority of cases fall in the mildly retarded group and some in the upper ranges of the moderately retarded.
3. Obesity. This is usually present and constant and is of the Frolich type (thick heavy hips and thighs and pendulous abdomen). These people have "tree trunk" legs—heavy and shapeless. There is no curve to the calf of the leg and no shape to the ankle. The legs taper down into the shoes like tree trunks.
4. Hypogenitalism. This may not be noticed in childhood but becomes quite apparent in adolescence.
5. Polydactyly and often syndactyly also. Polydactyly consists of one or more complete or rudimentary extra fingers and/or toes; syndactyly is a webbing or joining of fingers or toes.

The Laurence-Moon-Biedl Syndrome is a rare form of amentia, but a most interesting one. The pathological condition of the eyes is progressive and eventually results in blindness (destruction of the optic nerves).

It is classified as genetic or familial in origin.

Hydrocephalus—Congenital

Hydrocephalus is a condition characterized by an abnormal increase in the amount of fluid in the cranium, causing enlargement of the head, wasting away of the brain, and loss of mental powers. The cranial bones become widely separated and the veins greatly distended by the expansile force of the fluid.

While this is the typical picture, there are some instances where hydrocephalus may exist in a small skull, owing to premature ossification of the cranial bones, and the condition may then be revealed by x-ray or by examination of the brain after death. Such cases are usually profoundly retarded, with frequent convulsions. Death occurs early.

The onset of hydrocephalus usually takes place in the first few months after birth, though it may occasionally exist before birth or it may not become apparent for a few years. Usually, its late appearance is produced by environmental factors, while that appearing at birth, or shortly thereafter, is usually genetic in origin.

Generally speaking, we divide hydrocephalus into two types, depending upon the course it takes.

In the one type, the nature of the disease is active and steadily progressive. Such children are acutely ill, the body is wasted, convulsions are frequent, and severe paralysis is generally present. These children require total nursing care. They may be profoundly, severely, or moderately retarded, but the mental condition is of secondary importance in view of the steadily progressive nature of the disease. These patients may be blind or deaf from the pressure of fluid, and otopic atrophy is often seen. Their place is in the hospital ward rather than the special institution, and death is the usual and early outcome.

The second type—usually seen in special institutions—is that in which the hydrocephalus is either increasing very slowly, or has undergone spontaneous arrest. In these cases, the mental deficiency varies from severe to mild; in the latter type, a moderate amount of improvement can be achieved through special training.

Craniotomies have been performed to drain off excess fluid and to decrease pressure. However, they are only palliative and not curative. A shunt can sometimes be inserted by the neurosurgeon, allowing the cerebral spinal fluid to drain into the peritoneal cavity.

Mental Retardation With Chromosomal Abnormality

Down's Syndrome (Mongolism, Trisomy 21)

This is the only common form of mental retardation due to chromosomal abnormality, all others being relatively rare. About one out of each hundred retardates is a mongol. The name was given to this syndrome by Dr. Langdon Down of England in 1866. He thought the almond shaped eyes of these children looked quite oriental, but it is the only feature that does so. Today, we are increasingly using the term Down's syndrome in place of mongolism.

For years, doctors inquired into some of the prominent factors of Down's syndrome, trying to discover its cause. One of these factors, that seemed to need explaining, was the fact that most of these children are born late in the reproductive life of the mother. They are often the last-born of a family, and usually appear as the last member of a large family, all of the preceding children being physically and mentally normal.

Research into the fact that identical twins were both mongoloid if one was, but that in the case of fraternal twins, one could be mongoloid and the other normal but both were never mongoloid, brought close scrutiny of the chromosomes. It was found that there was an abnormality in the chromosomes of each and every mongoloid child's cells, that this abnormality seemed to be an accidental, abnormal splitting of the chromosomes at the moment of pairing in the new zygote cell. Most of the abnormalities center around chromosomal pair #21; instead of a single #21 of the maternal cell combining with a single #21 from the paternal cell to form the new pair of #21's in the zygote cell, one of the singles accidentally splits into two lengths and there is, therefore, a resulting number of three #21 chromosomes in each cell of the embryo.

The other accidental chromosomal abnormality is when #15 pairs off with #21, with two resulting 15-21 conjunctions.

In either case, the syndrome we now call Down's syndrome develops in this child. The embryonic damage seems to begin about the eighth fetal week. The endocrinal balance becomes upset and the results show up in numerous physical changes in the fetal body and brain. Three tissues are especially affected, the endocrine glands, the brain, and the heart. There is lack of growth of the brain, which appears small and rounded and has simple gyri and shallow sulci.

At birth, the baby usually presents some of these diagnostic features, but not necessarily all of them: the skull is small, rounded, and short from front to back (brachycephalic). In most cases, the eyes have a downward and inward slope similar to that of the Mongolian race. Commonly, there is an epicanthal fold at the inner angle. Myopia (nearsightedness) and convergent strabimus (eyes crossing inward) are very common, as is cataract. The tongue is very large and very long and is marked by deep transverse fissures; in most cases it is constantly protruded and withdrawn from the time of birth. The hands are stubby, broad, flabby, and clumsy looking; the thumb is abnormally short; the little finger is not only very short, but often looks deformed, as it tends to curve inward; the middle fingers spread out in trident fashion. The feet are often marked by a large cleft between the first and second toes and by a deep furrow running from this gap to the heel on the sole. The nose is short and squat, with a depressed bridge. The ears, in some cases, are small and badly developed; in others they are large and outstanding. The skin is soft and smooth in infancy, but later becomes dry and rough. The hair is soft and silky at first, but later becomes dry and scanty. The abdomen is large and tumid, and umbilical hernia is common. There is hypotonicity of muscles and ligaments, giving the joints an extraordinary range of motion.

Enough of these multiple abnormalities are apparent at birth so that the attending physician can usually make a diagnosis of mental subnormality based on them. Occasionally, he may have to watch the progressive maturation of the child to make a positive diagnosis.

The teeth are delayed, irregular in eruption, and are often peg shaped. The genital organs are small and rudimentary, and the descent of the testes and the onset of menstruation are usually delayed.

The circulation is usually poor and the extremities often look blue and feel cold. There is a great liability to sores. The heart is the site of numerous fetal abnormalities, such as patent foramen ovale, interventricular septal defects, patent ductus arteriosus, and aortic and pulmonary stenosis.

Respiration tends to be shallow and irregular in rhythm. The voice is usually harsh and guttural and the speech is of a peculiarly explosive character.

The stature is always below normal, but the body is proportionate. Knock-knee and flat foot are common, as are developmental dental lesions.

The lips are often thickened, everted, and cracked; the cheeks are frequently marked by a bright red flush.

In infancy, most children with Down's syndrome evidence mental subnormality and very slow physical maturation. They are slow in sitting up, standing, and walking. Speech is markedly delayed; some mongoloids do not talk until six years of age or older.

In disposition, they tend to be cheerful, happy, warm, outgoing children. They are affectionate, good-tempered, and easily amused; they are inquisitive, very observant, fond of drill and dancing, and have a remarkable fondness for music.

The degree of mental defect varies greatly. The majority belong to the moderately retarded group and are easily trained in the activities of daily living. They socialize well. A few belong to the profoundly and severely retarded group and need total care. A small group are mildly retarded; they may learn to read and write, and perform simple duties with a considerable amount of intelligence. Their poor muscular coordination and the clumsiness of their hands prevent them from doing work that requires dexterity. They are able to take part in family life very well, and truly belong there rather than in an institution.

Mental Retardation Associated with Prematurity

This diagnostic category is for retarded persons whose birth weight was less than 2500 grams (5.5 pounds) and/or whose gestational age was less than 38 weeks at birth, and who do not fall into any of the previously listed categories.

Mental Retardation Following Major Psychiatric Disorder

This category is used when there is no evidence of cerebral pathology and mental retardation follows psychosis or other major psychiatric disorder in early childhood.

Mental Retardation with Psycho-Social (Environmental) Deprivation

In spite of the great medical interest in the sometimes bizarre and usually rare syndromes already discussed, the majority of cases of mental retardation have no clinical or historical evidence of organic disease or pathology. In those cases where at least one parent and at least one sibling are mentally retarded, the retardation in the patient is identified as **cultural-familial mental retardation.** In those cases where there is early infant sensory deprivation (including that resulting from severe sensory impairment (e.g., a blind and/or deaf child), or deficient verbal stimulation, the resulting mental retardation is said to be associated with **environmental deprivation.** Most of these patients have borderline or mild retardation.

References

Carter, C. H.: Handbook of Mental Retardation Syndromes. ed. 2. Springfield, Charles C Thomas, 1970.

Gardner, L. I., ed.: Endocrine and Genetic Diseases of Childhood. Philadelphia, W. B. Saunders, 1969.

Tredgold, R. F., and Soddy, K.: Textbook of Mental Deficiency. ed. 11. Baltimore, Williams & Wilkins, 1970.

Valentine, G. H.: Chromosome Disorders: An Introduction for Clinicians. ed. 2. Philadelphia, J. B. Lippincott, 1970.

Epilepsy

Behavioral Objectives

The student successfully attaining the goals of this chapter should be able to:

- Explain the "electrical" malfunction of the brain underlying epilepsy.
- Describe the purpose of an electroencephalogram in the detection of epilepsy.
- Identify 3 physical causes of epilepsy and explain why most cases of epilepsy are referred to as idiopathic.
- List the 4 types of seizures.
- Describe the differences between a grand mal and petit mal seizure and between grand mal and status epilepticus.
- Identify the causes of a Jacksonian seizure and describe its occurrence.
- Give the 2 characteristics of a psychomotor seizure.
- Identify the specific drug treatment for each type of epileptic seizure.
- Discuss the type of psychological support needed by people who suffer from epilepsy.

Epilepsy is a very, very old disorder, it was described in ancient Persian and Egyptian records, in the Old Testament, and in Greek and Roman records long before the Christian era.

The word **epilepsy** is Greek and it means "to be seized." It has been known under a variety of names; some, which are still in common usage, are "falling sickness," "fits," "convulsions," and "seizures."

Epilepsy is the most common of all known, neurological disorders. It affects some 1,500,000 Americans. It is no respecter of age, sex, economic or social levels, degree of intelligence, or nationality. It may be present at birth or develop in infancy, childhood, adolescence, adulthood, and even in old age.

While a disproportionate number of the mentally retarded are also afflicted with epilepsy, by far the greater number of victims have normal, and often superior, intelligences. Many great personalities of history have been epileptic, among them Julius Caesar, Alfred the Great, Napoleon, Lord Byron, Algernon Charles Swinburne, Guy de Maupassant, and Paganini. In a great majority of the cases, the seizures do not seem to impair the intellect; in a small number they do cause deterioration of the mental processes. In other words, the majority of persons who are subject to attacks of epilepsy are in every other way perfectly normal human beings.

Superstition and ignorance still cause many persons to fear and dread this disorder. All through the ages, society has rejected the epileptic, the one shining exception being the Greeks at the apex of their culture. They believed that the person so afflicted was a favorite of the gods, that they "seized" him at intervals and acted through him. They gave him respectful and loving care in their temples. Many other civilizations have believed him to be "possessed," or seized, by evil spirits and have fled from him in fear during his seizure and have ostracized him in the community.

Even today, many look upon this condition as the "sins of the fathers being visited upon their children." An increasing number of persons are gradually becoming aware of the true nature, cause, and progress of this disorder, but society as a whole still rejects the person so afflicted as an undesirable citizen, some persons even treating him as a social outcast. Many old laws dehumanizing the epileptic citizen are still on our statutes; some of these strip him of all rights under the law; in some states, he cannot vote; in others he cannot marry; some will not allow him to own property; some place him under legal guardianship. Most employers will not hire him, partly due to their dislike of and fear of his affliction, their dislike of the possibility of his having one of his seizures in the presence of customers, and also due to the fact that insurance companies hike the premium heavily if a known epileptic is on the payroll. (Actually, statistics show that the incidence of injuries to epileptics, or those caused by him to others on the job is no higher than that of the nonepileptic workers. There are, of course, certain types of work that an epileptic should not be allowed to do such as construction work on high scaffolding where he might fall, and driving trucks. But the same limitations should also apply to the man with a bad heart, or one who is on heavy doses of tranquilizing or sedative medication.)

The person with epilepsy needs the understanding and warm acceptance of his fellow man. He needs to work, not only to earn a living for himself and for his family, but to experience self-fulfillment, pride in being and doing, and self-respect.

It is estimated that only one out of every five epileptics is under a doctor's care. The victim, or his family, is often reluctant to consult a physician about the seizures because of a dread of having the public know about the disorder.

Definition of Epilepsy

There are various definitions of this convulsive affliction. One is that "epilepsy is an impairment of brain function characterized by recurrent, periodic, sudden disturbances in mental function. There are also often changes in thought processes or behavior."

The brain might be compared to a complex computer engaged in receiving, sorting out, transferring, registering, and replying to messages of many types. All of these messages are flowing in and out of the brain in the form of electrical energy which is flashed over a very complicated network of sensory, motor, and mixed nerves. In a brain that is functioning normally, the electrical impulses travel to and from the special centers in the brain without interference or blocking.

In the epileptic, functioning may be comparatively normal for varying periods of time—hours, weeks, months, and even for years. But, at intervals that vary with the individual—that may be triggered by chemical, mechanical, thermal, or emotional stimulation—a "block" will suddenly build up in the brain, especially in the cerebral cortex, and the electrical charges will "pile up" at that point, and then discharge en masse, knocking out the functioning of the brain much like a bolt of lightning can knock out a transformer. In most types of convulsions that result from this abrupt discharge of impulses, the patient will experience loss of consciousness and may have a varying degree of mucular spasm.

The cerebral cortex is the most highly developed area of the human brain. It is composed of interconnected cells, some 13 billion of them. Each cell receives electrical impulses from other cells, and in turn "fires" or sends impulses to other parts of the network. The strength of the stimulus needed to produce "firing" is known as the cell's **threshold.** In normal persons, neurons have thresholds sufficiently high to control the passage of nerve impulses through the cortex. A normal nerve cell, or **neuron,** can be compared to a gun whose trigger requires a fairly firm pull. In the epileptic, some neurons have abnormally low thresholds and a relatively weak stimulus may cause them to "fire" as a group. They may be compared to guns with extremely sensitive triggers.

Many of the symptoms exhibited by the patient having a seizure depend on the cortical region, or regions, affected. Sometimes just a localized area is involved in this blocking and rapid mass discharge of impulses, and sometimes the entire cortex is involved.

Electroencephalogram

The **electroencephalograph,** which was introduced in the early 1940s, has given us much insight into the electrical activity emanating from normal and abnormal brains. This machine records the frequency and wave characteristics of the electrical activity of the various areas of the brain.

Taking an electroencephalogram (E.E.G.) is relatively simple. The patient either sits in an easy chair or reclines on a bed. A number of electrodes are attached to his head, over the various areas of the brain. Each electrode is attached to the machine by an individual wire, where the currents coming from the brain are amplified. These currents move a series of pens on a moving band of paper and the currents are recorded as a series of wave patterns.

The brain wave pattern is not the same when a person is awake as when he is asleep. If he moves abruptly, focuses his attention on something, or even breathes deeply, the waves change slightly.

When a seizure is recorded on an E.E.G., the wave length pattern will change abruptly and become a veritable storm of sharply pointed lines, tightly packed together on the moving band of paper. Depending on how much of the brain is involved in this rapid discharge of electrical energy, one, several, or all of the patterns drawn by the pens will show the seizure pattern.

If the E.E.G. and other evidence suggest the possibility of a tumor, scar, or other abnormality in the brain, the doctor may want to confirm it by a **pneumoencephalogram.** Air is injected into the spinal canal; the air will rise to fill the cavities of the brain. An abnormality such as scar tissue, or a tumor, can then often be located under x-ray. If it seems feasible to remove it surgically, its removal may terminate this type of seizure.

Causes of Epilepsy

While epilepsy is the oldest and most thoroughly investigated and written about of all our nervous system disorders, we must admit that, to date, the exact cause of most seizures is unknown. The etiology of this large group of seizures is simply listed as **idiopathic,** meaning "cause unknown." A small number of cases are genetic or familial, and then there is the group caused by organic brain damage or changes.

The ultimate factor in many bodily disorders seems to be a predisposition or susceptibility to that disorder. It would seem that while we do not inherit many diseases per se, we do inherit tissue weaknesses that do predispose us to develop these diseases as we progress through life.

Those who have a **low convulsive threshold** have a predisposition to seizures. Given certain chemical or mechanical irritations to the brain, the low-convulsive-threshold person will be apt to become a seizure patient, while the high-convulsive-threshold person will not do so.

We do know that organic damage to the brain can, and often does, result in seizures; such things as tumors, scar tissue, and vascular abnormalities in the brain are understandable causative factors. But, in the much larger idiopathic group there is no discernible pathology present. If there has been thermal, mechanical, or chemical damage to the brain at one time or another, there is no discernible evidence of that damage later on.

Brain injury may occur before birth, during birth, or after birth. It may result from prolonged hyperpyrexia (high fever), anoxia, kidney disease, liver dysfunction, or glandular dysfunction. It may result from infection that has settled in the brain after diseases like encephalitis, meningitis, measles, or whooping cough; it may arise from chemical imbalance.

All the factors mentioned above could, of themselves, be productive of seizures. But doctors are quite uncertain whether this is actually the case or whether it is the seizure threshold state that is basically to blame, with the above factors being chiefly **triggering** factors.

At any rate, the electroencephalograph shows that the form of an epileptic's brain waves when he is not in seizure are different from those of persons who are not subject to seizures. Work with the E.E.G. indicates that 1 person out of each 10 tested has some irregularity of his brain wave patterns. This may indicate that this person has a predisposition to seizures or allied disorders. But since only 1 person in every 200 who have been given an E.E.G. actually is an epileptic at the time of his testing, something more than a predisposition, or susceptibility to them, must actually be responsible for them.

Emotional upset is a noticeable triggering factor for seizures in the person who is epileptic. This is not to suggest that emotional upset is ever the sole cause of seizure, merely that emotional upset may precipitate a convulsion by acting on an already disordered part of the brain. Studies show that there may be an hereditary predisposition to epilepsy.

Types of Seizures

Seizures are infinitely varied in form. There are subforms and mixtures of forms. We shall limit our discussion to the four main types. They are called the **grand mal**, the **petit mal**, the **jacksonian**, and the **psychomotor** types.

Grand Mal Seizure

Grand mal attacks are more common in adults than any other form of seizure. The words are French and mean "big sickness." Some persons will have their convulsions only while they are asleep; these we term **nocturnal** seizures. Most persons have them more commonly during their waking periods, and many have them at any hour of the day and night.

The patient may or may not have a sensory warning of the oncoming convulsion. If he does (and about 50 percent do), this warning, which is called an **aura,** will involve the same sensation before each seizure. For example, he may have an auditory aura which takes the form of a sound like the ringing of a bell. He will hear this particular sound just prior to the convulsion and will learn to associate it with the fact that he is going into seizure. Occasionally the aura will precede the loss of consciousness sufficiently for the patient to lie down on the floor, or to indicate to others that he is about to convulse. More often the aura is so brief that unconsciousness engulfs him before he can protect himself or communicate with others.

The patient may or may not cry out as he passes into unconsciousness. If he does, the cry is usually a weird, high pitched bird-like cry that is easily identified by trained personnel as a seizure cry.

The convulsion is divided into two phases, the first or **tonic phase,** and the second or **clonic phase.**

Abrupt loss of consciousness and rigidity or spasm of all skeletal muscles characterize the **tonic phase.** The victim falls to the floor while in this state. The face usually turns a dusky color—a bluish grey—because of anoxia (the patient is not breathing). The tonic or rigid phase is the shorter of the two phases, lasting from a few seconds to as long as three minutes.

As the second, or **clonic phase,** sets in, the face may lose its dusky color and become pale. The skeletal muscles begin to alternately relax and contract; the eyes usually roll upward, and saliva appears on the patient's lips. If he bites his tongue (and this frequently occurs because his jaws are alternately opening and closing), blood will discolor the saliva that rolls from his mouth and he may seem to be hemorrhaging. Sometimes the saliva is so mixed with air as to look frothy. The patient may or may not lose control of his bladder and/or bowels.

His appearance in this second phase may be very frightening to onlookers who may think he is expiring. This second phase is considerably longer than the first one, lasting from a minute or two up to as long as ten minutes.

The convulsive movements slowly lessen and finally stop; the patient relaxes, his color normalizes, and then he will usually go into a deep sleep for a varying time, sometimes for several hours. When he does awaken, he often complains of a headache, and of his skeletal muscles being very sore.

Occasionally he regains consciousness at the end of the convulsion and will be disoriented and confused for awhile. More rarely, he regains consciousness abruptly and is quite able to get up and go about his business in an orderly fashion.

The dangers inherent in a grand mal attack are: injury due to falling to the floor or against furniture; the swallowing of his tongue if he is in the supine position, with complete blockage of his airway; the possibility of aspirating saliva or vomitus. Although biting the tongue produces a painful after-effect, it is not, as a rule, dangerous, and the tongue heals quickly. (First aid for the patient in a grand mal attack is discussed in Unit VI, under the care of the retarded and the epileptic.)

Status epilepticus is the term given to a rapid series of grand mal attacks so close together that the patient has no intervening periods of consciousness. Tonic and clonic phases succeed each other so quickly that the patient seems to be having an extremely long single seizure. This is a dangerous situation, for it can lead to complete exhaustion and death unless terminated. The status condition can usually be terminated by an I.M. (and especially by an I.V.) injection of a powerful sedative drug such as a short-acting barbiturate, paraldehyde, or Valium.

When seizures of the grand mal type start in adolescence, they are usually of the idiopathic type; when untreated they tend to keep recurring until the patient reaches his or her "change" in reproductive cycle. Then they will taper off and cease. This has led many physicians to feel that the glandular system is involved in this particular variety. However, no real proof of this has been established to date.

Petit Mal Seizure

Petit mal (pronounced petty-mahl) is almost always associated with childhood. It is thought of primarily as a children's disorder. The words mean "little sickness." These seizures are very short in duration—often lasting from two to five seconds, though they may occasionally last as long as half a minute.

There is no aura, no cry, and most often no falling. The patient loses consciousness abruptly and returns to it after a few seconds without any unusual symptoms or sensations. He is utterly unaware of having "blacked out" and goes right on with any activity he may have been engaged in.

If you are looking at him at the moment he goes into seizure, you will see the awareness in his eyes suddenly replaced by a blank stare. Occassionally, some slight muscular activity, such as the blinking of his eyelids, rapid swallowing, or a slight twitching of a facial muscle, is present. If he is walking, he may stumble (but it is rare for him to fall); if he is holding some object, he may drop it.

If you are not looking at him, and he is not talking, the seizure often goes unnoticed. Uninformed parents frequently think a child is daydreaming when he seems "far away." Petit mals vary from an occasional seizure up to as many as two hundred a day.

If a doctor suspects petit mal, he has a simple way of confirming his diagnosis; he asks the child to breathe slowly and deeply (hyperventilate) for about three minutes. This will produce a seizure in the person who is subject to petit mals.

The number of children with petit mal, especially when seizures are infrequent, cannot be accurately estimated. One of every three patients with petit mal later develops grand mal seizures; more than half outgrow the affliction.

Jacksonian Seizure

The jacksonian type of seizure was named for a London neurologist, Dr. John H. Jackson, who first made a study of it and described it. This is one form of seizure in which consciousness is usually present throughout the entire seizure, or if it is lost, it is lost late in the attack.

This type of seizure is associated with organic brain damage, usually scar tissue, a tumor, or abnormal blood vessels in the motor area of the frontal lobe of the cerebrum just anterior to the central sulcus.

It is characterized by skeletal muscle convulsion which usually follows a specifically progressive path. Let us suppose that a patient is sitting in a chair talking to you and he goes into a typical, complete jacksonian seizure. This is what you will see: suddenly the fingers of his right hand will start convulsing, then the convulsion will progressively involve his wrist, elbow, and shoulder. The patient cannot stop this progressive contraction though he will usually try to hold his right arm still by grasping it with his uninvolved left hand. The contractions now sweep up the right side of his neck and face; from there, they proceed downward to the muscles on the right side of the thoracic cage, the abdomen, right thigh and leg, to the right foot.

This is the typical, complete pathway of the seizure. However, it may stop at any point along this pathway. If this unilateral muscular convulsion is on the right side of the body, then the focal point of brain irritation is in the left hemisphere of the brain, and vice versa. Occasionally, the convulsions will spread from one side of the body to the other; in this event, the entire cerebrum has become involved, the patient will lose consciousness, and the convulsion will terminate as a grand mal.

Surgical removal of the scar tissue or tumor which is responsible for this type of seizure is often successful in terminating the disorder. It is, at least, often worth trying.

Psychomotor Seizure

The psychomotor type is the most difficult type of seizure to diagnose because of the great variety of forms it takes. In some patients with mild attacks, these may seem like petit mals; in others, with a more severe form, they resemble grand mals.

This type of seizure occurs in approximately one third of adult epileptics. If it is a "pure" type, that is, unmixed with other forms of epilepsy, it does have two distinguishing characteristics: **automatic behavior** and **amnesia** for the duration of the seizure.

Here we have a patient who will suddenly break into an automatic form of behavior inconsistent with his ordinary or preceding behavior. This automatic behavior has a purposeful appearance but is usually entirely unrelated to the situation. The most common movements are sucking and chewing movements of the mouth; others are running, jumping over objects, throwing objects around or breaking them, tearing up paper, pushing or striking people.

Let us suppose that a patient is standing in the day room talking to his doctor; suddenly he whirls around, runs over to a rocking chair, seizes it and throws it across the room. His eyes have a glazed look and he stands, trembling slightly. Then he walks back to the doctor and enters into meaningful conversation again. He is unaware of what he has just done (amnesia).

Many such attacks last only a few seconds, but others may continue up to 15 or 20 minutes in length. These seizures can look like temper tantrums if the patient stamps around, strikes out at people, or pushes them aside.

However, a temper tantrum has a cause; something leads up to this type of behavior. When a person changes his behavior abruptly and without cause, and this behavior is contrary to the patient's general pattern, and when this behavior is followed by amnesia, this is suggestive of psychomotor epilepsy.

Treatment

During the last part of the 19th century, the medical profession made real progress in studying the nervous system and its disorders. Doctors first used the bromides to treat their epileptic patients and made some headway in decreasing the frequency and severity of seizures. However, bromides made the patient feel "groggy" and often resulted in an irritating skin rash.

Then the barbiturates were synthesized and came into common use. They became the drugs of choice in treating epilepsy for many years. Their main disadvantage was that the patient was drowsy and in a state of mild mental confusion.

The first true anticonvulsant drug was dilantin sodium (it is thought that an anticonvulsant drug prevents seizures by raising the seizure threshold). Since its advent, many other anticonvulsant drugs, such as mysoline, mesantoin, tridione, and paradione have been manufactured. An anticonvulsant drug that works well on one patient for a particular variety of seizure may not be so successful on another. Doctors often have to try several of the anticonvulsants, in varying dosages, until they find one, or a combination of them, that will bring the seizures under control. Many doctors prefer to combine a nerve sedative (such as phenobarbital) with an anticonvulsant drug, as the combination of sedative and anticonvulsant often works better than either one alone. The most commonly used combinations used for **grand mal** are, in this order: (1) phenobarbital plus dilantin, (2) phenobarbital plus mysoline, (3) phenobarbital plus mesantoin. For treating **petit mal,** tridione or paradione seem to be the drug of choice. For **jacksonian** seizures, mysoline is often a first choice. Whatever the choice of drug or drugs, the goal of the medication is to either eliminate the seizures completely or, failing in this, to render them less severe and their occurrences much less frequent.

There is now available an anticonvulsive drug, carbamazepine (Tegretol). It is the first major advance in 20 years in the long-term treatment of grand mal and psychomotor epilepsy.

Today, 80 percent of epileptics are being kept seizure-free on a combination of anticonvulsants, nerve sedatives, and/or tranqualizers.

You sometimes read about the "epileptic personality." Is there really a "particular type of personality" that goes with epilepsy? Do all, or even most of them exhibit the same group of qualities or in-between-seizure behavior patterns? It seems not. It is true that many of them become resentful, frustrated, angry people. They may be sullen and hateful, refusing to cooperate with others. But many psychologists feel that it is the environment that has reacted upon the basic personality to produce this type of person, that they become sullen, angry, hostile people, not because of the effect of epilepsy upon their dispositions, but because of their rage at their treatment by members of society.

The main needs of the epileptic today are: the proper medication, understanding, social acceptance, kindness, a job in which he can function, efficiently, and the feeling that his is not a disorder that is repelling, disgraceful, or a cause for ostracism. He can become a very valuable member of society if he is given half a chance.

References

Gardner, L. I., ed.: Endocrine and Genetic Diseases of Childhood. Philadelphia, W. B. Saunders, 1969.

Schwartz, L. and Schwartz, J.: The Psychodynamics of Patient Care. Englewood Cliffs, N. J., Prentice-Hall, 1972.

Discussion Questions

THE SITUATION:

A student nurse is assigned to an ambulatory moderately retarded ward in a psychiatric hospital. This is her first contact with retarded patients. This is a children's ward, made up of youngsters three to twelve years of age.

A small girl runs up to her, wraps her arms about the nurse's body, smiles warmly up at her, and says, "Hi! How you?" The nurse bends over and the child raises her arms to be held. The student is very near to tears. What a delightful child to be institutionalized! Why isn't she in her own home with her family? The nurse thinks she must be six or seven years of age. Her head is small and round—her hair brown and cut in bangs, and her mouth is fairly large, with everted lips. Her eyes are very blue and merry, with a slight oriental slant and a fold of skin covering her canthuses. She speaks with a slight explosiveness to her speech and uses single words or, at the most, a two- or three-word sentence. It is her warmth, her lovingness that is so appealing. The music coming in over the loudspeaker changes to a polka. The child slips off the nurse's lap and dances in time to the rhythm, her face alight with pleasure.

A technician comes to take the child to an activity. She tells the student that this is Nancy Thomas, that she is nine years of age, has been at the hospital three years, and is a special ward favorite. Nancy goes off with the technician, waving and saying, "Bye" as she leaves the day room.

The student meets the senior technician and is taken into the nursing station. She wants to know more about Nancy, and the senior technician gets Nancy's chart out for her to go through. As the student reads Nancy's history, the technician tells her Nancy's parents are very concerned about her well-being and happiness, and that they come frequently to take her home for a weekend, and in nice weather, for a ride. Nancy loves riding in a car. They supply her with toys. When the student asks why they do not keep the child at home, the technician replies, "We've all asked each other that same question—why parents, who are so obviously accepting of their child, ever agreed to institutionalizing her. As far as we can learn, her parents have reared a large family of nine children, and Nancy was born when her mother was forty. The obstetrician who delivered the baby urged the parents not to take her home from the hospital, but to let him arrange for institutionalization for her. The mother would not hear of this and insisted on taking the baby home. None of us really know why they brought her here when she was six years of age, other than that there has been some reference to a prolonged illness of the mother before Nancy arrived. Perhaps she was so ill she could not look after the child and feared for her well-being, who knows? She seems very happy here and we all love her."

THE QUESTIONS:

1. From the description of Nancy's appearance, what variety of mental retardation does she classify under?
2. Why do you think the obstetrician advised the parents not to take the baby home from the hospital?
3. If the parents had been motivated by the illness of the mother to institutionalize Nancy three years ago, and if the mother's health is now much better, do you wonder why they do not take her back home again?
4. Can you think of any other reason, or reasons, why, after six years, they might have made the decision to institutionalize her?
5. Do you feel that these parents may have some guilt feelings over their decision?
6. If they brought her home, what community aid and/or resources might be available to them to help care for Nancy?
7. Do you feel the institution could give Nancy all the benefits she could derive from living with her family?

unit
Six

Therapeutic
Interventions

Milieu Therapy

Behavioral Objectives

The student successfully attaining the goals of this chapter should be able to:

- Explain how the introduction of the tranquilizing drugs has helped change the manner of treating mentally ill patients.
- Identify the members of the hospital team dealing with emotionally ill patients.
- Describe the type of atmosphere and the attitudes which help establish a therapeutic milieu.
- List the 8 aims of staff members working with patients who are hospitalized for mental illness.
- Explain why counseling family members is important in the treatment of mentally ill patients.
- Describe the role of half-way houses in the rehabilitation of patients with emotional problems.

The past three or four decades have seen a tremendous change in many of our mental hospitals and in the care of the mentally ill. Bars have been removed from windows, long-locked doors opened, drab, stark rooms redecorated, and comfortable furniture and colorful draperies installed. The old prison atmosphere has changed.

These changes in the surroundings can be attributed to a greatly changed concept of mental illness on the part of hospital staffs and the public in general, to a deeper insight into the needs of the mentally ill, and, especially, to the response of patients to new therapies.

Under the old concept of custodial care for the mentally ill, which caused the patients to relinquish their responsibilities and to regress, a great many of these persons were relegated to "back wards." Here, they were provided with minimal physical care, locked in, and left essentially alone. Most of their decisions were made for them. They were dehumanized, garbed in unattractive clothing, and placed on a rigid institutional routine. When they acted out their hostility, they were subdued with sedative drugs, harsh commands, and at times manhandling. If they did not respond to these methods and "behave," they were put into restraints such as strait jackets or hand and ankle cuffs. Even those living on the "better wards" had to submit to the regimentation, the total loss of freedom, the locked doors, and lack of privacy and personal belongings. The staff members who cared for these patients often had little, if any, training in psychology or psychotherapy. The "attendants" or "guards" were hired and placed on the wards without in-service training and learned to cope with the behavior of their patients to the best of their ability.

Some of these attendants were kind and motivated to do their best; others were ignorant and brutal persons. Even the registered nurses were without much training in the care of the mentally ill. It was amazing that anyone, under these circumstances, ever regained mental health, but some did. A great many, however, regressed and deteriorated into a state of chronic derangement, and were moved to the back wards to live out their lives.

The convulsive therapies brought new hope in shortening episodes of mental illness. Insulin coma, metrazol shock, and then electroshock (E.C.T.) were used. The latter became widely acclaimed, but, after a few years of experience with it, physicians were convinced that it had an important but limited usefulness. It seemed especially effective in mental depressions, but did very little for our largest group of mental illnesses, the schizophrenias. Actually, just how and why shock treatment improves the mental processes is still unknown.

The introduction of the tranquilizing drugs had the greatest impact on the mentally ill patient. These drugs have added another dimension to psychiatric therapy. They have the ability to lower the anxiety level, thus producing sustained relief of the symptoms of many disturbed mentally ill patients, without inducing marked sedation.

As these drugs became more widely used, much of the disturbed behavior on the wards lessened or ceased entirely. The patients became less disorganized and more compliant. Their destructiveness decreased greatly. Thus, it became possible to improve their physical surroundings and to gain their cooperation in efforts being made for them.

While the severity of the patient's symptoms was yielding to the ataractic drugs, great strides were also being made in the psychiatric field. Training was begun at all levels to acquaint hospital personnel with psychiatric care. We began to look at the patient's behavior as an indication of his needs. More and more staff members began to pool their knowledge and efforts in assessing the needs of the patient. Thus, the psychiatric team was born. It came to include all levels of professional and para-professional persons who had actual patient contact. Today, in many hospitals, these teams include psychiatrists, psychologists, physicians, social workers, therapists (vocational and physical), teachers, counselors, pastors, nurses, and technicians—in short, anyone who will be working with the patient.

When a new patient comes on the admission ward, he is made to feel welcome and is introduced to all his fellow patients. He is usually apprehensive, upset, and disturbed. This is a strange new world he is entering, and often he has been admitted against his wishes and will. Every effort is made to convey to him the fact that, at the hospital, he will be accepted just as he is, that no one will criticize him, reprimand him, or judge him. An attempt is made to explain his legal rights to him. He is evaluated physically, mentally, and emotionally during the first few days after his arrival so as to ascertain his needs as a complete person. On the basis of these evaluations, the team outlines a treatment program for him. If he is rational enough to participate in this planning, he is involved in it and thus becomes aware of what forms of treatment are being scheduled for him and why. Where this can be done, the patient's cooperation is usually much better.

On many wards, the patients are encouraged to set up their own council and form their own ward rules and regulations. Where it is possible for them to do this, they are also expected to enforce these rules. When a resident breaks one of these rules, or shows grossly unacceptable conduct, the entire ward then exerts social pressure on this person, and this has proven much more effective in reshaping behavior than when the staff has enforced the hospital rules.

The patient is encouraged to accept as much responsibility for himself and his behavior as he possibly can and is not required to assume responsibility which he cannot handle. As he improves, more and more responsibilities are offered him. Patients should be encouraged to help other patients as much as possible so as to experience responsibility and satisfaction in tasks that hold real meaning.

Patients who tend to withdraw should be placed in a unit which has as one of its primary goals the interaction of its members. The staff should continually reach out toward these withdrawn persons and allow them plenty of time to respond. A one-to-one relationship may be advisable.

We are becoming more and more aware of the profound effect that staff can have on patients. In the past, staff was cautioned not to become involved in the patients' problems. Their role was that of observing, recording, and controlling the patients' activities. Thus, a wide gulf existed between the controlled patient and the controlling staff. Today, emphasis is being placed on the necessity of becoming involved with the patient, of participating with him on the wards so as to positively influence the course of his illness. He must learn to trust, to feel that his rights as an individual are respected, that his treatment needs are being explored with him, that all efforts are directed toward helping him; that there are genuine expectations of his improvement.

These changed attitudes, plus a realistic social setting on the wards, add up to what is called a **therapeutic milieu** for the patient. Milieu is a French word meaning "total environment." When the environment acts constructively on the patient to help him function comfortably and be himself, and yet will encourage him to improve his behavior, regain his self-confidence, enable him to assume responsibility, and to socialize effectively, we say we have established a therapeutic milieu for him.

One of the most important elements in a patient's hospital environment is the nursing staff. It is the nurse and those working under her supervision who are largely responsible for creating an environment that will be health-producing for the patient. Of much importance are the interactions that exist among the patients and between the patients and staff members. The patient must become the focus of interest and concern to the staff so that they may help him to handle stressful situations better. He must be encouraged to become an active participant in all aspects of ward living. He should be given the opportunity to discuss his fears, his problems, his observations, his successes, and his failures openly and frankly with the staff and also with other patients. This can be handled best in group therapy sessions and also informally in small spontaneous interchanges.

With a therapeutic staff trained to understand the dynamics of behavior, each member of the staff should reinforce the patient's strengths and help him reduce his weaknesses. He often needs help in re-establishing contact with reality. This can be done by encouraging him to participate in ward activities. Work and play can be used therapeutically for him, helping him to work off pent-up emotions. He can be encouraged to satisfy his creativity in the making of objects of beauty and utility; and the social interchange on the wards tends to pull him back into reality.

The staff directs its efforts in the hospital to:

1. Convince the individual that he is a person of worth and dignity.
2. Convince him that the staff has realistic expectations that he can and will improve.
3. Provide him with a therapeutic milieu which will act as a realistic social setting for his therapy.
4. Meet the patient's needs physically, mentally, and emotionally as much as possible.
5. Emphasize and provide meaningful tasks and experiences for the patient.
6. Reduce the social distance between him and the hospital staff.
7. Reduce his anxiety and fear.
8. Bring the patient slowly but steadily closer to reality and to the community.

While the patient is undergoing therapy in the hospital, it is highly advisable that his family be counseled also. They should be made aware of his problems and his anxieties. Since the patient became ill within the family, work, and social settings, these settings should be examined and obvious areas of stress identified. Above all, a deeper understanding of the patient's feelings and the reasons for his behavior must be achieved by those persons who are most significant to him—relatives, friends, employer, fellow-workers. This is necessary if they are going to be able to accept and assist him when he returns from the hospital.

As the patient improves, he should be allowed short visits home to help him rebuild the emotional ties he may have broken there and to help him progress toward eventual complete recovery.

If most of his emotional stress appears to arise within the family setting, it may be advisable, when he is well enough not to need around-the-clock care, to move him to a halfway house. Here, he can live for weeks until he is able to adjust better to his home setting. Some hospitals have set up special living units where patients may room in and go out daily to their work, or may go out to a halfway house to spend their evenings and nights and return daily to the hospital for therapy.

References

Almond, R.: The therapeutic community. Sci. Amer., 224:34 (March) 1971.
Burton, G.: Personal, Impersonal and Interpersonal Relations: A Guide for Nurses, ed. 3. New York, Springer, 1970.
Huey, F.: In a therapeutic community. Amer. J. Nurs., 71:926 (May) 1971.
Isler, C.: T.L.C., or a punch in the nose? RN, 35:46 (January) 1972.
Kyes, J. and Hofling, C. K.: Basic Psychiatric Concepts in Nursing. Philadelphia, J. B. Lippincott, 1974.

General Principles
of Therapeutic
Intervention

Behavioral Objectives

The student successfully attaining the goals of this chapter should be able to:

- Describe how mental health personnel can help establish a low-pressure environment for psychiatric patients.
- Indicate the importance of providing proper explanations to an emotionally disturbed patient and describe the type of explanation that should be given to a patient with a limited attention span, an apprehensive patient, and an indecisive patient.
- Demonstrate the correct manner in which a mental health worker should react to an emotional outburst by a patient.
- Explain how the dynamic approach is used in establishing a therapeutic relationship.
- Discuss how the importance of consistency and the setting of limitations is part of the therapeutic milieu.
- Explain why mental health workers should not try to impose logical explanations on patients who are emotionally ill.
- Describe the ingredients of a therapeutic relationship that are most conducive to a therapeutic environment.

Regardless of the pattern of behavior that may characterize a patient's illness, there are certain general principles that apply to the care of all who show behavior disorders. Everyone has certain basic and psychosocial needs that must be met, no matter how different the surface behavior may be.

Acceptance

The patient needs to be accepted exactly as he is, as a person of worth and dignity. An emotionally ill person cannot be expected to meet normal standards of behavior, nor should he be punished or rewarded as his behavior approaches or recedes from such standards.* All of us have certain standards of conduct which we strive to maintain. When others fail to meet our standards, we tend to pass judgment upon them and to punish them in one way or another for their transgressions. This is acceptable behavior between normal individuals. But the emotionally ill person needs a *very low-pressure social environment* in which he can learn to live again with others, in much the same manner as a person who has been paralyzed must learn to walk again. To accept a patient as he is does not mean we sanction or approve his behavior; but neither do we judge or punish him for it. We should not call attention to his defects nor show him by word, action, attitude, or expression that we disapprove of him. We must show an interest in him as a human being, as an individual possessed of dignity and worth.

Explanations

Routines and procedures should always be explained at the patient's level of understanding. Most of us like to be informed concerning what to expect in any given situation. Mentally ill patients are no exception. What is being done and why it is being done should always be explained, and in such a way that full allowance is made for the limitations placed on the patient by his symptoms. A patient with a limited attention span needs a brief, clear, pointed explanation; an apprehensive patient needs a firm explanation that assumes he will accept the procedure; an indecisive patient needs someone to make his decisions for him and to outline procedures for him so that he is not faced with the necessity of deciding. The purpose behind an explanation is to reduce anxiety whenever possible by preparing the patient for what is to come.

Expression of Feelings

The patient needs to be able to ventilate his feelings without fear of retaliation. He should be encouraged to express his feelings. This allows him to lower his own frustration level and it assists us in being able to assess his real feelings and the motivation for his behavior. Staff members must both talk and *actively listen* to the patient. Conversation should center on the patient, on his needs, wants, and interests—not on the listener's. The patient should be encouraged to express emotions such as anxiety, fear, hostility, hatred, and anger. The ability of a patient to express a negative emotion can be a very healthy sign, for strong emotions, bottled up, are potentially explosive and dangerous. Strange as it may seem, hospital personnel can frequently be of more help to a psychiatric patient if they are the objects of his

* When a behavior modification program (See Chapter 32) is in operation, however, this tenet no longer holds.

hostility than if the patient likes them. Their quiet acceptance of his dislike permits him to discharge his emotion without retaliation. One of the real dangers of hatred and hostility to the person who feels them is the fear of retribution they carry. Therefore, the patient needs an atmosphere in which his behavior is calmly accepted and no threat is present for him.

Understanding

Staff personnel need to increase their own self-understanding so as to be better able to understand the whys of patient behavior. Each person needs to analyze his or her own feelings and motivations, and usually needs considerable help in developing skills in interpersonal relationships. Group discussions on emotions and their effects are very valuable in deepening self-awareness. Staff personnel will become comfortable in their relationships with patients only when they feel secure about their ability to respond appropriately to patient behavior.

When we are able to analyze a patient's behavior and find the underlying motivation, then, and only then, can we organize these findings into a truly therapeutic care plan designed to meet his needs. We must then constantly evaluate his behavior to see if his needs are being effectively met. This is what is called **using the dynamic approach.** Using professional knowledge and skill in such a manner that they are constructive to the well-being of the patient leads to a **therapeutic relationship.** It is important to try to place ourselves in the patient's position and to understand whatever he is experiencing. At the same time efforts must be made to establish and improve communication, especially in the field of "active" listening.

Consistency

Consistency is a measure that contributes much to patient security. All mentally ill patients are insecure and uncertain. Not knowing what to expect produces anxiety. Consistency in all areas of experience is valuable to the psychiatric patient, for it builds into his environment something upon which he can depend. A consistent hospital routine with firm limit setting is tremendously important to him. It reduces the number of decisions he must make daily and he learns what he can expect from his environment. The attitude of the entire hospital staff toward him must likewise be consistent; this consistency in attitude should extend from person to person and from shift to shift. When he is continuously exposed to an atmosphere of quiet acceptance, his anxiety lessens and he becomes increasingly aware of the friendliness of the staff.

Setting Limits

We have been stressing the acceptance of patient behavior and the value of a permissive, therapeutic atmosphere. However, permissiveness must have a limit. The patient cannot be allowed to do exactly as he pleases. The actual limitations on a patient's behavior should be determined by the entire team to whom he is assigned, and those limitations should be consistently enforced by everyone who comes in contact with him. It stands to reason that if, through his suspiciousness, he refuses food and tries to starve himself, this cannot be permitted; if he tries to take his life or the life of another on the ward, this must be prevented; if he is overactive, he must not be allowed to exhaust himself. We accept the fact that the patient has a right to feel the way he feels. But certain limitations must be drawn and his behavior kept within these limits, for if these limits are enforced in a consistent, quiet, matter-of-fact way, they contribute to his security.

We should avoid physical and verbal force if possible. Force always traumatizes. None of us likes being forced to comply with the wishes of another. But, in spite of every precaution, occasions may arise in which the use of force cannot be avoided. When it must be used, adequate help should be secured and the action carried out quickly and efficiently. While you are employing force, you should never show annoyance or anger toward the patient. Your own self-control in this situation is very important.

Reassurance

All of us need reassurance occasionally; the psychiatric patient needs it constantly. However, we should make every effort to see a situation as the patient sees it. Reassurance is effective only if it does not contradict a false concept that the patient holds (i.e., a concept or defense mechanism he is using to protect his ego). The best way to reassure a patient, in addition to well placed verbal assurance, is by giving attention to matters that are important to him, and by doing things for and with him without asking anything of him in return, such as a show of appreciation for an improvement in his behavior. We do not change a patient's behavior by reasoning with him. Simply telling him why he ought to do something is not an effective way of getting his cooperation, especially when he has emotional difficulties. The patient has developed his pattern of behavior to defend himself from anxiety-producing stress, and he uses what reason he is capable of using to bolster his defensive patterns of thinking. If his false belief is based on strong emotional needs, the more we challenge it, the more the patient will defend it. We should work at helping him develop emotional security. With an improvement in this area, he will tend to slowly develop some insight into his behavior and the forces behind it. However, insight can be a threat as well as a help to the emotionally disturbed patient. Thus, interpretation of his behavior should be done only when the patient is ready for it, secure enough to tolerate it, and able to apply it to alter his behavior. This help is best left in the hands of the psychiatrist.

We should not try to meet our own emotional needs through our patients. With mentally ill patients, each of us should be trained and prepared to understand their needs and to meet them, with no thought of return to ourselves other than to see our patients recover. Whenever we find ourselves evaluating a patient's behavior in terms of right or wrong or are critical of a patient, or defend or justify ourselves, we are in danger of letting our own emotional needs take precedence over those of the patient.

The relationship between each staff member and the patients is founded on a realistic basis. We must be warm and understanding and the relationship we offer to our patients should be dynamic. This relationship is based on mutual respect and trust. It must be able to tolerate mistakes and be able to bear the strains and stresses of termination. Mental health personnel, in order to build the trust of patients, should never deceive or lie to them. Their attitudes should be consistently friendly, accepting, permissive, yet firm. Promises should always be kept.

A patient who believes that any staff member is untrustworthy will not share his true thoughts and feelings. In order to help the patient to trust us we must be trustful of ourselves; we must be aware of personal integrity, be able to see our own goals and motivations as constructive, be comfortable in our own increasing self-awareness, be able to accept these differences without experiencing an intense need to change them. It is so true that as we become more self-aware and accepting of our own limitations and weaknesses, we become more accepting of the different behavior of others. But the patient may have been conditioned by his own life experiences to be very doubtful of trustworthiness in others, and so, if we are going to be able to earn his trust, we must be very careful that what we are doing to, for, and with him is absolutely consistent with what we are feeling and saying.

References

Abdella, F. G., et al.: Patient-Centered Approaches to Nursing. New York, Macmillan, 1960.

Burton, G.: Personal, Impersonal and Interpersonal Relations: A Guide for Nurses. ed. 3. New York, Springer, 1970.

Horney, K.: Our Inner Conflicts: A Constructive Theory of Neurosis. New York, Norton, 1945.

Kyes, J. and Hofling, C. K.: Basic Psychiatric Concepts in Nursing. ed. 3. Philadelphia, J. B. Lippincott, 1974.

Manfreda, M. L.: Psychiatric Nursing. ed. 9. Philadelphia, F. A. Davis, 1973.

Matheney, R. V., and Topalis, M.: Psychiatric Nursing. ed. 5. St. Louis, Mosby, 1970.

Mereness, D.: Essentials of Psychiatric Nursing. ed. 8. St. Louis, C. V. Mosby, 1974.

The Therapeutic Relationship

Behavioral Objectives

The student successfully attaining the goals of this chapter should be able to:

- Examine, for a day, his or her own negative reactions and feelings to other people's behavior, noting where possible the reasons for these feelings.
- Describe the way to assess an emotionally ill patient and set up a patient care plan and intervention program for such a patient.
- Discuss the suitable manner of terminating a therapeutic relationship with a patient.
- List the 4 main components of a therapeutic relationship and discuss the most effective method of establishing each.

Before being exposed to the psychiatric unit, the student should have acquired a general knowledge of normal growth and development, the psychology of normal behavior, and at least an introduction to psychopathological behavior.

She should have attended classes in behavior analysis and behavior shaping conducted by a psychologist or by a nurse-therapist skilled in this area. In these special classes, she should have developed some small degree of skill in analyzing behavior—the behavior of her medical and surgical patients, of her classmates, and especially her own behavior. She should have become able to assess her own strengths and weaknesses and to have become fairly comfortable with herself as she really is. Until she has become aware of her negative feelings and behavior and has learned to accept them and live comfortably with them, she will find it difficult, even impossible, to accept her patients' negative behavior with understanding.

Each person brings to her work her own integrated personality. She is the unique product of her own particular environment. Her attitudes and the way she feels about things have been formed in her early childhood and have intensified slowly over the years. It is not easy to change one's concepts, but everyone must work hard at overcoming prejudices, fixed attitudes, and the need to sit in judgment of others.

It is mainly the behavior of the psychotic patient that tends to disturb the student. Many students come from middle-class families with firm moralistic backgrounds. When patient behavior violates all that they have been taught to believe in, or to expect as decent behavior in others, their own anxiety tends to increase.

One of the best outlets for this anxiety is for the student to be assigned the task of writing down her feeling-reactions to any behavior that is up-setting to her, be it the behavior of patients, nurses, staff members or mem-bers of other hospital disciplines—and especially when it is her own behavior that has distressed her. Students can then discuss this behavior and their feeling-reactions toward it in class and try to discover why that particular be-havior caused them to react emotionally as they did. Was it because their self-images felt threatened by the incident? Did it make them feel angry? Afraid? Defensive? Hostile? Ashamed? Jealous? Guilty? Inadequate? Much insight can be gained in this way that will help us understand our own mo-tivations.

When the student first comes on the psychiatric ward, she is usually quite apprehensive about patient behavior. How will the patients receive her? Will any of them become unmanageable? Harm her? Will she be able to "handle" them appropriately if they become upset? Will she become upset by their behavior and show this? These and many other anxious thoughts crowd in upon her.

Her first few days are spent in becoming oriented to the ward and its residents. She is kept busy helping her patients, reading their charts, dis-cussing their behavioral patterns with other ward personnel, attending team meetings, and watching ward interactions. She becomes aware that, while some of the patients are showing unacceptable behavior in a frank, overt way, others are showing their maladaptations in more covert ways, and still others seem to be behaving in such a normal way that it is hard for her to believe they are sick enough to need special psychiatric care.

Each day, after her ward experiences, she carefully writes down her ob-servations and reactions. She takes these notes to class, reads them to her instructor and classmates, and participates in the group discussion concerning them.

After several days spent in the ward milieu, the instructor will determine when each student is ready to try a one-to-one relationship with a particular patient.

This is not a social relationship. Rather, it is a professionally therapeutic relationship set up between her and a patient for the primary purpose of encouraging that patient to exchange his psychotic pattern of behavior for one that will help him adjust to his real life situation. This relationship is, in effect, a contract or agreement between the patient and the staff member that they will work together at a specified time and place and for an approximate time interval to improve his ability to deal with his problems.

Assessment

As a prelude to assessment the student chooses her patient and explains to him in simple, clear sentences what she proposes to do—that she is going to devote special time to him daily to help him with his problems. She sets up a certain time to meet with him each day and tells him just how long each visit will last. To ease his anxiety about these "visits," she tells him he can discuss his problems with her if he chooses; she also explains that what they discuss will be treated confidentially by her unless it involves information his doctor or another therapist might need to have in order to help him.

The student must now gather all the information she can obtain about her patient and from her patient.

She reviews his chart, history, diagnosis, and treatment plan. She checks what drugs and therapy he is on and why. She discusses him with his team and with members of his family, if possible, learning all she can about the onset of his illness, his pattern of behavior, his diagnosis, and his possible prognosis. She checks his involvement with various hospital disciplines and what his response has been to various therapies.

She assesses the environmental pressures and stresses he is encountering on the ward; his reactions with other patients and staff; his response to ward rules and regulations. A mentally ill person is seldom functioning at a mature developmental level. This handicaps him in establishing a good relationship with himself and others, which, in turn, limits his ability to adjust to his environment. One of the assessments a student makes is to determine, from her patient's verbal and nonverbal responses, the level at which he is functioning. Another important assessment is the degree to which he functions in reality.

She tries to ascertain how he feels about himself (his self-image) and how he thinks other people feel about him. She is especially concerned about his behavior because his behavior is the key to his needs, and determining his needs is the primary purpose of her assessment.

How does he feel about his hospitalization? About his family? How does he view his sickness?

She endeavors to assess his personality strengths and weaknesses, to pinpoint areas in which he lacks insight or needs support or correction. Her powers of observation and her ability to record her perceptions are very important. She tends to steadily improve in this area as she analyzes her patient's reactions and describes them. She describes how he looks, what he says, how he responds verbally or nonverbally to her presence and comments. Her ability to communicate may be highly tested. She may frequently become irritated, angered, or upset. She will have to try to control her emotions carefully while with the patient, and must honestly record her own negative reactions in her notes whenever these occur.

As her assessment of her patient proceeds, she should have brief interviews with her instructor, with whom she should discuss the information she is gathering, as well as her own feeling-reactions to the patient's behavior.

Patient Care Plan

The patient care plan covers his physical needs, mental needs, emotional needs, and spiritual needs. Most students will need considerable help from their instructors in setting up their care plans. Since her own personality is her most effective tool in attempting to change her patient's behavioral pattern, she analyzes her potentials and makes the very best possible use of them in her intervention plan. She realizes that the ward environment, other patients, other staff members, and members of other disciplines, are also all reacting with her patient. She takes into account the hospital's various resources, the resources of the community and those of the people who are significant to the patient (members of his family, friends, fellow workers, employer, etc.). She utilizes every avenue of help she can find in trying to fill the needs of the very complex person who is her patient.

She should submit her patient care plan to the psychiatric team for their consideration and evaluation before putting her care plan into effect. If they feel that the forms of intervention she has set up to try to change his behavioral pattern are logical and workable, they will tell her to try out her plan; if they feel that the way she is planning to handle a particular form of behavior is not going to be effective, or that it is psychologically unsound, they can discuss this possibility with her and perhaps suggest another form of approach to the problem.

Intervention

To be accepted, intervention must be seen by the patient as an effort to help him with his problems. If he cannot slowly come to understand that whatever is done to and with him is for the primary purpose of helping him improve his emotional and behavioral state, intervention will not be effective. Thus, whatever methods are used to change his behavior should be constantly evaluated. Are the methods producing the desired result or results? Is there no behavioral change? Is there, perhaps, a worsening reaction? If one of the latter two results appears, the care plan must be re-studied fully and the plan of intervention possibly changed. The hoped-for changes will not always be successfully made, which at times may be discouraging and disheartening. At times, the patient may cooperate toward achieving a common goal, then suddenly refuse to cooperate.

Termination of Relationship

The therapeutic relationship is a very close, delicate, and intimate relationship between two people. During the course of interaction, if the patient fully accepts the nurse or health care professional and cooperates with her toward an improved mental health goal, he tends to become quite dependent on her and to become emotionally attached to her. It is not easy to terminate an emotional dependency. It is usually quite traumatic for the patient, and it may also be hard on the staff member. If she has given deeply of herself and of her professional skills, she often approaches termination of the relationship with a genuine feeling of regret and loss.

It is not easy to determine, at the start of a therapeutic relationship, just how long it may take to help a patient back to a level where he may gain enough insight so as to be able to manage his feelings, and his behavior, in an acceptable way.

Yet, the staff member must indicate, both at the initiation of the relationship and at intervals during it, that, hopefully, the day will arrive when the patient will no longer need specific help from her, that he will reach a plateau of emotional stability that will enable him to handle his own problems without her intervention.

The patient is often fearful of his inability to make his own decisions and to act responsibly. He may fear the approaching time of his return to family and job, concerned that he may not be well enough yet to carry on his work and family responsibilities. He may be fearful about his acceptance by family and friends. He may wonder on whom he may call for help if he needs it. He may feel quite threatened by the withdrawal of help from the one person who has earned his trust, helped him to face up to his own needs and to adjust his behavior to an acceptable level.

In anticipation of many of these fears, these problems can be discussed long before the relationship is terminated. Ways should be found to handle the patient's fears and other members of the treatment team slowly included in preparing him for discharge or for further therapy in or out of the hospital, as his needs may indicate. As the nurse or other staff member slowly withdraws from the relationship, she should include other patients on the ward in an enlarging circle to help promote her patient's socializing.

She should discuss his fears with members of his family and help them to adjust to his return.

To make termination easier, she can assure the patient that she intends to return, from time to time, to visit with him and that he may call for her, or other staff members who have become close to him, whenever he feels the need.

Components of Therapeutic Relationship

Let us examine a few of the basic ingredients that are so necessary for a successful therapeutic relationship. High on such a list are mutual acceptance, mutual trust, integrity, consistency, good two-way communication, and some ability to differentiate between reality and unreality.

Acceptance

Acceptance often starts out one-sided. Frequently, the patient wants no part of the nurse or other staff member nor of their help. He may be fearful of any closeness and suspicious of their intentions toward him. If much of his previous interpersonal experiences have convinced him that he is not acceptable to others, he may have real difficulty in changing this self-concept. However, it is important to convey to the patient that he is a worthwhile person, and that even though some of his behavior may be unacceptable, he—as a person—is acceptable. If limits are set on his behavior so as to help him behave more appropriately and he is supported warmly all the while, he will slowly begin to feel that he is accepted and viewed as a worthwhile person.

However, he may need to test the sincerity of the therapeutic relationship over and over again before his fears and doubts are all swept away. Acceptance is a way of expressing belief in the fundamental worth of another person. We all have need for acceptance; the mentally ill have a very great need for it.

Mutual Trust

As with acceptance, the need for mutual trust is vital to a therapeutic relationship. If we have found our world a friendly and trustworthy place in which to live, we will bring this ability to trust to our work. But, if the patient has suffered from a series of experiences that have convinced him that he cannot trust others, we must start at the bottom to establish a basis for trust, building slowly and carefully. Honesty, integrity, and consistency are all building blocks in laying such a foundation.

The nurse or staff member working with the patient, after explaining in clear, simple language what she intends to do with and for the patient, must let nothing interfere with her carrying out her contract or pact with him. She has promised to visit him daily. In order to build up his trust in her, she must arrive at the appointed time, stay just the length of time promised, and leave when her time is up. Should something unavoidably cause her to be late, or to prevent a visit, she must get word to him, explaining her inability to keep that appointment, but assuring him that she will be with him on time the following day.

She has promised him that he may discuss his problems with her if he so chooses; therefore, she must truly listen to him when he talks to her. If he chooses to remain silent, she will sit beside him, relaxed and quiet, respecting his wishes. She must answer any question he asks her honestly. If she does not know the answer, she should tell him so, but she should also assure him that she will try to find out the answer for him. When his behavior becomes unacceptable to her, she must tell him that it is unacceptable, but that she will help him set limits to behavior so that he may become able to express his emotions constructively instead of destructively. In this way, he can become aware of when his behavior is unacceptable and needs changing, that he is not being rejected for this behavior but that, in fact, someone is offering to help him control it. This also assures him that she has genuine confidence in his ability to improve his behavior and that she is a person on whom he can depend and rely.

Communication

Communication often gets off to a one-sided start. If the patient is uncommunicative, if he neither replies to her greetings nor volunteers any verbal remarks, she will have to rely heavily on nonverbal communication until he starts contributing to a two-way flow of words. Good communication is a two-way process in which the participants alternate as sender and receiver. When the conversation is not two-way, it is necessary to assess the patient's facial expression, eye messages, posture, action of body parts, and tone of voice in order to help determine his feelings. Sometimes his silence speaks very loudly.

Many times, because of fear or embarrassment, the patient may decide to conceal or distort information. If he is aphasic, he may be unable to convey his thought content in correct words; if he is a withdrawn schizophrenic, he may ignore all attempts to communicate with him, refusing to react in any way. He may give the impression of being unaware that anyone is present. However, he is usually keenly aware of and ordinarily understands exactly what is being said. He may invent his own words (neologisms), making it very hard to understand his meaning; if he has a loose association of words (fragmentation or word salad), the order of the words may confuse the communication; if he is hallucinating, he may be talking quite out of line with reality. Thus, it is very important that all questions and answers be recorded as accurately and as quickly as possible after their occurrence so that his statements can be examined and their meaning arrived at as closely as possible. If a patient has agreed to having his conversation taped, replaying the tapes is wonderfully helpful although time-consuming. However, many patients are so highly suspicious of any recording of their conversation that this is often not feasible, at least in the early stages of the relationship.

If the patient is manic, he may be so restless and distractible that it may be hard to hold his attention. He may chatter constantly, moving rapidly from one partially expressed idea to another (flight of ideas).

If he is deeply depressed, he may present facial immobility, and his dull, slow, low speech may make him difficult to understand.

The patient may be constantly reading his own meaning into any and all of the other person's communication, also. If he is paranoid, he may develop a very false concept of her meaning, due to his habit of projecting and his tendency toward referring all he hears to himself (ideas of reference).

Then, too, no matter how clearly or factually a message is presented to him, he may only "hear" what he wishes to hear, especially if the subject is one that is stressful to him. However, normal persons also often block out that portion of a message that is hurtful to their self-image, and hear only that portion that is comforting or acceptable to it.

Other factors such as poor enunciation, language barriers, differences in ethnic and environmental backgrounds, hearing disorders, distractions and environmental noises can all add to the difficulties of communicating.

Therefore, skillful observations must be made, based extensively on nonverbal messages to determine the feelings of the patient. Negative emotions such as fear, shame, hostility, suspiciousness, loneliness, worthlessness, apathy, guilt, and unreality may coexist together, and it is not easy for the observer to sort them out and to identify them correctly. The patient may also alternate between negative and positive emotions so that his feeling world may be very ambivalent. He may deeply desire these therapeutic visits, yet fear the motivation behind them or his involvement in such an intimate relationship until a bridge of trust can be built.

If the patient's self-image is faulty, it is necessary to try to help him correct it so as to enable him to find real worth in himself. The patient should be persistently encouraged to clarify, explain, and describe events that seem important to him and to help him to communicate his views of the world and the significant people in it.

Communication should be such that both parties comprehend what each is trying to say.

Because consistency is so important in the therapeutic relationship, other members of the staff on the ward should be informed of just what is being attempted with the patient, including plans of intervention. Their cooperation should be sought in every possible way. Any limits set should be carried out by others on all shifts. With consistency of treatment, the patient learns what he can expect from his environment and feels more secure.

Reality

The ability to differentiate between reality and unreality is often seriously affected in a mentally ill person. What he observes and hears may be very distorted. If he is hallucinating, what he hears and sees may cause him to respond to his own unconscious motivation and he may interpret and respond to the behavior of others in a very inappropriate way because of his faulty perception. The person who gains the trust and acceptance of such a patient is in a position to help him validate his concepts of reality, and to gently and slowly bring him back into the real world. While making her assessment, she should always try to establish the approximate degree of his distortion and of his ability or inability to respond to reality.

References

Aguilera, D. C., et al.: Crisis Intervention—Theory and Methodology. St. Louis, C. V. Mosby, 1970.

Ashley Montagu, M. F., ed.: Man and Aggression. New York, Oxford University Press, 1968.

Burton, G.: Personal, Impersonal and Interpersonal Relations: A Guide for Nurses. ed. 3. New York, Springer, 1970.

Carlson, C. E., et al.: Behavioral Concepts and Nursing Intervention. Philadelphia, J. B. Lippincott, 1970.

Kyes, J. and Hofling, C. K.: Basic Psychiatric Concepts in Nursing. ed. 3. Philadelphia, J. B. Lippincott, 1974.

Ulrich, R., et al.: Control of Human Behavior, Vol. 2: From Cure to Prevention. Glenview, Ill., Scott, Foresman, 1970.

Psychopharmacology

Behavioral Objectives

The student successfully attaining the goals of this chapter should be able to:

- List the 4 groups of major tranquilizers, indicate the side effects of each and name one prominent drug under each category.
- Identify the 2 major types of antidepressants and the dangers that may result from the use of each type.
- Name the kind of mental disorder for which lithium carbonate may be prescribed.
- List the 4 chemical families that constitute the minor tranquilizers and indicate why their use should be limited.
- Explain why antiparkinsonian agents are frequently prescribed along with tranquilizers.
- Explain why drugs alone cannot be viewed as the major component of treatment for mental illness.

General Considerations

The importance of drug therapy in the treatment of mental illness today cannot be overestimated. Since 1955, when phenothiazines were first introduced, the entire practice of psychiatry has been changed and the course of major mental illnesses drastically altered because of them. The emptying of state mental hospitals and the success of community-based treatment would not have been possible without modern psychopharmacology. The role of the nurse and mental health worker in this quiet revolution is central and indisputable. It is usually they who first perceive the need for medication in a particular patient; or the need to change the drugs he is receiving. It may be the team who first recognizes side effects or adverse reactions and calls them to the physician's attention. It is the nurse who instructs the patient in precautions to observe with certain medications. It is often the nurse practitioner who takes the medical history and alerts the physician to important medical illnesses, family history, and tendencies to drug and medication abuse. The psychiatrist working together with the mental health team in the area of psychopharmacology delivers a safer, more comprehensive service to their patients.

Major Drugs

The three groups of drugs used most frequently are the major tranquilizers, antidepressants, and antiparkinsonian agents. The major tranquilizers alleviate psychosis, the antidepressants alleviate depression, and the antiparkinsonian agents alleviate the extrapyramidal symptoms that develop as a side effect to the major tranquilizers.

There are subtle differences in the action of various members of the group of major tranquilizers with regard to whether they are more "alerting" or more "sedating," what particular side effects they have, and the likelihood of their causing a "parkinsonian" effect. The differences in the group of anti-depressants have to do with their tendency to cause more or less drowsiness initially. However, the patient's individual reaction, particular situation, and preference almost always casts the deciding vote as to which drug to use.

Patients remember difficulties with drugs as well. The man who has experienced disturbed sexual functioning on thioridazine (Mellaril) will ask for something else. The person who has a tendency to pseudoparkinsonism and has had great difficulty in this regard with haloperidol (Haldol) or fluphenazine (Prolixin) may be apprehensive of this reaction with other drugs.

In certain patients, their reporting on drugs is qualitatively different from the example given above. The patient who objects to any medication that lessens his psychotic manifestations has to be overridden.

If the patient's last medication experience was as an inpatient, the doses he remembers may be out of line for outpatient care. Too much sedation could make traveling dangerous or might result in the patient staying at home in bed. The chlorpromazine (Thorazine) that successfully aborted a psychotic episode in the winter can surprise the unwarned patient by causing a nasty sunburn in the summer.

Nonetheless, whenever possible, the patient's wishes are honored, and his comments about his drug experiences always listened to. If there is a clear contradiction to the patient's drug or dose choice, or if the nurse/physician feels there is great importance in using a different drug, all of the facts are explained to the patient and his full cooperation sought. Exercising traditional "medical authority" with psychotic and suicidal outpatients is only occasionally helpful when it comes to medication.

When a patient is started on psychotropic drugs *for the first time* more caution is required, and a careful history for drug sensitivities in both the patient and the family must be obtained. A family history of success with a particular psychotropic drug in a blood relative with a similar disease is con-

Portions of this chapter have been adapted from *The Practice of Mental Health Nursing: A Community Approach* by A. J. Morgan and J. W. Moreno, J. B. Lippincott Company, Philadelphia, 1973.

sidered as presumptive evidence that the present patient may do best with the same medication. For example, we know that amitriptyline (Elavil) is more sedating than imipramine (Tofranil), and usually a best bet when depression is accompanied by considerable anxiety, agitation, or insomnia. However, if two sisters in a family developed agitated depressions within a few years of each other and the first did well on Tofranil and less well on Elavil, using Tofranil in the second sister from the beginning should be considered. Both constitutional factors and family suggestibility play a role in drug response and information about family drug experience is sought and valued.

Major Tranquilizers (Antipsychotic Agents)

These most valuable drugs are divided chemically into four groups: (1) phenothiazines; (2) thioxanthenes; (3) butyrophenones; and (4) rauwolfia alkaloids. Of these the phenothiazines are the largest and most important group.

(1) PHENOTHIAZINES

Most major tranquilizers fall into this group. The oldest and most widely used drug in this category is chlorpromazine (Thorazine). It also has the highest incidence of allergic reactions, affecting the liver, skin and blood, although these can occur with any in the group. Promazine (Sparine) has a cross-sensitivity with chlorpromazine (allergy to one will occur with the other) but switching to other phenothiazines will usually diminish the allergic reaction. The most serious *liver* complication is obstructive jaundice, usually reversible if noticed in time and the offending drug is withdrawn. The *skin* complications include hypersensitivity to sunlight and various skin eruptions and edema. Nurses who handle Thorazine concentrate, in particular, may develop a contact dermatitis, in which case further direct exposure of the chemical to the skin must be avoided. *Blood* dyscrasias are not strictly dose-related, occurring most frequently in white, elderly, debilitated women, the most serious form being agranulocytosis. The onset of this reaction is very rapid and occurs usually in the sixth to eighth week of treatment. Symptoms are sore throat, fever, chills and weakness. Treatment of agranulocytosis should take place in the hospital and if not promptly undertaken there is considerable risk of death. Following recovery, patients should never again be given any phenothiazine, tricyclic drug (see antidepressants) or diphenylmethane derivatives (see minor tranquilizers). The nurse should be keenly aware of this most dangerous of all adverse reactions to psychoactive drugs and act quickly if sore throat or any other symptoms of infection occur, especially in the population at risk (elderly, debilitated, etc.). Of the other phenothiazines, one is of exceptional value in the outpatient setting, and that is fluphenazine enanthate (Prolixin enanthate). Given I.M. every 10 days to two weeks in a

Table 30-1
Drug Therapy for Psychosis
(Listed in order from the most to the least sedating)

DRUG	INTENSIVE-TREATMENT DOSE (mg—t.i.d.)	MAINTENANCE DOSE (mg—b.i.d. or t.i.d.)	AVAILABLE DOSAGE SIZE (mg)
Butaperazine (Repoise)	25-60	5-10	5, 10, 25
Chlorpromazine (Thorazine)	150-500	50-100	10, 25, 50, 100, 200 (30, 75, 150, 200, 300)*
Triflupromazine (Vesprin)	50-150	25-50	10, 25, 50
Thioridazine (Mellaril)	200-300	20-60	10, 25, 50, 100, 150, 200
Mesoridazine (Serentil)	50-100	10-25	10, 25, 50, 100
Chlorprothixene (Taractan)	50-100	25-50	10, 25, 50, 100
Loxapine Succinate (Loxitane)	25-50	10-50	10, 24, 50
Promazine (Sparine)	200-600	50-100	10, 25, 50, 100, 200
Carphenazine (Proketazine)	50-100	25-50	25, 100
Thiopropazate (Dartal)	20-30	5-15	5, 10
Fluphenazine (Permitil, Prolixin)	2-8	1-4	1, 2.5, 5
Perphenazine (Trilafon)	4-16	2-8	2, 4, 8, 16
Prochlorperazine (Compazine)	50-150	25-50	5, 10, 25 (10, 15, 30, 75)*
Trifluoperazine (Stelazine)	10-20	1-10	1, 2, 5, 10
Haloperidol (Haldol)	2-5	1-2	.5, 1, 2, 5
Thiothixene (Navane)	10-20	5-10	1, 2, 5, 10

* Delayed-release form.

dose of 0.25 to 2 cc (25 mg/cc) this drug can effectively handle most psychotic symptomatology. It is widely used in outpatients where there is some question as to the patient's reliability regarding the taking of oral medications. Prolixin enanthate has a higher than average incidence of extrapyramidal reactions and usually the patient is instructed to take an antiparkinsonian agent by mouth concurrently and is warned about the possibility of such reactions. If the reaction is severe, 50 mg of diphenhydramine (Benadryl) or 1-2 mg of benztropine mesylate (Cogentin) can be given I.V.

The other phenothiazines (see Table 30-1) differ somewhat as to dose and severity of adverse reactions, chief among these being drowsiness, hypotension (especially postural), extrapyramidal reactions, appetite and weight increase, depression, atropine-like effects (dry mouth, blurred vision, amenorrhea) and allergic reactions (see chlorpromazine).

(2) THIOXANTHENES

Chlorprothixene (Taractan) and thiothixene (Navane). Navane appears to cause less drowsiness and more extrapyramidal effects than Taractan and also, like Thorazine, may produce lenticular pigmentation. Other side effects are similar to the other major tranquilizers.

(3) BUTYROPHENONES

Haloperidol (Haldol) is similar in effect and side reactions to the other major tranquilizers. It may, however, produce very severe extrapyramidal effects but tends to cause less appetite enhancement and weight gain than the others.

(4) RAUWOLFIA ALKALOIDS

Reserpine (Serpasil) is rarely used today in psychiatry but is excellent for schizophrenics who do not respond well to the other major tranquilizers. Reserpine rarely produces allergic reactions, but notable side effects include nasal stuffiness, abdominal cramps, diarrhea, nausea, aggravation of peptic ulcer and depression in some patients.

(5) DIBENZOXAZEPINES

Loxapine succinate (Loxitane), chemically related to the tricyclic antidepressants, has recently been introduced for treatment of the symptoms of schizophrenia. It comes in three strengths—10 mg, 25 mg, and 50 mg, and the starting dose ranges between 20–50 mg per day with a maximum dose of 250 mg per day suggested. Twenty mg of Loxitane is roughly equivalent to 200 mg of Thorazine. In its sedating qualities, it appears to be somewhat on the order of Stelazine.

Antidepressants

There are two chemical groups of drugs with marked effect on depressive syndromes. They are the dibenzazepines (the tricyclics) and the monoamine oxidase inhibitors (MAOI). The tricyclics include imipramine (Tofranil), amitriptyline (Elavil), protriptyline (Vivactil), desipramine (Pertofrane, Norpramin), nortriptyline (Aventyl), and doxepin (Sinequan). The MAOI's are represented by isocarboxazid (Marplan), nialamide (Niamid), phenelzine (Nardil), and tranylcypromine (Parnate).

Thioridazine (Mellaril) has recently been promoted for the treatment of moderate to marked depression with variable degrees of anxiety in patients with depressive neurosis, even though its primary effect is as a major tranquilizer. Dosage range for depression is 20 to 200 mg per day.

It generally takes one to three weeks for the antidepressant effect to be noticed with any of these drugs, and the patient must usually be encouraged to continue taking his medicine even though there is little improvement at first. Indeed, the patient's psychomotor retardation, often part of the depressive picture, may seem enhanced by the drowsiness that the medication causes at first.

Once the depressive symptomatology is relieved, there is a tendency to discontinue the medication prematurely. However, the patient should ordinarily continue on the antidepressant for three to six months, and then undergo gradual dosage reduction for up to a total of one to one and one-half years.

TRICYCLICS

The side effects of the tricyclics closely resemble those of the phenothiazines, to which they are related, with the exception of extrapyramidal symptoms. Notable is the tendency to aggravate or precipitate narrow angle glaucoma, and before starting tricyclics the patient should be asked if he has this condition, whether he has experienced eye pain, or seen halos around lights. He should be examined for the presence of injected conjunctivae (reddened eyes). The hypotensive effect is the most serious side effect in the elderly and they should be told (as with the phenothiazines) not to stand up too quickly. Tricyclics also tend to produce withdrawal symptoms upon abrupt discontinua-

Table 30-2

Drug Therapy for Depression

(Listed in order from the most to the least sedating)

DRUG	INTENSIVE-TREATMENT DOSE (mg—t.i.d.)	MAINTENANCE DOSE (mg—b.i.d. or t.i.d.)	AVAILABLE DOSAGE SIZE (mg)
TRICYCLIC AND RELATED DRUGS			
Doxepin (Sinequan)	25-100	25	10, 25, 50
Amitriptyline (Elavil)	25-100	25	10, 25, 50
Nortriptyline (Aventyl)	25-100	25	10, 25
Imipramine (Tofranil)	25-100	25	10, 25, 50
Desipramine	25-100	25	25, 50
(Pertofrane, Norpramin)			
Protriptyline (Vivactil)	5-20	5-10	5, 10
MONAMINE OXIDASE INHIBITORS			
Isocarboxazid (Marplan)	10-30	10	10
Phenelzine (Nardil)	15-45	15	15
Tranylcypromine (Parnate)	10-30	10	10

Source: Nathan S. Kline, M.D.

tion of a dose over 150 mg per day for six to eight weeks. Withdrawal consists of nausea, vomiting, abdominal cramps, diarrhea, chills, insomnia and anxiety; it begins in four to five days and lasts three to five days. It is avoided by gradual withdrawal over three to four weeks.

Toxic mental effects of tricyclics are of two types. The first consists of a shift from the original depression to a state of manic-like excitement and the second resembles an organic brain syndrome, especially in the elderly, being anything from a transient defect in recent memory to delirium.

MAOI's

The MAOI's, while quite useful in some patients not affected by the tricyclics, carry with them such potentially serious side effects as to be considered by some authorities to be unacceptable for general usage in a community mental health setting. If a physician insists on using them, the nurse should definitely caution him in cases where the patient's reliability or ability to understand and follow directions is in any way questionable. The dangers are two. (1) *Hypertensive crisis* may occur in patients on MAOI's who eat foods that contain tyramine or dopa. Such foods include aged cheeses, broad beans, beer, yeast products, Chianti wine, pickled herring, chocolate, or chicken livers. The symptoms of such a crisis are: sharp elevation in blood pressure, throbbing headache, nausea, vomiting, elevated temperature, sweating, and stiff neck. Chlorpromazine 50 to 100 mg. I.M. is often effective in aborting the episode. (2) *Potentiation of other drugs.* The list is long and contains many drugs in common use in medical problems such as C.N.S. depressants (downs), sympathomimetics (ups), ganglion blocking and anticholinergic agents (used in peptic ulcer and other G.I. conditions), antihistamines, opiates, diuretics, chloroquine, hypoglycemic drugs, corticosteroids, antirheumatic compounds, and the tricyclic antidepressants.

Other Drugs

Included here are: (1) lithium carbonate (an antimanic agent); (2) the minor tranquilizers (antianxiety agents); and (3) sedatives and hypnotics. While extremely important in selected patients, these drugs have a very limited use in outpatient care as compared to the major drugs discussed above, with the exception of lithium carbonate.

Lithium Carbonate (An Antimanic Agent: Eskalith, Lithonate, Lithane)

This drug is the treatment of choice in acute manic episodes which it can terminate within ten days in 90 percent of patients. It is also tried in other forms of cyclic illness whether or not there is a manic phase, with varying success. Because the effective therapeutic dosage is fairly close to the toxic dosage, it is important to monitor the lithium blood level regularly.

Six hundred to 1,800 mg of lithium carbonate per day in divided doses usually produces a serum lithium level of between 0.6 and 1.5 mEq/L, which is within the therapeutic range and not significantly toxic. Because lithium is excreted at far different rates in various people, a serum determination must be made frequently at the beginning to be sure the 1.5 mEq/L limit is not exceeded. In the presence of febrile illnesses or any situation that causes a loss of fluids (including administration of diuretics), the lithium level must be very closely watched.

Side effects are commonly nausea, occasional vomiting and mild abdominal pain, fatigue and thirst. These gradually subside and later recurrence may signal impending intoxication.

Intoxication generally occurs when serum levels exceed 2 mEq/L and it produces confusion, coarse tremor, muscle twitching and difficult speech. More severe effects include ataxia, muscle twitching, nystagmus, hyperreflexia, stupor and coma. Fatalities are rare.

Lithium should be avoided in pregnant and nursing mothers until its safety in this situation is known.

Minor Tranquilizers (Antianxiety Agents)

These drugs can be divided into three chemical families: (1) propanediols, which include meprobamate (Miltown), and tybamate (Solacen, Tybatran); (2) benzodiazepines, which include chlordiazepoxide (Librium), diazepam (Valium), and oxazepam (Serax); and (3) diphenylmethane derivatives—hydroxyzine (Atarax, Vistaril).

The antianxiety agents have a limited usefulness in the outpatient setting. Anxiety normally accompanies growth and change and is an important ingredient in providing the motivation for most psychotherapeutic work. Unless anxiety is incapacitating, most patients can tolerate a good bit of it without medication, and find that it diminishes rapidly as their energies are directed toward therapy and growth. Further, pharmaceutical company advertising notwithstanding, these drugs are more similar to the barbiturates and other C.N.S. depressants than not. They have a high potential for habituation and addiction and carry the same danger on withdrawal (convulsions and delirium tremens) as the other C.N.S. depressants. Of the three groups, the benzodiazepines carry the least risk of the above.

As long as we have a society where so many people tend to get "high" on "downs," it seems wise to sharply limit the use of these drugs.

Sedatives and Hypnotics (C.N.S. Depressants)

Chemically these are divided into (1) barbiturates and (2) nonbarbiturates. These drugs have a very limited but important place in psychiatry. They are all frequently used as "recreational chemicals." They have withdrawal effects (convulsions, etc.) when abruptly stopped, especially when a high dosage was used, and withdrawal from a severe abuse situation should always be carried out in a hospital. When severe sleep disturbances are a problem and cannot be handled by the sedating phenothiazines, either paraldehyde or chloral hydrate are recommended because they carry the least abuse potential. A listing of popular sedatives is given here for completeness, and not as a recommendation for use.

(1) Barbiturates: amobarbital (Amytal), butabarbital (Butisol), pentobarbital (Nembutal), phenobarbital (Eskaphen, Eskabarb, Luminal), secobarbital (Seconal).

(2) Nonbarbiturates: ethchlorvynol (Placidyl), ethinamate (Valmid), glutethimide (Doriden), methyprylon (Noludar), methaqualone (Quaalude), chloral hydrate (Felsules, Rectules, Noctec), paraldehyde.

Antiparkinsonian Agents

Benztropine (Cogentin), biperiden (Akineton), procyclidine (Kemadrin) and trihexyphenidyl (Artane) are used most frequently. If one does not work well enough after a trial, the patient is switched to another. More and more physicians use these agents only after dystonic effects appear, while others prefer to start them simultaneously with the major tranquilizer. After accommodation to the tranquilizer (six to eight weeks) the antiparkinsonian dose can usually be lowered or a milder agent used (Cogentin is the most powerful). Some patients remain convinced, however, that the antiparkinsonian is the real tranquilizer and will not be without it. The atropine-like effect of these agents adds to the similar effect of the tranquilizers and causes blurred vision and dry mouth. If the vision is not improved with dosage reduction, dime store reading glasses are recommended (especially for patients who must read), and hard candy for the dry mouth.

The extrapyramidal effects which the antiparkinsonian agents are used to treat can be produced by all the major tranquilizers in large enough doses. These drug-induced effects can be divided into three classes: (1) dystonic effects, which occur the first day of treatment, up to one week; (2) akathisia, which begins during the second week of treatment; and (3) pseudoparkinsonism, which appears after three or four weeks of treatment.

Dystonia is manifested by muscle spasms of the head, neck, lips and tongue and appears as torticollis, retrocollis, opisthotonus, oculogyric crisis, trismus (lock jaw), slurred speech, dysphagia (difficult swallowing) and laryngospasm (which can be life-threatening).

Akathisia, or motor restlessness, is seen as constant pacing and inability to sit down.

Pseudoparkinsonism is characterized by a masked face (immobile) and shuffling gait with pill-rolling movements of hands, coarse tremor, drooling and waxy skin. Also seen are weakness, diminished drive and muscular rigidity.

It may often be impossible to tell except by trial and error whether the

Table 30-3   Common Adverse Effects of

MAJOR TRANQUILIZERS ....

Phenothiazines	Fluphenazine (Prolixin, Permitil) Trifluoperazine (Stelazine) Butaperazine (Repoise) Promazine (Sparine) Triflupromazine (Vesprin) Chlorpromazine (Thorazine) .... Perphenazine (Trilafon) Prochlorperazine (Compazine) Acetophenazine (Tindal) Carphenazine (Proketazine) Thioridazine (Mellaril) ....
Thioxanthenes	Chlorprothixene (Taractan) Thiothixene (Navane)
Butyrophenones	Haloperidol (Haldol) ....
Rauwolfia alkaloids	Reserpine (Serpasil) ....

ANTIDEPRESSANTS ....

Dibenzazepines (Tricyclics)	Amitriptyline (Elavil) Desipramine (Norpramin, Pertofrane) Doxepin (Sinequan) Imipramine (Tofranil) Nortriptyline (Aventyl) Protriptyline (Vivactil)
Monamine oxidase inhibitors (MAO inhibitors)	Isocarboxazid (Marplan) Nialamide (Niamid) Phenelzine (Nardil) Tranylcypromine (Parnate) } ....
Lithium	Lithium carbonate (Eskalith, Lithonate, Lithane) ....

MINOR TRANQUILIZERS

Propanediols	Meprobamate (Equanil, Miltown) Tybamate (Solacen, Tybatran) }
Benzodiazepines	Chlordiazepoxide (Librium) Diazepam (Valium) Oxazepam (Serax) } ....
Diphenylmethane derivative	Hydroxyzine (Atarax, Vistaril) ....

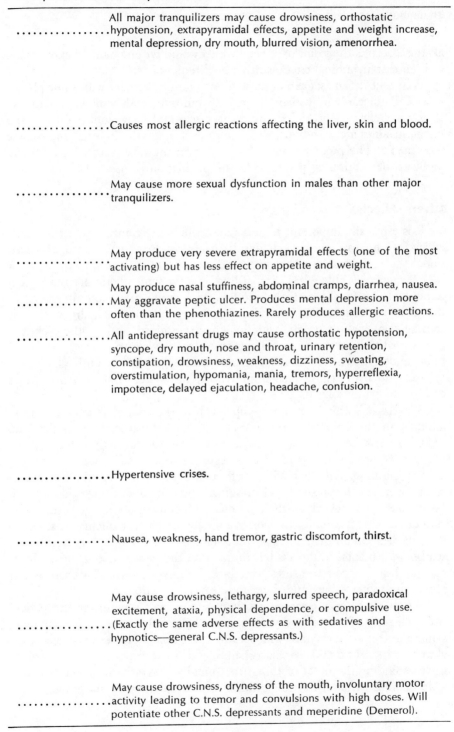

.................All major tranquilizers may cause drowsiness, orthostatic hypotension, extrapyramidal effects, appetite and weight increase, mental depression, dry mouth, blurred vision, amenorrhea.

.................Causes most allergic reactions affecting the liver, skin and blood.

.................May cause more sexual dysfunction in males than other major tranquilizers.

.................May produce very severe extrapyramidal effects (one of the most activating) but has less effect on appetite and weight.

.................May produce nasal stuffiness, abdominal cramps, diarrhea, nausea. May aggravate peptic ulcer. Produces mental depression more often than the phenothiazines. Rarely produces allergic reactions.

.................All antidepressant drugs may cause orthostatic hypotension, syncope, dry mouth, nose and throat, urinary retention, constipation, drowsiness, weakness, dizziness, sweating, overstimulation, hypomania, mania, tremors, hyperreflexia, impotence, delayed ejaculation, headache, confusion.

.................Hypertensive crises.

.................Nausea, weakness, hand tremor, gastric discomfort, thirst.

.................May cause drowsiness, lethargy, slurred speech, paradoxical excitement, ataxia, physical dependence, or compulsive use. (Exactly the same adverse effects as with sedatives and hypnotics—general C.N.S. depressants.)

.................May cause drowsiness, dryness of the mouth, involuntary motor activity leading to tremor and convulsions with high doses. Will potentiate other C.N.S. depressants and meperidine (Demerol).

akathisia seen is the result of anxiety which would require more phenothiazine or is an extrapyramidal effect which would require less.

Persistent dyskinesia can occur with long-term treatment with some phenothiazines, especially in women, the elderly and those with some brain damage. It is not relieved by antiparkinsonian drugs and may continue after the phenothiazines are withdrawn. It is recognized by rhythmic facial and tongue movements. The problems with this side effect must be weighed against the problems of continuing psychosis in the population at risk.

Adverse Effects

It is especially important to be aware of the more common adverse or side effects of the psychotropic chemicals. Many of these have been discussed under the individual drug headings and are presented here in chart form for easy reference (Table 30-3). Some drugs elicit a sympathetic nervous system response (as for fight or flight) and cause a group of symptoms related to this such as tachycardia, high blood pressure, dry mouth, a dry G.I. tract causing constipation, excitement, hypomania and so forth. Others elicit a parasympathetic nervous system response (more vegetative) with a slowed pulse and hypotension, drowsiness, etc. Still others bring forth allergic responses and many cause such primitive nervous system responses as tremors and pseudoparkinsonism.

Also drugs within a certain group (such as the tricyclics) vary, one from another, in the severity of the adverse effects they cause. Finally, the individual patient's response can cause a great difference in both a drug's therapeutic effectiveness and the type and degree of adverse effect seen.

For the most part these adverse effects are little more than bothersome to the patient, are dose-related and diminish when the dose is reduced, and can be handled satisfactorily without discontinuing medication. However, these side effects are the most common reason for patients' reducing or stopping their medication and it falls upon the nurse, more than any other health care worker in a mental health center, to question the patient about these effects, reassure him, suggest measures to reduce the annoyance, and recognize and report the more serious and dangerous adverse reactions.

When there is a clear choice between having a nonpsychotic patient with blurred vision and a dry mouth, or a psychotic patient without these symptoms, almost everyone will opt for the former. Not every choice is as clear and the nurse and psychiatrist must weigh the various choices together, each reminding the other of things that one has forgotten until the best possible solution is found for the particular patient at the particular time.

Clinical Responsibilities

What are the nurse's duties in administering tranquilizers and mood-elevating drugs to her patients? First, she must be well acquainted with their actions, dosages, forms, characteristics, and complications. She must take great care and caution in administering these drugs, observing the patient closely, both as to his behavioral and his physical reactions. Any failure of the drug to produce the desired effect should be recorded and reported. Any sensitivity or toxic reaction should be reported immediately. Since the physician usually must adjust the dosage to the individual's physical and emotional requirements, and since each person's tolerance or reaction to these drugs is specifically his own, it is especially necessary for the nurse to judge if the dosage is achieving the hoped-for results. The physician must rely upon her close observations to decide whether he should maintain the dosage, decrease it, or increase it.

But in spite of the excellent response of psychotic patients to our modern drug therapy, we must realize that drugs, no matter how effective, are by no means the final answer to mental health problems. They cannot in themselves repair personality disorders, nor can they take the place of meeting sociological needs. Their major contribution is symptom removal from the patient. This, in turn, enables him to respond to other therapies, such as psychotherapy and sociotherapy, in a much more effective way.

Reference

Detre, T. P. and Jarecki, H. G.: "Psychotropic Agents" *In* Modern Psychiatric Treatment. Philadelphia, J. B. Lippincott, 1971.

The Physical Therapies (Somatic Procedures)

Behavioral Objectives

The student successfully attaining the goals of this chapter should be able to:

- Briefly describe the 2 types of hydrotherapy, pointing out the purpose of each and the precautions which must be taken whenever these therapeutic procedures are used.
- Explain why prefrontal lobotomies as a form of psychosurgery are rarely performed today, by noting the irreversible physical changes inherent in the procedure and the possible harmful effects that may result.
- State the purpose of narcoanalysis and explain the basis of the procedure.
- Indicate the reasons for the possible use of insulin shock treatment and briefly summarize the procedure.
- Define E.C.T. and E.S.T. as therapeutic modalities and indicate the types of emotional illnesses that respond to this type of treatment.
- Explain the effects which psychopharmacology has had on the use of physical or somatic therapies in the treatment of mental illness.

Introduction

Over the years, before the advent of the era of psychopharmacology in the mid-20th century, a number of different physical procedures were used, or experimented with, in the hopes of bringing a return to sanity to those who were mad (i.e., psychotic, manic, or exhibited hebephrenic or paranoid schizophrenia).

In the 18th and early 19th centuries, bloodletting, spinning chairs, isolation, bondage, whipping, and other measures were used in the treatment of psychosis.

Hydrotherapy

Among the most humane of the physical therapies used were the various forms of hydrotherapy, the two most popular being the prolonged bath and the complete-body wet sheet pack. They are rarely used today and there is divided opinion as to whether the hydrotherapy technique was the therapeutic principle, or whether the additional care and solace these patients received helped to bring them back to reality. In any event the combination of hydrotherapy and care worked and may well return some day as an adjunct to psychotherapy and chemotherapy. The considerations and descriptions of the hydrotherapies are presented for interest:

The **wet sheet pack,** usually given cold, is used for its sedative effect; it combats restlessness, tension, insomnia and fatigue. When the entire body is suddenly cooled, the immediate action is to contract the cutaneous blood vessels; the reaction is a feeling of comfortable warmth and relaxation which results in decreased restlessness and drowsiness.

The procedure consists in wrapping the patient in two wet sheets thoroughly wrung out of water between 45 and 50° F. The sheets are so placed that no two skin surfaces touch and no pockets of air are left in the pack. After the sheets are in place, one under and one over the patient, he is then wrapped, mummy-fashion, in a woolen blanket and then in a plastic sheet.

The treatment should always be explained to the patient, who should be undressed and toileted before being placed in the pack. The patient should warm up within fifteen to twenty minutes. His physical condition, as indicated by color, pulse, and general reaction, should be checked. Should he fail to become warm (react), he should be removed from the pack and wrapped in heated blankets with a hot water bottle at his feet.

The patient should be protected from injury by the use of bed rails. The overhead light should be turned off and the blinds drawn so as to induce rest and sleep. When the pack is removed, he should be encouraged to rest another hour or so.

When sheet packs have been scheduled for a hyperactive patient, whenever he becomes very restless and agitated, it is wise to place him in the pack at regular intervals and not only when he is hyperactive. Thus, he will learn to associate the pack with therapy and not feel that it is a form of punishment for him when he is excited or misbehaves.

The **continuous tub bath** is a favorite method of treatment for overactive, excited, or agitated patients. It is ordinarily a much longer treatment than the pack; the patient remains in the tub for from three to twelve hours. He must be under competent observation at all times. The tub has the advantage of permitting the patient to move his body about in the water with comparative freedom. He is suspended in a hammock with an air pillow placed behind his head in order to permit him to sit comfortably. He is submerged to the shoulders in continuously running water at the neutral temperature of 92° to 96° F. A canvas cover, with a cut-out for his neck, is fastened over the tub and a soft bath towel folded about his neck to prevent the skin from chafing from the canvas. The water should be checked frequently and kept well regulated at all times. The physical therapist or the nurse should check the patient's pulse at the carotid artery at regular intervals. The attitude of the personnel should contribute to the relaxing, sedative effect of the bath.

Should a series of these baths be indicated, and should they tend to have a deleterious effect on the patient's skin, lavish application of cold cream or lanolin before and after the treatment will prevent the skin from breaking down.

The cold sheet pack and the continuous warm bath may be given by physical therapy personnel in the physiotherapy department, or they may be given on the patient's ward by nursing personnel (in the event the tub baths are to be given on the ward, a special free-standing type of tub must be available).

A record is kept on the patient's vital signs and his reactions while under treatment. The continuous whirlpool bath is a newer type of bath and is a most pleasant form of therapy. Since the patient cannot be as readily restrained in it as in the older type of tub bath, it is not usually used for the very aggressive person, but for persons who are nervous or mildly agitated.

Electrical forms of heat to the body, followed by soothing tissue massage, are also relaxing adjuncts.

Psychosurgery

Although used with success in some otherwise intractable patients and criminals to remove symptoms (as with severe obsessive-compulsive neurosis) or to control behavior (as with violent criminals—often at the inmate's request), surgery on the brain (the selective destruction of brain tissue) has come under attack on medical and ethical grounds, and is rarely performed today.

Prefrontal lobotomy was introduced by Antonio Egas Moniz, a Portuguese psychiatrist, in 1935. In 1936 this procedure was introduced in the United States by Freeman and Watts. While it is still occasionally used in intractable cases, it has decreased with the advent of the ataractic drugs.

In prefrontal lobotomy, the association fibres between the frontal lobes and the hypothalamus (midbrain) are severed. There is general agreement that the thalamus is the area where ideas and sensations are invested with emotional responses. The severing of the association fibres detaches the emotional charges that result in uncontrollable behavior.

The operation is performed by drilling holes in the skull and cutting the association fibres in the plane of the coronal suture, or by severing the association fibres from above the eye.

Patients with agitated depressions, severe withdrawals, and pronounced projective patterns have tended to show improvement with psychosurgery, but because there is very apt to be some deterioration of the mental processes, it should be tried only when all other forms of treatment have failed.

Nursing care should follow the rules of all postoperative care. Danger signs are a pulse under 60 or above 120 and a temperature over 102° F; a sudden drop or sudden rise in blood pressure; continuous vomiting; failure to regain consciousness in three or four hours; or, if after a return to consciousness, there is a marked restlessness, again followed by unconsciousness.

Following the operation, most patients are regressed, some to a greater degree than others. The major task is resocialization through habit training. Incontinence, which is exceedingly common, gradually comes under control through regular toilet training. The patient may have to be retrained in self-feeding, table manners, and dressing himself. In other words, he must relearn his habits of living.

Narcoanalysis

Narcoanalysis consists of the intravenous injection of either sodium amytal or sodium pentothal, given very slowly. It is injected by the physician; as the patient relaxes and his defenses lower, the physician gently questions the patient in sensitive areas, either to elicit desired information for his own use in planning therapy or to help the patient recall to consciousness very painful experiences.

The physician reassures the patient at the end of the session. The treatment may be used only once, a few times, or a series of injections may be given. The nurse usually prepares the injection for the treatment. If she remains in the room during the treatment, she must be careful to maintain a positive and reassuring attitude. She should not bring up any of the material discussed between the doctor and the patient in later patient contacts. If the patient wishes to discuss these matters and brings them up himself, then the nurse should be very discreet, tactful, and reassuring to the patient.

Insulin Shock Treatment

Shock treatment may be administered by drugs or by electricity. Back in 1933, Manfred Sakel, of the University Clinic in Vienna, devised a method of treating psychotic patients with insulin. **Insulin shock treatment** is usually used as an adjunct to psychiatric therapy; its primary function is to make the patient accessible to psychotherapy and other forms of psychiatric treatment. It hastens recovery and helps reduce the length of hospitalization. It consists of the production of a state of coma in fasting patients by the injection of a fairly large dose of insulin (from 60 to as much as 400 units, depending on the patient's reaction to it), in the buttock, I.M.

The usual procedure is to start the patient on a small dose of insulin and build it up daily until coma results. This may take from seven to ten days. The first coma is terminated after one minute by the administration of glucose, I.V. In the daily treatment, given early in the morning before breakfast, the coma period is gradually extended to an hour; then this period is continued until the patient has had a total of fifty hours of coma time.

Since insulin shock treatment can be dangerous, it must be performed in a fully equipped unit within the hospital. Specially trained physicians, nurses and attendants should be with the patients at all times. Alert observation, frequent checking and charting of vital signs, and facilities for prompt emergency treatment are required. If the patient tends to have convulsions in his coma, preventive measures can be taken by giving the patient dilantin sodium or one of the barbiturates. Besides convulsions, hyperexcitability, cardiac collapse, and prolonged or irreversible coma may result.

During coma, the patient's head should be slightly elevated and turned to one side to prevent aspiration of mucus. Suction should be used to clear the patient's throat if necessary.

After termination of the coma, the patient should be wrapped in a warm, dry blanket and fed a substantial meal. Then he should be showered and dressed.

In many hospitals today, group therapy is carried on in the unit after breakfast, with all of the patients participating from their beds. They seem to be especially amenable to group or individual psychotherapy immediately after they regain consciousness.

Orientation to the procedure to help the patient to know what to expect is essential; otherwise, the symptoms of hypoglycemia may frighten him when they occur.

Insulin shock therapy has been on a steady decline during the last few years. Yet insulin shock, plus the use of an antidepressant drug, appears helpful for some schizophrenic patients who are depressed.

Insulin subshock, an insulin treatment short of shock therapy, is sometimes employed for its sedative effect in the reduction of anxiety and hyperactivity.

Electroconvulsive (Electroshock) Therapy (E.C.T. or E.S.T.)

In 1937, Cerletti and Bini suggested the use of an electric current passed through the brain to produce a convulsion, to replace the use of camphor, metrazol and insulin shock therapy.

Great hopes were entertained for its effective use in all forms of mental illness. However, time proved that except in the treatment of agitated and retarded depressions, it was not as uniformly effective for other forms of psychoses.

What the electric current actually does is to produce a typical grand mal convulsion in the patient. Since the convulsive threshold varies from patient to patient, a minimal dose of current is administered and increased until the convulsive threshold is found.

All metal objects are removed from the patient's body and hair; all his clothing is loosened. Two small metal electrodes, which are connected to the machine by cords, are lubricated and then bound to the temples by an elastic strap. A rubber covered mouth gag is inserted in his mouth and held firmly in place. Four attendants hold the patient's extremities lightly against the treatment table. A nurse stands at the head of the patient with emergency treatment close at hand (oxygen, suction, heart stimulant).

The physician turns on the low voltage, low amperage current for a very brief time, less than a second in some cases. The patient's body arches upward from head and heels as long as the current is passing through the brain. (typical tonic stage of a grand mal), and when the current is turned off, the body lowers and heaves on the table (clonic stage of the convulsion). He finally relaxes on the table, usually remains unconscious for several minutes, then slowly recovers consciousness. He is typically dazed and confused for a while. When his mind has cleared sufficiently so that he can answer simple questions, he is helped off the table, showered, dressed and taken to the breakfast table.

Physicians vary in the number of treatments they include in a "course." Some give from 6 to 20 treatments, with 10 being about average. They are given at the rate of 2 to 3 treatments a week; often, after a resting period, another course is given.

One rather frequent complication of electroshock treatment has been fracture of the spine, humerus and femur. To prevent this, muscle relaxant drugs such as succinylcholine dichloride (Anectine) may be used in conjunction with sodium pentothal.

Patients undergoing E.C.T. repeatedly need a great deal of reassuring to persuade them to continue on with their course of treatments. They may be upset at the idea of having electricity passed through their brains, having been conditioned to fear it all of their lives, and they also fear loss of consciousness.

References

Kolb, L. C.: Modern Clinical Psychiatry. ed. 8. Philadelphia, W. B. Saunders, 1973.

Kyes, J. and Hofling, C. K.: Basic Psychiatric Concepts in Nursing. ed. 3. Philadelphia, J. B. Lippincott, 1974.

Manfreda, M. L.: Psychiatric Nursing. ed. 9. Philadelphia, F. A. Davis, 1973.

Matheney, R. V., and Topalis, M.: Psychiatric Nursing. ed. 5. St. Louis, C. V. Mosby, 1970.

Behavior Modification

Behavioral Objectives

The student successfully attaining the goals of this chapter should be able to:

- Describe the ways that a patient's behavior may be modified or changed by the techniques of relaxation and desensitization, condition avoidance and operant conditioning (token economy).
- Explain the limitations of behavior modification as a therapeutic modality.

Behavior modification consists of the *systematic* application of learning principles with the purpose of bringing about change in the patient. What the patient *does* is the focus, rather than how he feels, or why he is as he is.

A classic use of behavior modification techniques is in the treatment of phobias by **relaxation** and **desensitization.** For example, if a patient is afraid of flying, the therapist will compile a series of slides or photographs in hierarchial order from the most anxiety-provoking scenes to those that are completely neutral. Such a series may include: (1) a picture looking out of the window of an airplane on take off (most anxiety-provoking), (2) a picture of the inside of the airplane, (3) the airport waiting room, (4) the airport ticket counter, (5) the airport parking lot, (6) the road to the airport, (7) the patient's own car, (8) the patient's driveway, and (9) the patient's living room (least anxiety-provoking).

In an actual therapy situation there may be 20 or 30 items in the series. Then, the patient is taught to relax by a method that is fairly similar to self hypnosis. While the patient is relaxed in the therapist's office, usually on a couch or in a lounge chair, the least anxiety-provoking scene is projected on a screen. The patient learns to *pair* (associate) the feeling of relaxation and the picture he is viewing. Then the patient works his way up the series of pictures until he comes to one that causes him to feel anxious. The series is then stopped, the patient returned to a state of relaxation, and the series continued (going back a few pictures to a non-upsetting one). After many "tries," the patient will learn to pair the feeling of relaxation with what was formerly the most anxiety-provoking scene.

Following this **desensitization** procedure, the patient will usually be taken on a field trip to the airport by the therapist. If at any time the patient feels anxious, he is encouraged to practice relaxation and the steps are retraced to a non-anxiety-provoking stage. Finally, when the patient is ready, he may be taken for an actual airplane ride. However, the pattern of relaxation that occurs during the symbolic representation of the feared event usually **generalizes** to the real-life situation itself, making a "field trip" unnecessary.

The behavior treated in this example was the fear of flying. It is not necessary for the patient to ever know *why* he became afraid of flying. It is only required that the fear be stopped.

Another technique of behavior modification is termed **conditioned avoidance.** Here the habit pattern of the patient is paired to an unpleasant stimulus so that the patient learns to avoid both the stimulus and the habit. The classic example of this technique is the use of disulfiram (Antabuse) in the alcoholic (See Chapter 21).

Yet another area of behavioral modification involves modifying the environment of the patient in such a way that desirable behaviors are rewarded and undesirable behaviors punished. An example of this is **operant conditioning** (see Chapter 39) as seen in **token economy.** Here, each patient on a small psychiatric inpatient unit or partial hospitalization unit, has a **problem oriented record,** on which problem behaviors are listed (such as pacing, excessive smoking, not socializing, "talking to voices"). A schedule is then drawn up to provide the patient with "tokens" for desired behavior. For example, a patient may be entitled to a token for every half-hour in which he does not pace the floor, or for every 15 minute conversation he holds with another patient. These tokens are used to "purchase" desired things. Perhaps the group is planning a picnic or a trip to an amusement park, and each patient desiring to go will be "charged" 30 tokens. If a patient does not have enough tokens, he is not permitted to go on the excursion. A token economy obviously takes a lot of staff and involves a lot of record keeping, but it does produce desired behaviors.

In a completely developed behavior modification program the staff, too, are rewarded for desired behavior (such as coming to work on time, and getting the patients to cooperate). In this situation, there is usually a minimal base salary, and the staff can "earn" a lot more if they produce a lot more.

While these techniques appear to work on almost anyone, a patient with a host of problem behaviors (e.g., a chronic paranoid schizophrenic) presents too formidable a task for any behavior therapist. The approach is best with phobias, some sexual disturbances, and some obsessive-compulsive neuroses.

References

Burley, E., et al.: Behavior modification: Two nurses tell it like it is. JPN, 10:9 (January-February) 1972.

Fullerton, D., et al.: Motivating chronic patients through a token economy. Hosp. and Comm. Psych., 22:287 (September) 1971.

Yates, Aubrey J.: Behavior Therapy. New York, John Wiley and Sons, 1970.

33

Group Therapy

Behavioral Objectives

The student successfully attaining the goals of this chapter should be able to:

- List the 3 ways that group therapy may help patients with emotional problems.
- Describe the differences between group therapy and psychotherapy and guidance therapy.
- Describe the role of the leader in group therapy.
- Explain why the members of a therapy group should share a certain degree of similarity in outlook and attitudes.
- Indicate the method by which a qualified member of the health team would go about setting up a group therapy session in the hospital.

There are many definitions and many concepts of **group therapy.** In fact, there are many concepts of just what constitutes a "group," and just what "therapy" is. Actually, a group may consist of as few as three persons interacting together; the upper limit is indefinite.

Obviously, the one-to-one relationship we have discussed in earlier chapters cannot be classed as a form of group therapy. But when a nurse, a therapist, or another health team member is working with two or more patients simultaneously, and they are interacting not only with her, but also with each other, we have the basis for group therapy.

We become members of many groups throughout our lives. At birth, we become members of the family group. Then come the play groups, groups in school, in church, and the important teenage peer group; then the social groups, business groups, political groups, and parent groups. We remain in some of these groups temporarily, some permanently; some directly, and some indirectly; some voluntarily, and some involuntarily. But always, along life's way, we are involved in group activities. Truly, "Man lives not to himself, alone."

We are told that our behavior is formed, influenced, and controlled by the dynamic forces existing within groups. If the child's first group—his family —fails to provide him with positive, gratifying interpersonal learning experiences, his psychosocial development may well become impaired. For instance, if the child has never learned how to obtain satisfying feelings of approval from his mother and father, he tends to develop insecure relationships with authority figures, such as his teachers and his employers, in later life. If he fails to relate well with his peers in the latency period, and is unable to extract pleasure from his association with them, he may have trouble in competition and with leadership skills, for it is during this period that leadership and the ability to compete are formed.

Understanding, then, the profound effect that people have on one another, be it constructive or destructive, it has slowly come to be recognized that a structured group interaction can be used to promote well defined therapeutic objectives.

The word **therapy** indicates treatment of some sort, and **therapeutic** refers to any form of treatment or relationship in which the actions, techniques, and practices are purposefully planned and directed toward goals that offer a beneficial effect to the patient.

The first patients treated in groups in America were tubercular patients; later, others with various psychosomatic conditions were treated; then the neurotic, the socially maladjusted, and the psychotic.

In the early stages of group psychotherapy, it was considered necessary for the therapist to be a psychiatrist. Later, the clinical psychologist was considered sufficiently trained to conduct such sessions. Eventually nurses assumed this role.

Today, there is little controversy as to the nurse's role in group psychotherapy. Some feel that she is beyond her educational depth and abilities in this field. Others feel that if she has at least a master's degree in psychiatric nursing plus specialized instruction in group dynamics, that she can be classed as a Nurse Therapist and conduct such sessions.

Some feel that the nurse needs the co-presence of a psychologist, or psychiatrist at each session. Others feel that she is able to conduct the meetings "on her own," but that it is essential that she make careful notes after each meeting on the various interpersonal reactions that occurred, and discuss these regularly with a staff psychiatrist so as to receive his help and guidance in the matter.

Still others feel that the personality of the nurse and her familiarity with group dynamics are more important than her academic preparation. Some even feel that certain psychiatric technicians on the wards would be quite capable of carrying on group therapy if supervised by a well-trained nurse therapist.

But, regardless of the differences of opinion and the controversies over who is qualified to conduct group therapy, more and more hospitals are involving their nurses in conducting group therapy sessions. This is being prompted in part by the limited staff in all disciplines, the need for nursing to reinforce treatment programs, and the need for nurses to involve themselves more with patients than they have been doing.

Group therapy is a method of treatment through which a number of patients with emotional problems meet with the therapist in an organized, structured situation for the purpose of arriving at a better understanding of themselves and others, to learn how to modify their behavior to a more socially acceptable form, and to enable them to develop more satisfaction in their relationships with others.

There are many varieties of therapy included today under the general term of group therapy. Among those most commonly used are: rehabilitation therapy, remotivation therapy, occupational therapy, physical therapy, play therapy, (for children), work therapy, activity group therapy, psychodrama, family therapy, the program of Alcoholics Anonymous, as well as therapy groups established for narcotic addicts, for homosexuals, for the parents of cerebral palsy children, and the parents of retarded children. There is no question that there is some (and sometimes much) overlapping in these various therapies.

There can also be variations and overlapping in group therapy. There are differences in the types of patients involved, in the goals established, and in the methods used. Some group therapists may establish themselves as the authority figure in the group. This might be advisable if the group were to consist chiefly of withdrawn schizophrenics, where the primary goal would be to get them to interact with other members of the group and where a great deal of direct intervention might be needed.

However, the method becoming more and more popular is the method by which the group leader, or therapist, sits quietly in the background, controlling the interaction by indirect guidance, sometimes so indirectly that it would seem as though the patients were "running the whole show." The leader invites them to air their grievances and explain their problems to the entire group, and leaves much of the reaction in their hands. If and when the behavior tends to get a little out of hand, she will quietly redirect their focus to a better solution of the problem, often saying only a word or two.

Unlike psychoanalysis, counseling, or guidance therapy, this form of patient interaction does not aim to solve a single, specific situational problem. Rather, its aim is to bring people with similar problems together to help them ventilate their feelings to each other, explore common emotional problems, face their traumatic memories together and to face up to their unacceptable feelings. The leader rarely directs their conversation or suggests remedies for their problems, but rather acts as a catalyst, helping the ebb and flow of high emotional feelings, of group approval or group criticism that results from the discussions. The leader encourages them to express their real feelings about people and situations, about themselves and their families, about their fears and hopes, their hospitalization and their "illness." Only when violence threatens to break out does the leader take the ball directly into her own hands.

Often a patient will express deep hostility toward society, toward a family member, an employer, a fellow worker, and even toward another member of the group. The other patients can realize, through this exploding anger, that other people can hate and plot revenge and desire to kill, even as they do. They can identify with this destructive form of hate. In assuring the angry patient that they, too, entertain similar "bad" emotions, they help restore his self-confidence and help channel his destructive impulses without harm to others.

Sometimes a group member will be met by hostility from his fellow members. They may tell him in no uncertain terms that his feeling, behavior, or thinking is wrong. This may result in a behavioral change or a changing concept in the person thus judged by his peers.

Slowly, a sense of "belonging" develops in the group. An increased sense of self-identity becomes noticeable in most of the participants. Eventually, the patients in the group start behaving like members of a strongly knit "family." What threatens one, threatens all. When one member rejoices over a problem worked through there is a personal sense of elation in the entire group.

This is truly a patient administered form of therapy—patients administer therapy to each other. This form of patient-acting-on-patient is therapy at its best. And it has a strong deterrent force on unacceptable behavior and acting out.

Here are some of the suggestions that have come to be widely accepted in setting up group therapy on a ward:

1. The group should be composed of not less than 8 nor more than 18 persons for most effective interaction.
2. The intelligence level and the age factor should be relatively comparable in the group.
3. The group should be relatively stable in order for the feeling of togetherness to develop. However, it can be "open-ended"; that is, when one or two members leave the group, another one or two can start with the group, just so the majority of the group has not changed.
4. The length of the therapy is variable. In some instances, it goes on year after year with a few entering and leaving it from time to time. In other instances, if the goal for which it was set up is reached, it may be disbanded.
5. The meetings should last from one to one and a half hours.
6. They should be held from once to as often as three times a week, with most of them being conducted twice weekly.

The leader should assume the responsibility for making all the arrangements for the group meeting. She should set a goal for her therapy, and work out plans for its implementation. She should then go to the treatment team and explain her plan, asking for their cooperation in her project. The team members can help her choose a balanced group of patients for her sessions, as they are usually quite familiar with the behavioral patterns of the patients under their care.

Her next step is to involve one of the staff psychiatrists (preferably the psychiatrist on the team whose patients are to be involved in the therapy) in her project, as she will need his guidance and suggestions in all crisis intervention. He can be of great help to her in her growth as a therapist.

Then she should discuss her plans with the nursing staff on the wards, and what she hopes to accomplish with her group. They can be of valuable help in rounding up the patients for their sessions, seeing that they are on time and seated comfortably in the therapy room.

The leader should choose a room for the therapy that will accommodate the size of the group she wishes to handle; one that is well lighted and ventilated and that is comfortably and cheerfully furnished. The chairs and davenports should be arranged in a circle or semicircle. If possible, such a setting should be close to the ward on which the patients live so that they can find it readily.

She is now ready, with the team's help, to choose those patients who will participate in the therapy. There should be some uniformity in social values, outlook, and philosophical points of view in order not to hamper social interaction between the group members. There should be some similarity in the behavior pattern of several members of the group so that they can reinforce each other. There should also be some dissimilarities and groups of other behavior patterns. Generally, groups react well when some of the patients are activators, some are pacifiers, and some are passive recipients.

The leader must also decide whether she wants to handle the group alone and do her own recording after the meeting, or whether she wants a nurse-recorder to sit in on all sessions to keep records for her.

She will make arrangements for plenty of hot coffee, and some cigarettes for those who smoke, to be placed in the therapy room on session days, so as to add to the relaxing quality of the meetings.

She should now personally go around and invite those agreed-upon patients to become members of the therapy class, informing them that the purpose of the meetings will be to help them to arrive at a better understanding of their problems and their needs, and to provide them with the opportunity to discuss their problems with the therapist and with each other. She must arrange with other disciplines that other therapies do not interfere with the bi-weekly group meetings.

Each invited member should feel that the invitation is a very special one and that he will be welcomed into the group and accepted as a very important member of it.

Not all of those invited always accept the invitation. Now and then, one who starts will drop out of therapy. Some persons do not tolerate well the increased intimacy that such a group formation engenders. Some become overwhelmed and oppressed by shame when they yield to the invitation to disclose the disturbing facts in their past lives. Some cannot tolerate the criticism of their fellow members and may develop a keen antagonism toward those who so criticize them.

Yet, on the whole, once a patient joins such a therapy group, he usually will persevere in it and very often members of the group, working out their problems together, become deep friends and will carry on these friendships after they leave the hospital.

References

Aguilera D. C., et al.: Crisis Intervention—Theory and Methodology. St. Louis, C. V. Mosby, 1970.

Berne, E.: Principles of Group Treatment. New York, Oxford University Press, 1966.

Kolb, L. C.: Modern Clinical Psychiatry. ed. 8. Philadelphia, W. B. Saunders, 1973.

Kyes, J. and Hofling, C. K.: Basic Psychiatric Concepts in Nursing. ed. 3. Philadelphia, J. B. Lippincott, 1974.

Mereness, D.: Essentials of Psychiatric Nursing. ed. 8. St. Louis, C. V. Mosby, 1974.

Morgan, A. J. and Moreno, J. W.: Practice of Mental Health Nursing: A Community Approach. Philadelphia, J. B. Lippincott, 1973.

Care of the Patient With Special Patterns of Behavior

Behavioral Objectives

The student successfully attaining the goals of this chapter should be able to:

- Identify the underlying psychological causes of withdrawal and the basic need of a patient displaying such behavior, and explain how hospital personnel can fulfill this need and help the patient progress toward a more acceptable form of behavior.
- Indicate the type of feelings which underlie aggressive patterns of behavior and list and describe 3 ways in which this behavior can be manifested and the type of treatment and care needed in each instance.
- Discuss the type of feelings which would lead a patient with projective patterns of behavior to display superior attitudes, delusions of persecution, delusions of grandeur and ideas of reference and influence, indicating the best manner of handling such a patient.
- Explain the importance of providing activity and social interaction for the patient who uses physical symptoms as a pattern of behavior.
- Describe how hospital personnel should react to and treat patients who display ritualistic behavior.

Care of Patients With Withdrawal Patterns of Behavior

Withdrawal may vary widely in degree and in its method of expression. Basically, its essential feature is failure or inability to expend emotional interest on persons or objects outside the self. This failure to respond to his environment appropriately leads the patient to respond inappropriately to situations and persons, and leads to inconsistencies in behavior that appear to the viewer as a rather complete disorganization of the personality.

Let us examine the behavior of a severely withdrawn patient. He is sitting on a chair, pushed into a corner of the day room, head bent, eyes closed, and face expressionless. His hands are tightly clasped; they open briefly while the fingers of one hand rub the knuckles of the other. He seems unaware of all that is going on around him. When someone walks up to him and speaks to him, he does not raise his head, glance at the speaker, nor answer him. If a nurse approaches him with his medication and water, she must ask him several times to raise his head and take his medication. Eventually he does open his mouth to accept the medication and swallow it, followed by a sip of water, but without glancing up. He passively lets ward personnel bathe him, shave him, dress him, feed him. If and when he responds to a request, he does so dully, slowly, and without interest.

Why is he behaving like this? What need, or needs, is his behavior serving?

His behavior tells us that he is very fearful of people and that he is isolating himself as much as possible from them. His attitude is geared to get rid of them as quickly as possible.

He is dwelling in a fantasy world of his own making. While he may be avoiding the hurts of the real world, he is also very isolated and lonely in his imaginary world. Since man is a social being, his need to socialize is very deep seated. When he defies this need and refuses to relate socially with his fellow man, it shows that he is deeply insecure in his interpersonal relationships and is suffering from a feeling of great inferiority. His need for reassuring relationships with others is very great. His outstanding need is for a friend, a true friend whom he can trust, someone who can accept him without criticism or judgment, someone who can support his ego needs and who will make no demands upon him.

If someone offers him a therapeutic relationship, he may be unable to accept it at first. Even though he hungers for a deep relationship with another human being, he is so distrustful of his fellow man that he cannot respond to that offered friendship until he has overcome his distrust, and until he has become convinced that he is a person of real worth.

As the staff member assigned to work with the withdrawn patient tries to bridge the abyss of his loneliness and fear, the patient will slowly reach the stage where he can glance briefly at her, then away again, and a little later on she can hold his gaze and he will watch her face more carefully. At about this same time, he gives evidence of anticipating her visits and begins to show open interest in his new friend and will await her arrival on the unit. The day when he can start communicating verbally with her is a red letter day for him. One day, when the time seems appropriate, she can suggest a walk together; later, if he has enjoyed card playing before his illness, she can suggest a simple game of cards. As his ability to socialize with her increases, she can expand their activities to include any of his special interests. By now, the patient will have become quite attached to and dependent on her, and it is time to help him to begin to socialize with others. He will probably be quite reluctant to admit other persons into the "twosome" that has developed between them. In fact, he may so resent the intrusion of others that he may show real anger. But, slowly and carefully, she will invite other patients to join them in their walks, games, and activities to extend his ability to socialize. Because of the possibility of acute jealousy at this point, the inclusion of others in the circle should be done carefully, gently, and tactfully. When he has adjusted to the admission of others into the group, the staff member should begin to gently withdraw from it, eventually leaving her patient reacting with other patients on the ward. The relationship has gone through first, recognition, then acceptance, and finally, pleasure in interaction. It is terminated as soon as the goal of social participation with other people on the ward has been satisfactorily accomplished.

Care of Patients With Aggressive Patterns of Behavior

Patients with aggressive patterns of behavior generally function on a more organized level than do those who show withdrawal. Aggression may take one of three forms: that of **explosive excitement, agitated depression,** or **retarded depression.** It is also seen in manic excitement.

While these forms of behavior may appear to be quite different, they all have two basic characteristics in common, *hostility* and *guilt*. These patients have, as their central problem, the handling of their hostility and its accompanying feeling of guilt.

The aggressive patient is usually strongly ambivalent. He is very vulnerable to criticism and is deeply wounded when anyone seems to slight him. Yet, one of his prominent faults is his highly critical attitude toward others.

In the first form of aggression, explosive excitement, he vents his hostility on the environment, expressing it in ridicule, sarcasm, outbursts of destructiveness, and in rage at any restrictions or obstacles. He rebels against authority in any form and tries to dominate his environment through sheer activity. He seems constantly torn between hate and love, between his dependence on others and his fear of being dependent. This patient needs an atmosphere that is calm, accepting, and non-challenging. He needs a "quiet room" near the ward, to which he can be taken when he becomes too explosive. He must be watched to see that he does not exhaust himself with his overactivity.

It is necessary for him to discharge his hostility on the environment. He needs personnel who can accept his stream of abuse in a calm, collected fashion and who can overlook his offensive behavior, crudity of manners, and vulgarity of speech.

Because of his great feelings of guilt, he needs constant reassurance as to his personal worth. We must provide outlets in work and play for his aggressive energy. Some excellent involvements for him are punching a punching bag in the gym, playing a fast game of volleyball, tennis, or badminton, jumping on a trampoline, taking a fast jog along a country road with personnel and pounding metals with a hammer or mallet. These activities will channel his energy. Finger and brush painting supply him with a good medium in which to express and to dissipate emotions such as anger and hate.

Agitated depression is the second way in which the patient may express his hostility. He is burdened with an overwhelming anxiety about his hostile feeling and he experiences a very great feeling of worthlessness. This person turns his aggression inward upon himself rather than on the environment. His self-punishment is based on delusions of himself as a person of unpardonable sinfulness; he sees himself as guilty of the gravest crimes and as possessing loathsome qualities. He feels himself to be so despicable that he is sure it is impossible for anyone to approve of him and like him, much less love him.

He becomes so steeped in self-pity that it becomes difficult to divert him from his misery. He will accuse himself of his worthlessness over and over again in a low, dull, but agitated voice. We must patiently allow him to accuse himself, then assure him repeatedly that he is much too harsh with himself, that we love him because we know that he is a good and constructive individual. We must constantly support him with our acceptance, understanding, and warmth.

Because he is unable to sleep and eat properly, we must supervise his intake of food and medications, see to his elimination, and activate him to take some programmed exercise each day.

Last, but not least, we must constantly be alert to any signs of self-destruction and take all means to prevent suicide.

The third form of aggression is still more passive and is called retarded depression. Here, the patient is accepting his poor self-estimate by centering on his failures and inadequacies rather than his crimes and sinfulness. His emotions are those of sadness, hopelessness, and unworthiness. His thinking and body activity slow down, his face takes on a deeply sad and hopeless expression, and he tends to sit or lie quietly for hours at a time. He also is a potential candidate for suicide and should be under vigilant supervision at all times.

He needs much interaction and stimulation; he should be placed on a ward where the environment is stimulating and challenging and not allowed to withdraw from participation in ward activities. The staff should keep him involved in work and activities that will give him scant time to indulge his sense of worthlessness. If, however, he asks for menial tasks to do as an expression of his need for self-punishment, this should be allowed without comment. Above all, the staff should maintain a very positive attitude toward his ability to improve and should constantly convey to him their concept of him as a very likeable and truly worthwhile person.

Care of Patients With Projective Patterns of Behavior

Projective disorders are characterized by the attribution of one's own unacceptable thoughts, self-inadequacies, and wishes to others. These persons are highly suspicious and denial is a mechanism extensively used.

A prelude to projective behavior as an adult is a childhood in which hate, suspiciousness, chronic insecurity, and the forming of poor social skills all contribute to a hostility-laden outlook. The child becomes afraid of his hostile feelings toward others and tries to hide them. Because he cannot bear to acknowledge his own faults and inadequacies, he denies them to himself and projects them out on the people around him.

He accomplishes two things by doing this: he feels more comfortable with himself, and he can feel superior to those on whom he has projected his faults.

He subconsciously misinterprets events that tend to show up his own inadequacies and hostility.

As this child grows up, his projection becomes second nature with him. Since he can admit no fault in himself and no virtue in others, he irritates those about him and arouses aggression in them. His superior attitude implies that all others are inferior. This superior attitude fills a deep-seated emotional need—it is a "self-esteem builder."

When accumulating anxiety threatens to overwhelm him, he tends to develop a delusion of persecution. He comes to feel that the environment is aligned in a plot, or plan, to harm him. This concept bolsters his ego, since it both makes him important enough to be persecuted, and gives him a solid alibi for failure.

In time, his inflated ego will usually develop a second delusion, a delusion of grandeur. He may come to believe himself the wealthiest man in the world, a person of great power and authority, some great historical person such as Napoleon. While he is given to strong delusions, he rarely hallucinates.

Always a suspicious person, his suspiciousness and brooding sensitivity become marked. He begins to show ideas of reference (he refers all happenings in his environment to himself and feels that everything that goes on has a special relationship to him). Then come ideas of influence and he believes that his behavior is being caused and influenced by outside forces.

By this time, his behavior is such that there is often need for psychiatric hospitalization and treatment.

In assessing his needs, we must take into account his pronounced insecurity, poor self-esteem, inability to admit his hate and hostility, his failures and inadequacies, plus his poorly developed social skills.

Since he is extremely proud and sensitive, we must use tact and courtesy in dealing with his negative emotions and behavior.

His sarcasm and ridicule should be met quietly by us with no retaliation. We should listen to his story, no matter how out of line with reality it is, courteously and without either agreeing or disagreeing with it. We should note carefully what he says and record it. As his anxiety and hostility decrease and his self-confidence increases, there will be less and less need for exaggerated self-praise and for caustic criticism of others. Whenever he does show accomplishment and reliability, we should praise him for it. Since he is badly in need of acceptance, we should accept him, just as he is; as long as he needs to pretend to be a superman, we should allow him this pretense, but we should not reinforce nor contribute to his delusions.

Since large groups either overwhelm him or afford him a screen behind which he can evade coming to grips with his problems, he should be encouraged to work or play with only a limited number of other patients to start with. He should be helped in acquiring skill in social relationships. Since he has a need to seem important, we could fill this need by encouraging him to help in the care of a more helpless patient, or perhaps to help give physical care to a withdrawn patient. Anything that can help build up true self-esteem in him should be tried. Our remarks to him should always be kind and accepting and should reassure him that we respect him as a person of worth and integrity.

Because of his delusional symptoms, he might become potentially dangerous to someone on the ward if he thought his own life was in danger. We must never overlook this possibility but should watch his behavior carefully and guard against any semblance of attack. Should he show indications of becoming unable to cope with his environment, of being overwhelmed by it to the point of showing deep depression, we should take precautions against possible suicide.

Care of Patients Who Use Physical Disability as a Pattern of Behavior

A person who uses physical symptoms as a means of channeling his anxiety actually has need of his symptoms and does not want them alleviated. However, he is quite unaware of this fact. Usually his reliance on symptoms of illness to bring him love and attention stems back to a childhood in which his needs for love and attention were not fully met. When an accident or a sudden bout of illness caused him to become the center of attention, when deep concern and anxiety on the part of his family filled his need for attention and affection, he was reassured as to his importance and he delighted in the sympathy with which he was showered. When his need for love, reassurance, and security mounted again, he unconsciously sought fulfillment of these needs through complaints of feeling sick. Repetition of this cycle caused him to become overly concerned with body symptoms, and this habit became firmly ingrained in his personality. It is interesting to note that people using physical symptoms as a defense mechanism do so with an odd mixture of anxiety and calmness.

One important factor in the pattern of body overconcern is that it supplies a rationalization for inadequacies and failures. Another is that it seems to be quite acceptable socially. It is difficult to help a patient of this type change his behavioral pattern. Since he has need for his symptoms, he actually does not want to give them up.

This person is rarely found in a psychiatric hospital. He is much more commonly found in a general hospital, undergoing endless rounds of examinations and tests. The physician often has genuine difficulty in differentiating between true symptoms and those being used as a method of behavior adjustment, especially when, through unconscious suggestion, certain tissues and organs malfunction. The system most commonly involved is the gastrointestinal tract, but the cardiovascular, the neuromuscular, the respiratory, and the urinary systems are also frequently involved.

What are his special needs in the hospital? First, we should try to convey to this patient a feeling of his real worth and complete acceptance as a person. We must listen attentively to his description of his ailments. Even though he presents these to us daily, and in detail, we must listen without interruption. When he obviously waits for our comments, our best handling of the situation is to refrain from commenting as much as possible, and then merely limiting our comments to repeating the feelings just expressed by the patient. After having listened to him sufficiently so that he is assured of our interest in him and his problems, we should try to involve him in discussions and in activities which seem of interest to him but which do not encourage him to launch forth in further elaborations of his symptoms. The more we can involve him in social activities on the ward, the less time he has to dwell on his "troubles." The patient has a right to his feelings, however annoying they may be to others, and he has the right to tell us about his troubles. We should calmly accept his complaints but not give any indication of pity or of feeling sorry for him, for pity will encourage him to bid for more sympathy. He especially needs involvement in recreational play upon the ward, he needs to learn to play and to enjoy himself more.

Care of Patients Who Control Anxiety Through Ritualistic Patterns of Behavior

A child cannot tolerate rejection. Stern, exacting parents are so threatening to a child that he often develops ritualistic behavior to handle the guilt and anxiety they produce in him.

Ritualistic behavior is an attempt to reduce a threatening environment by a "sameness" of thought and action. The ability to do a certain thing in the same learned pattern reduces the necessity of judging and choosing. Learning to do something well actually requires a certain degree of "sameness," or repetition. But when one develops the necessity of exactly and immediately repeating a certain pattern of behavior in order to reduce anxiety, we say this person has become ritualistic—rigid—in his inability to handle his anxiety in some other way. Ritualistic behavior is compulsive behavior. Unless the patient can reduce it by a particular repetitive action, his anxiety will mount and become intolerable.

It does present therapeutic difficulties on the ward. The staff must accept the compulsion, knowing that it is very necessary as a safety valve for the patient's tension. Efforts should be directed, at first, to making the patient feel thoroughly accepted, compulsion and all. The patient must be furnished with an environment that is not handicapping, one in which he will not feel conspicuous nor isolated by his behavior. Full allowance should be made for the problem of adjusting to ward routine. Ritualism is time consuming, and he should not be forced to feel criticized or pressured. The patient is very anxious and he fears new experiences.

We must reduce his anxiety, build his confidence that his compulsion will not prevent him from entering into personal relations with others on the ward and bolster his security. The routine we set up for him should be as consistent as possible.

As his self-confidence improves and he realizes that we have realistically accepted the limitations imposed by his behavior, that no one is punishing or rejecting him for it, and that any handicap his compulsion produces in him is being allowed for, his anxiety should lessen. He should be assured that as his mental health improves, he must, and will, acquire more and more control over his behavior. As he improves, we should warmly encourage him for the real improvement he evidences.

The symptoms the patient is exhibiting should be concentrated on rather than his diagnosis. If an accurate assessment of his behavior is made, his needs can be diagnosed and a care plan set up to meet his needs. If his behavior fluctuates, the intervention methods used also must fluctuate. Therefore, it is necessary to constantly evaluate how successfully the patient's needs are being met. The improvement in the patient's behavioral pattern serves as the standard in this regard.

References

Aguilera, D. C., et al.: Crisis Intervention—Theory and Methodology. St. Louis, C. V. Mosby, 1970.
Ashley Montagu, M. F., ed.: Man and Aggression. New York, Oxford University Press, 1968.
Carlson, C. E., et al.: Behavioral Concepts and Nursing Intervention. Philadelphia, J. B. Lippincott, 1970.
Duvall, E. M.: Family Development. ed. 4. Philadelphia, J. B. Lippincott, 1971.
Erikson, E. H.: Insight and Responsibility. New York, Norton, 1964.
Horney, K.: Neurosis and Human Growth. New York, Norton, 1950.
Kyes, J. and Hofling, C. K.: Basic Psychiatric Concepts in Nursing. ed. 3. Philadelphia, J. B. Lippincott, 1974.
Menninger, K. A.: Man Against Himself. New York, Harcourt, 1956.

Care of the Very Young Who Are Mentally Ill

Behavioral Objectives

The student successfully attaining the goals of this chapter should be able to:

- Identify the major form of psychogenic psychosis seen in childhood.
- Describe the behavior of a marasmic infant and identify the cause and treatment of this disorder.
- Explain why early infantile autism develops and describe the manifestations of this behavior as well as the patient care plan, therapeutic goals and treatment of such children.
- List the basic considerations which should be taken into account in the assessment of the adolescent schizophrenic and indicate the type of care needed.

Caring for the young child who is mentally ill calls for some modification in his treatment as compared to the mentally ill adult.

The child's personality is less structured and formed than the adult's. He is living through his most active phase of development and shows rapid modification in behavior from one stage of growth to another. The environmental pressures leading to his disordered personality functioning are either present in his immediate environment or in his very recent past.

We know that the child's emotional life revolves primarily around his mother, father, and siblings, and that his emotional problems most often arise from his family's interpersonal relationships.

The psychological fate of most children is, to a considerable extent, determined by the emotional health of his parents and by the complex forces interacting within the family group. Let us review some of the forces capable of blocking the normal psychological development of the small child. They include: a rejecting mother; an indifferent or an absent father; the arrival of a new child; sibling rivalry and jealousy; conflicts; aggression and abuse between parents or between parents and children; sexual abuse between parents and children; antisocial behavior on the part of parents; mentally ill parents (neurotic, psychotic, or psychopathic behavior on their part); inconsistency caused by one parent being overpermissive and the other overly strict; rigid, overdemanding and punishing parents. These and many other factors may distort the parent-child relationship and lead to defects in the personality development of the child. Failure in normal personality development will handicap the child by producing an inability to deal effectively and realistically with the business of living.

Some of the milder manifestations of emotional difficulties in the child show up under the guise of undue apathy, undue excitability, and disturbances in feeding and sleeping; in habit disturbances such as nail biting, thumb sucking, enuresis, prolonged masturbation, temper tantrums, and somnambulism; in conduct disorders such as excessive shyness, seclusiveness, worrying, undue submissiveness, irritability, and unsocialized aggressiveness; in delinquencies such as stealing, lying, defiance of authority, habitual truancy from school, fire setting, defacing of property, and in unacceptable or inappropriate sexuality.

While all of the above behavioral manifestations are commonly encountered, it is to the much rarer child, one whose behavioral problems are so severe that he must be hospitalized for psychiatric treatment, that we now turn our attention.

Causes of Mental Illness

Mental illness in a child is thought to be due to one of two causes, or to a possible combination of both. Either he has been subjected to organic brain damage, or his psychosis is of psychogenic origin (having no known physical cause although several are suspected). It is the latter type that we shall discuss.

His pattern of behavior closely follows the pattern exhibited by the schizophrenic teenager and adult. Thus, we say that schizophrenia is the one form of psychogenic or functional psychosis seen in childhood. While its onset is more often seen in the eight- to fifteen-year-old group, it may appear in the child as early as the two- to three-year-old level, and occasionally in a child under one year of age.

The symptoms will vary with the age level at which they appear. The smaller child will show a varying degree of withdrawal and regression, with progressive loss of affect, diminishing interest, and increasing apathy. Children eight years old and older will add delusions and hallucinations to the picture, and behavior may show either apathy or aggression.

The behavioral changes seem to be a reactive response to a deep, inherent, threatening danger to the ego-structure of the child.

The newborn infant is characterized by extreme helplessness, both bodily and intellectually. He cannot distinguish self from environment. His most prized source of comfort is his mother's breast, followed by the deep pleasure of being cradled and rocked in her arms, held against her body, caressed by her hands and lips, and soothed by her soft words and songs.

Everybody needs such comfort and encouragement from a maternal figure. When the infant is not given this evidence of being loved and wanted, it feels disturbed and insecure.

Marasmic Infant

It has been postulated by a number of researches that there exists a genetic predisposition to schizophrenia. In studying the disorder in twins, F. J. Kallman found that if the disorder existed in one of monozygotic (identical) twins, it occurred also in the other twin in 85.8 percent of the cases, while in dizygotic (fraternal) twins, there was only a 14 percent expectancy. If this concept should be true, it could account for the fact that some infants, when completely deprived of mothering, develop **marasmus,** or early autism, while others, though showing signs of emotional impairment, seem able to weather the bleakness of early months without love and survive, albeit emotionally handicapped.

The marasmic infant seems to lose the will to live. It becomes dull, apathetic, inert. It loses its sucking reflex and takes less and less food. It frequently dies in a few months of time.

The therapeutic care for such an infant is love and more love. This baby needs to be cuddled, caressed, nuzzled, and spoken to softly and lovingly, played with, held tenderly for long periods of time, and rocked to sleep. If intervention of this type is instituted and the infant's vitality is not too low, there will be a slow but steady "quickening" of affect in the child and he will begin to respond to the feelings of the therapist.

Autism

More commonly, the emotional deprivation begins to manifest itself toward the end of the first year or the beginning of the second year of childhood. Here the child is older, has more adjustive capacity, and is less vulnerable physically. The two main symptoms of schizophrenia developing in the second and third year of life are extreme withdrawal and obsessiveness. This syndrome is called **early infantile autism.**

The child develops a severe disability in interpersonal relations; his peculiarities of language and thought take on the general features of schizophrenia. The child becomes less and less able to relate to people and to form affective (emotional) ties. He often becomes mute. If interfered with, he tends to develop temper tantrums. Although the child has no interest in people, he usually does have a good relation to objects and he may play happily with them for hours. His obsessiveness shows in his need for a maintenance of "sameness." He cannot tolerate change.

Though he shows his hate and frustration by kicking, biting, and striking at those who try to break through his protective shield of withdrawal, he often also drives his frustration in upon himself, and self-punishment in the form of head banging, flesh tearing, and pounding of the head and body, biting of fingers and hands, and pulling out of hair is not uncommon.

Often, this child is diagnosed as retarded, due to his limited responsiveness. In actuality, he has an average, or even superior, intellectual potentiality. His facial expression, though serious and perhaps tense, is usually strikingly intelligent. Frequently, those who do speak have an extensive vocabulary and a surprising memory.

INTERVENTION

Assessment should list extreme insecurity, deep fear, distrust of people, and deep loneliness. There is usually impaired self-image and maldevelopment of the ego and superego structures. The child fails to adapt to reality. He is highly suspicious of the friendly intentions of adults or of other children. His developing self-concept shows impairment of a clear body image, personal identity and lack of beginning polarization of sexual identity.

A patient care plan for an autistic child should be geared to his inability to tolerate change in his environment and upon his need to insulate himself from it. A therapeutic milieu should be set up for him, establishing an environment that will be consistent, accepting, yet firm, and able to convey to him some sense of security. He is so very insecure—so lonely—and yet he cannot accept physically expressed affection. It terrifies him. He needs a small room of his own, off the day room, where his belongings, toys and furnishings are not moved or disturbed.

The immediate therapeutic goal is to help him slowly develop a tolerance for physical closeness to the mental health worker. She takes over his bathing, feeding, dressing, and toileting, handling him kindly but impersonally at first. She accepts his temper tantrums without comment. She plans his care in a routine that he can adjust to. At intervals, she brings him out on the ward to be "exposed" to the interaction going on there, but does not force him to play with the other emotionally disturbed or hyperactive children. She takes him back to his own secure room when he shows mounting anxiety. He may have a few toys, or perhaps only one, that he is attached to. He will play with his toy, or toys, for long periods of time.

She should leave him alone by himself for a certain length of time, then go in and sit quietly by him, thus helping him associate her with the environment of his "sanctuary."

Eventually she should say a few words about his toys; then she should pick one up and talk about it; in time she should pick it up, talk to the child about it, then hand it to him. At first, he may refuse to accept it from her, but in time he will accept it. Later, she can play with the toy and then involve him in the play. He will still resent her touching him physically. Then, the day will come when he can tolerate her touching him without his resisting her or striking at her. It is a passive acceptance, but it is a step in the right direction.

She should now start to play records for him, choosing those he seems to enjoy. She may read children's stories or poems to him, and eventually recite or sing them to him and try to involve him in saying some of the words.

He may slowly start communicating with her, nonverbally, then verbally. The day will arrive when he will questioningly reach out his hand and touch her on the hand, arm, face, or body. After he has accepted her, she may venture to put her hand on his or gently stroke his cheek or hair. It will take a while longer before his fear will be reduced to where he can lay his head against her or welcome her arm around him.

She must move very slowly with him to earn his trust and to enable him to open up emotionally. He must find that she can be depended upon, that she is consistent in her contacts with him, and that he can trust her. As his behavior improves, she should praise each gain in conduct as he exhibits it. When he reverts to unacceptable behavior, she should ignore him.

Her long-term goal is to earn his trust and love, to help him back into the reality of normal living, to improve his own self-concept, develop his self-confidence, and eventually to improve his ability to communicate and to socialize with other children on the ward. As his behavior improves, she should make him increasingly responsible for it, correcting and directing him gently but firmly.

Few of these children become warm, outgoing personalities. Most of them, with therapeutic care, achieve moderate social adjustment, learn to communicate verbally, improve in affective ability so that they can accept and shyly return affection, and improve in their self-esteem and use of personal resources. They may even learn to participate in environmental activities, although most will remain "loners." That the autistic child can emerge at all from his severe withdrawal pattern and adjust to the reality of living is related in large measure to his age level. His is a stage of high developmental change characterized by rapid modification in behavior.

Adolescent Schizophrenia

The adolescent who begins to show a definite schizophrenic reaction has usually had a pre-schizophrenic type of personality and a childhood spent in a seriously disturbed family group. The precipitating factor is often the loss of an only friend.

The boy has probably been having difficulties in self-identification, in identifying his sex role, and in determining aims and goals. As a rule, his ability to socialize is poor. His childhood has usually been an unhappy one and he is hostile toward his parents and siblings. His self-esteem is very low. He has been having trouble adjusting to and controlling his sexual and aggressive drives.

He makes a friend, a real friend, with whom he feels free to discuss his problems and share his dreams. The friendship breaks up or the friend moves away. The loss of this outlet for his emotions is a crushing blow to him. He is forced back upon his family for socialization. His loneliness, daydreaming, hating, and fearing increase. His feelings dull; his interests narrow; emotional impoverishment increases and he becomes secretive, negativistic, and isolated. He may be irritable or flat emotionally. He may become preoccupied with his body or he may develop a severely defective body image. His thinking, feeling, and behavior tend toward disorganization, and delusions and hallucinations appear.

Upon being hospitalized, fear, anger, and resentment may control him or he may show deep apathy.

INTERVENTION

The major considerations in the assessment of the patient's needs, are his extreme loneliness, misery, fear, ambivalence (so common to the teenager), and his great need of an understanding, accepting friend. Also included are his poor and uncertain self-concept, his intense fear of failure and rejection, his inability to handle aggression and, especially, fear of handling his emerging sex drive. Very probably he has a deep need to identify with an accepting, wholesome father-figure.

If this last need is strongly indicated, a male member of the team should be involved to help fill this need. (It could be a male technician, orderly, nurse, social worker, therapist, or teacher.) In working through his intense feelings of guilt and shame, he would probably react better with a male figure.

A female mental health worker or nurse should first play the mother role with him, assuring him of love, acceptance, understanding, and positive support. He needs nurturing and maternal concern, for he still has much of the small child in his personality make-up.

Later, she must gradually become friend rather than mother. Then her major interventions should be similar to those she would use for the withdrawn adult male. She can be of much help to him in assisting him to grow up emotionally, become more independent, and to see himself as a worthwhile person. She must bolster his ego, strengthen his battered self-confidence. and help him to control his behavior, especially his sexual behavior. He needs help in learning to socialize with his own peer group. Involving him in adolescent group therapy can reap rich rewards.

His family is in need of counseling and therapy also. His parents need to be made aware of what effect the home environment has had upon the boy, and of how they can help him when he returns home again.

References

Bettelheim, B.: The Empty Fortress. New York, Free Press, 1967.

Freud, S.: Normality and Pathology in Childhood: Assessment of Development. New York, International Universities Press, 1965.

Goldfarb, W.: Childhood Schizophrenia. Cambridge, Harvard University Press, 1961.

Kolb, L. C.: Modern Clinical Psychiatry. ed. 8. Philadelphia, W. B. Saunders, 1973.

Usdin, G. L.: Adolescence: Care and Counseling. Philadelphia, J. B. Lippincott, 1967.

chapter
36

Care of the Geriatric Patient Who Is Mentally Ill

Behavioral Objectives

The student successfully attaining the goals of this chapter should be able to:

- Define the terms cerebral atrophy and senile brain disease, explaining the cause and mental effects involved.
- List 4 types of emotional strains which are frequently encountered by the elderly and give an example of each.
- Explain why patients suffering from senile dementia frequently are disoriented and tend to live in the past.
- Identify the considerations which should be taken into account in the following areas in the care of the elderly: appetite and diet, fluid intake, elimination problems, sleep patterns, mobility, hearing and vision defects, pain, and skin care.
- Describe the type of psychological and emotional support that can be provided for the elderly patient who is depressed and plagued by feelings of uselessness.

Each period of life is beset with its own particular stresses. In old age, several special stresses appear.

First, there are the physical disabilities and limitations that come with aging; second, there are special emotional problems attached to this stage of life; and third, there is the need of adjusting to new conditions and situations (economic, social, familial and sexual) at a time when a man or woman's physical energies are waning.

Today the United States has a far greater "older" population than any other country has ever had in all history. Age sixty-five is generally considered the beginning age for geriatrics. In 1950 there were 10 million people in the United States over age sixty-five. In 1970 there were 20 million (10 percent of the population). In spite of unfortunate stereotypes, less than 5 percent of persons over sixty-five require custodial care.

As medical advances continue to conquer killing diseases, a life span of

90 to 100 years may not be far distant. Back in the days of the Roman Empire, man had a life expectancy of some 23 years!

The shift of the age make-up of our population has given rise to a great many psychological, sociological, and medical problems, and we are giving them increasing attention as their importance is being realized. It was to be expected that as man's longevity increased, so would the problems of the mental disorders of old age increase—and they have. Psychoses associated with old age now constitute about 20 percent of all first admissions to mental hospitals.

There are various theories about why man ages; but regardless of the whys, the undeniable fact is that man does age. He ages physically, emotionally, and mentally. We accept reality of a slow and inevitable breakdown of man's body and mind and consider that these aging changes are normal insofar as they happen to some extent to all of us. But we should differentiate between these so-called normal changes and those that are pathological; in other words, those biological, psychological and sociological changes that are associated with abnormal behavior.

Physical Changes

First, let us discuss the usual physical changes of old age. Physical changes are apt to affect anyone's personality as a whole. As a person ages, his eyesight tends to dim, his hearing to become impaired, his digestion to become poor or easily upset, and the majority of individuals will develop moderate to severe limitations in locomotion, balance, and the ability to get around and to care for their own personal needs. He may lose good control over his bladder and bowel sphincters; have difficulty in mastication due to missing or poorly aligned teeth, or to poorly fitting dentures. If tremor develops, he may have difficulties in handling his food, dressing himself, or holding objects. He may develop acute or chronic inflammation of joints and organs as tissues break down. This can seriously interfere with his comfort and his locomotion. Bones lose their dense structure and are easily fractured; if he falls and sustains a fracture, healing is very slow. The skin becomes dry and wrinkled and loses its elasticity; the hair becomes thinner and grey; the internal organs undergo a gradual atrophy.

The vascular and nervous systems are among the first to be involved in the aging process. Fatty deposits form in the cerebral arteries; calcium is deposited in this layer and the result is cerebral arteriosclerosis (hardening of the arteries). With the narrowing of the lumen of the cerebral blood vessels, less blood reaches the brain. Many of the neurons of the brain die and there is a tendency of the brain to become smaller as the tissues artophy; this is called **cerebral atrophy and degeneration** or **senile brain disease.** Senile brain disease and cerebral arteriosclerosis (involving either blocking or rupture in the cerebral arteries) are the two major pathologies leading to psychotic conditions. However, psychoses in the aged are not wholly due to neurological damage, but also depend heavily on longstanding neurotic patterns of personality.

The individual who has a well-adjusted, balanced personality, who has enjoyed a healthy maturity, who maintains good contact with the outside world, who has built up emotional and intellectual resources and who has a cheerful outlook on life, is not prone to develop a severe mental illness in old age; he may well escape the dementia of senility, unless there is a profound organic neurological breakdown.

Persons who have always had difficulty in adjusting to the demands of life are prone to react to the emotional and social changes of old age rather badly. The more immature and maladjusted the adaptations of earlier life have been, the less stress it takes to produce disorganized or disturbed behavior.

Emotional Problems

Now let us think through some common emotional problems associated with aging. *Loneliness* is usually a serious problem in old age. By the time we reach sixty-five years of age, most of us will have lost a number of persons who have been highly significant to us, persons to whom we have been deeply attached. These may include parents, brothers and sisters, many of our friends, and perhaps our spouses. Loneliness tends to result in depression if we have few personality resources.

Another factor that is very important is that aging persons often feel unneeded. Their children are grown and have reached maturity and independence. Most have married and have homes and families of their own. Often they have scattered to distant places and seldom return to the parental home. They have little, if any, emotional need for their parents. Thus the parent tends to feel unimportant to his children, and he feels unneeded, unwanted, and neglected.

In the event circumstances make it necessary for him to go and live with a son or daughter, he may feel unwanted and unwelcome. Or, he may desire, and have expected, to live with one of his children only to be relegated by them to a geriatric home, a nursing home or a retirement home.

Another common problem is *loss of productivity*. Enforced retirement at age sixty-five is very common in today's business world. Many, many persons who are still quite able and capable of doing an excellent day's work are forced to retire from work that was a source of pride, accomplishment and deep interest to them. Unless they have prepared for this day and have developed areas into which they can channel their abilities and industriousness, they find themselves frustrated and their lives without purpose.

When there is sudden *cessation of income*, unless the individual has earned well, and saved and invested wisely, he finds that living on an inadequate pension and social security is most difficult. He may have to sell his home and move away from old neighbors and friends because he cannot afford the upkeep on his home and the problem of constantly rising living costs and taxes. The majority of our older people find themselves trying to adjust to small, and often meager, incomes. Should they be forced to go on old age assistance, this may hurt their pride and their self-esteem.

If they must move to a poorer neighborhood, among strangers, renting smaller, less comfortable living quarters, or perhaps just a room in a rooming house, their sense of helplessness and hopelessness increases.

Also there is a *loss of status* as they move from a position of social productiveness and responsibility to the ranks of the unemployed. They are troubled by their apparent uselessness, by the fact that no one seems to appreciate that they have a lifetime of experience and wisdom to contribute to the world.

Add to this the very real fear that many of them have of future invalidism and approaching death and you have a terrific build-up of negative feelings. In their intense anxiety they turn to the defense mechanisms that have served them well in the past, often overusing them in their effort to reduce stress.

And thus it happens that one will regress further and further into his past, seeking to recapture the pleasures and satisfactions of his youth; another may become very dependent; another may become highly suspicious of the motives and actions of others; another may become self-assertive to the point of being domineering; another may, because of his feelings of inadequacy and insecurity, become ill-natured, argumentative, and demanding; still another will become delusional and hallucinative as he rejects reality.

Senile Dementia

Dementia may be defined as a chronic, typically irreversible deterioration of the intellectual capacities. The onset of this deterioration is ordinarily gradual, involving a slow physical and mental letdown. The transition into the psychotic state is so imperceptible that it is most difficult to determine just where neurosis becomes psychosis.

The symptom pattern may vary greatly from one patient to another, depending much upon the pre-psychotic personality of the individual, the nature and extent of the brain degeneration, and the particular stresses in his life situation. However, there are some general symptoms that are common to many aging psychotic persons.

First, there is a gradual withdrawal into the self, a narrowing of interests (both social and intellectual), a lessening of mental alertness and adaptability, a resistance to changes in routine and to new ideas.

The patient tends to become preoccupied with physical symptoms, with his habits of eating, digestion and excretion. Periods of confusion and impairment of memory for recent events make their appearance. Although he may be able to clearly remember the events of his childhood, he may not remember what happened yesterday, or even what he just had for lunch. He lives more and more in the past. He tells the same story over and over again and is not aware that he just finished telling it. He becomes disoriented as to time, place and person. For instance, he may not remember whether he is married or not, whether he has any children or not; he may ask for a mother or a father who has been dead for many years; he may think you are his grandmother; he may think it is morning when it is bedtime, or that he is in his own home instead of a hospital ward; he cannot remember where he left various objects and often accuses others of moving or taking them.

Some patients become very careless and untidy in their appearance and personal habits. There is increasing impairment of judgment. As the patient's inhibitions lessen, he may act out sexual impulses that result in unacceptable behavior.

His ability to comprehend lessens, his confusion increases and his speech becomes rambling and often incoherent; delusions, hallucinations and delirious episodes may gradually make their appearance. Eventually many of these patients are reduced to a vegetative state.

Cerebral Vascular Accident

If the patient, instead of being the victim of senile brain disease (with its slow onset and procedure), suffers a major stroke (cerebral vascular accident–CVA), his progression is quite different. The onset is sudden. First there will be coma or an acute confusional state immediately following the brain hemorrhage. In the acute confusional state, there is a marked clouding of consciousness, incoherence, disorientation, and often paralysis of one side of the body (hemiplegia).

Convulsive seizures may precede the acute attack, occur at the same time, or appear at a later point in the illness. In severe brain hemorrhage, there may be a total loss of consciousness ending in death. Where the damage is less severe, the acute confusional state may last for only a few days or weeks, with eventual remission of acute symptoms. But in such cases there may be varying degrees of residual brain damage and impairment in physical and mental functions. In many of these cases, special rehabilitative measures may alleviate physical handicaps and clear up possible aphasic conditions.

But in many of these patients progressive personality deterioration occurs. There is also a strong tendency toward additional strokes that may leave the patient permanently paralyzed and bedridden. Death usually occurs from pneumonia, heart attack, or from massive CVA within three to five years.

Whether or not to hospitalize the aged, mentally impaired patient is a real problem. It seems so much more humane if the patient can remain at home, providing it is a good home and his family is genuinely concerned about his welfare and happiness. Home is where his roots are deeply sunk and where his interests and affection are centered.

Many authorities advocate that hospitalization in a psychiatric hospital be used as a last resource, feeling that the sudden change in environment and manner of living is too hard on the older patient and may lead to a feeling of hopelessness and complete breakdown.

If he can be under the care of his own physician and the family can be helped to use the services of a visiting psychiatric nurse, a social worker and the mental health clinic, he can often be handled very well at home. But if he becomes very confused and wanders about, getting lost, or if he becomes very noisy, violent, severely depressed, badly disoriented, or exhibits antisocial behavior, he may have to be hospitalized. First the physician will usually place him in a geriatric nursing home to see if they can handle him there. If not, he may have to be moved to a psychiatric unit. Here he will be treated, today, as an acute admission and if his behavior improves he will again be moved back to the nursing home. Today's tendency is to care for our mentally impaired citizens in the community rather than in an institution. However, some of them eventually reach the geriatric ward of the mental hospital to live out the remainder of their lives.

Mental Health in the Aged

We have been discussing the aged psychotic patient. It is a sad and depressing picture. But we should remember that severe mental deterioration is not the fate of all persons over sixty-five, nor even the fate of the majority of old persons. While there is a strong tendency for man's body to slowly break down, he may have several of the complaints of old age and still possess an alert, clear mind far into his eighties or even his nineties. Then there are those rarer souls who show little of the wear and tear of physical deterioration and who have clear, sparkling intellects and excellent senses of humor and who are a delight and an amazement to their children's grandchildren.

More and more of the "older generation" are striving to enjoy their leisure. They are traveling and seeing much of the world; they are "trailering" over the country, joining clubs and organizations designed for their instruction and their recreation. Yet it takes a substantial income to be able to do this. Federal, state and local funds and grants are going into the building of "high rise" apartments for the use of old persons who live on a very limited income. Here they can live among others of their age group, with next door neighbors, have privacy, and yet enjoy programmed activities and social functions; and someone is always close in the event that they become ill. Their self-respect can be retained and they need not be lonely. This type of community living is springing up everywhere across our country in the metropolitan areas, though it is not developing as quickly in rural areas. For the well-to-do there are lovely "retirement villages," although most elderly do best in their own homes.

Physical Needs

Treatment of the mentally ill older person must include caring for him as a complete person—physically, emotionally and mentally. Let us assess some of his physical conditions first. Is his appetite poor? Is he depleted in vitamins? Does he have trouble chewing and digesting his food? Is he suffering from constipation or diarrhea? Does he sleep poorly? Is his locomotion unsteady or quite handicapping to him? Is he incontinent? Is his hearing or his vision poor? Is he untidy about his personal appearance? Is he in pain? Does he have a severe tremor? Is his circulation poor? He may have some or all of the above complaints.

Each patient on the geriatric unit must be completely assessed. The evidence of all physical disabilities must be carefully checked against the overall care plan as set up by the team. If various rehabilitative plans made for him prove to be ineffectual or are not producing results, this information should be conveyed to the team and permission asked to try other methods or adjuncts.

Intervention

1. If the patient's appetite is poor, it is important to inform his physician who may then prescribe digestants and/or vitamins to improve his appetite; the diet, itself, might need revising, or it might need to be served more attractively.
2. If he has difficulty in chewing his food, it may need to be finely cut up, ground or blended for him. His dentures also should be checked to see if they fit snugly. If they fit poorly, the team should be notified of this fact.
3. If his bowel action is sluggish, he may need a gentle laxative; if peristalsis is too rapid, he may need medication to slow it down.
4. If he is sleeping poorly (and this is a very common affliction in the aged) he may need a sedative at bedtime. Since these aged, psychotic patients do not tolerate barbiturates well, the physician may order a phenothiazine, instead.
5. If his locomotion is very unsteady, he should be assisted to walk across rooms or down hallways; if he has a cane, it should have a rubber tip and a rubber-covered grip. Falls, resulting in fracture of the neck of the femur, are an all too common occurrence. If

he is in a wheelchair, he must have help in transferring to and from bed, in and out of a tub, and on and off the toilet seat.

6. If he is having trouble with either his bladder or rectal sphincter, special care must be given him whenever he voids or defecates. If he "dribbles" constantly, the physician might perform a prostatectomy if an enlarged prostate is the causative factor, but his age and general physical condition might be contraindications for surgery. In this event, the patient must be diapered and be put in rubber pants. If he is completely incontinent, an indwelling catheter might be helpful. If he cannot control his rectal sphincter, again, diapers and rubber pants are indicated. Whenever the patient wets or soils himself, his clothing or bedding must be changed, the soiled skin washed and dried carefully, and the patient kept as nonirritated and odor-free as possible.

7. If his hearing is poor, he should be spoken to slowly and clearly. Many aged persons need hearing aids but few of them will consistently wear one. (Their most common complaint is that the hearing aid intensifies all the background noises, which have been absent so long, and that these noises annoy them greatly.)

The patient's vision may be dim. Since his night vision is especially poor, a night light that will softly but clearly illuminate his room should be placed where it is most effective; many of these older people who sleep so poorly, will get out of bed, sometimes several times each night and wander around. If they cannot see to orient themselves, they become frightened and may panic.

8. If he is messy and untidy, he must be persistently kept clean. Often this is a source of annoyance to him, so we try to do this gently, frequently and without comment. If he has a severe tremor, he will tend to spill food and drink over himself. He may have to have help in carrying food to his mouth.

9. If he is in pain, he should be comforted and his physician made aware of his discomfort; the physician will usually order some form of relief for him. Since rheumatoid arthritis is very common in old age, the salicylates plus heat and gentle massage and passive exercising of a painful joint will usually give relief.

10. If the patient is dehydrated, his liquid intake and output should be carefully measured and adjusted.

11. His skin is usually very thin, dry and wrinkled. It breaks down easily. Ointments or lotions should be applied to the skin after the daily bath.

12. Various baths and exercises can be used as rehabilitative therapy, to provide comfort and to increase range of motion.

One of the big problems in caring for the aged physically, is the large
number of drugs they may be taking; since the aged are subject to much
tissue breakdown, many different medications must frequently be prescribed.
An analgesic, a diuretic, a mild laxative, a digestant, a chologogue and a
vascular hypotensive drug may be ordered simultaneously. Add to this one
or two tranquilizers, and perhaps a mood elevating drug, and the nurse's job
of administering these, charting them and listing the patients reactions and/or
side effects is a big one. If the patient is paranoid and suspicious of the intent
of the drug, the time involved in persuading the patient to take them, short
of force, may be considerable.

Psychological Needs

Psychologically, the primary effort is to convince the elderly psychotic
patient that somebody *cares* about him. Even though his physiological or
even his psychological problems cannot be changed much, the very fact that
someone *listens* to his complaints and then tries to do all that is possible to
make him more comfortable is usually very comforting to him. The second
objective should be to gain his confidence by a respectful acceptance of him
despite his regressed functioning. The third effort should be to help him
rebuild his badly injured self-image. He needs to feel that he is still a very
worthwhile person, and that age, instead of being just a process that will
put him on the discard heap, carries with it a dignity, and rich experience,
and wisdom garnered from many years of living. He needs to realize that he
still has much to contribute to life. This assurance of his worth is a priceless
possession. If the patient expresses feelings of depression, hopelessness and
helplessness, the message conveyed to him should indicate that while his feeling and his distress are understood, his sense of despair is not shared and
that he is considered to be a worthy person who will be cared for and assisted
so that he can adjust to the hospital and be happy there. Much of this
"caring for" attitude is conveyed nonverbally by a willingness to stay with
the patient, to tolerate silence, to allow weeping, and to do for the patient
those tasks which he is unable to accomplish for himself. The verbal responses
to the patient should be appropriate and firm. To such a statement as, "I
have nothing to live for," the following reply could be made, "I know you
feel this way right now Mr. A." This tells the patient that his feelings are
recognized and that he is not being judged for feeling depressed. The idea is
conveyed that his feelings that he has nothing to live for are not shared.

Since time hangs heavy on the hands of the aged, every effort must be
made to occupy the patient's time constructively and to provide experiences

that will be stimulating and pleasure producing to him. Any abilities or talents that he has should be explored. Occupational and Rehabilitative Therapy should be utilized as fully as possible.

The patient care plan should include ways and means to accommodate the patient's environment to his physical and mental limitations. In spite of childish behavior and attitudes, complaints and often unrealistic demands, bitterness, irritability and petulance, he must be handled with tenderness and warm support.

Caring for the mentally ill geriatric patient, requires a deep well of patience and compassionate understanding. The patient's feelings must always be considered and a tender and loving concern for his problems and needs conveyed to him. He needs to be treated as a human being worthy of our concern, our respect and our love.

We need only to reflect that there could sit our own mothers or our fathers, or perhaps, some day, ourselves.

References

Blumberg, J. E., and Drummond, E. E.: Nursing Care of the Longterm Patient. ed. 2. New York, Springer, 1970.

Kyes, J. and Hofling, C. K.: Basic Psychiatric Concepts in Nursing. ed. 3. Philadelphia, J. B. Lippincott, 1974.

Kolb, L. C.: Modern Clinical Psychiatry. ed. 8. Philadelphia, W. B. Saunders, 1973.

Care of Patients With Special Problems

Behavioral Objectives

The student successfully attaining the goals of this chapter should be able to:
- Summarize the characteristics of a compulsive personality and explain how anxiety can be reduced when the obsessive compulsions result in debilitating ritualistic behavior.
- Explain why firmness is an important aspect of the therapeutic milieu in the care of antisocial personalities and alcoholics.
- Describe the role of tolerance, compassion, and understanding when dealing with most emotionally disturbed people.
- Compare and contrast the manner of withdrawing alcoholics and drug addicts from their representative addictions.
- Explain how society can help former alcoholics and drug addicts from returning to deviant behavior, noting the role of A.A. and Synanon type houses in this program.
- Indicate how best to guide young people away from drugs.

Persons with personality disorders are relatively rare in the mental hospital. They are much more likely to wind up in our penal institutions if their behavior runs afoul of the law. However, more and more judges are tending to institutionalize certain members of this large group in an effort to change their behavior patterns. Thus we find some of the compulsive types, the antisocial types, and the sexual deviant types on our psychiatric units.

Alcoholism and drug addiction have become such a threat to our modern civilization that many hospitals have developed special units for those afflicted.

Care of the Compulsive Person

The compulsive person, as described in Chapter 16, has an over-developed superego which results in severe inhibition, perfectionism, self-doubt, rigidity, an exaggerated sense of duty, and a lack of normal capacity for relaxation; he is a scrupulous, overly responsible person who has difficulty in making decisions, and he is introverted and tends to daydream. He is quite ritualistic.

When his compulsion develops into a full-blown neurotic obsession his need to carry his obsessive ideas out in ritualistic action seriously interferes with his pattern of living. He is so busy with his compulsive action that he is unable to socialize, cannot earn a living for himself and family, and may become so anxious about his inability to function normally that panic may develop. Thus, it is not at all unusual for him to be institutionalized temporarily; he may even voluntarily seek hospitalization in an effort to change his pattern of behavior. This patient is in good contact with reality. He is suffering from a neurosis, not a psychosis. He is able to understand that the urge which drives him to compulsive action is not normal. It is not found in the other people he knows, but he has no insight as to the cause of his uncontrollable urge, and is quite unable to repress it.

Let us take a specific compulsion, the compulsion of handwashing. A young man of thirty-five is admitted to the ward with this form of obsessive-compulsion. How should his needs be assessed, what type of care plan should set up for him, and what forms of intervention would help effect a change in his behavior?

Assessment. First, his behavior is indicative of a form of extreme anxiety. His ritualism of handwashing is a defense he is using to overcome, or to help channel, his deep, chronic anxiety. He is unconsciously using this mechanism as a comparatively safe way to defend himself against his unconscious aggression, hostile impulses, and his guilt feelings. Because these feelings are being experienced on the unconscious level, he is not aware of them nor able to identify them as the source of his anxiety.

Care Plan. The first goal, in the care plan, should be to lower his acute anxiety level. During the panic stage of his reaction, a milieu should be set up for him that will allow him to comfortably indulge his compulsion without further loss of self-esteem. The patients, and those working on the ward, should be informed that this is a form of sickness with him and that he cannot control his impulsive behavior at this stage, that they must all accept his behavior for as long as he needs it as a means of catharsis for his anxiety.

He should be supplied with a ready source of water, bland soap, soft towels, and, if his skin shows signs of irritation or of breaking down, healing lotion or ointment to apply after each drying.

Intervention. The patient should slowly be included in more and more of the ward's activities, and as he learns that his handicap is not interfering too markedly with his involvement in ward activities and that he does not have to explain his frequent trips to wash his hands, he will gratefully participate; for he is lonely and his handicap has caused him to be embarrassed so often in the past that he has withdrawn from all but the most necessary interpersonal contacts.

As his anxiety level decreases, both from drug therapy and the accepting attitude on the ward, he can become involved in group therapy, where he should slowly gain some insight into his basic aggressive problems. He should also be involved in other activities in which he can channel his aggression, and for longer and longer periods of time.

It is important to acquaint him with the fact that he must slowly take over more responsibility for his actions, that he must become deeply involved in reducing his aggression and guilt drives and must learn to handle them in ways that are socially acceptable and less harmful to him (i.e., he must face reality).

The final goal is helping him return to normal activities and normal socialization, able to control his anxiety and to channel it more constructively.

Care of the Antisocial Person

The antisocial person is devoid of a sense of responsibility, lacks social judgment, and turns his frustration upon society. He tends to attack society repeatedly and, because of this is habitually in trouble. He is given to uncontrollable outbursts of temper and rage, is quarrelsome, destructive, deceitful, defiant, boastful, shameless, and erratic. His behavior indicates psychosocial inadequacy and indifference to social mores. He spends most of his life in jails and reformatories and never seems to profit from his experiences.

When he is sent to a hospital for evaluation and treatment, little can be accomplished toward his rehabilitation. Person-to-person and/or group therapy appear to yield poor results.

Since he is a very manipulative character, the staff must always be on guard against his blandishments. Basically, treatment of him must be watchful, firm, kindly, and decisive. He should be accepted as he is, and given the respect due any human being. His treatment schedule must be enforced firmly. He may present a very charming attitude and seem to be very sincere, but it is necessary to be aware, at all times, of his attempts to get his own way through manipulative methods.

Care of Patients With Sexual Disorders

Persons suffering from sexual disorders present much resistance to behavioral changes.

Many persons with sexual disorders function on an immature psychosexual level. They often have severe fear and doubts as to their maleness or femaleness, feeling inadequate or unable to function normally in a relationship. In many cases, they are unable to handle their aggressive, hostile drives. Some are deeply troubled people.

Homosexuals who are disturbed or in conflict with their homosexuality, seem to respond better when treated in a group. Male homosexuals should have a male psychiatrist or clinical psychologist to lead the group. In group therapy, they can discuss their feelings and emotional problems, and in many cases, becoming aware of some of the factors that have influenced their behavior, they become better able to handle their drives. Some of them may become able to control behavior that is socially objectionable.

If a sexual deviate develops remorse and guilt feelings about his sexual behavior and desires help and voluntarily seeks such help, psychoanalysis followed by psychotherapy, individual or group, can do much for him.

It is important to accept the patient with warmth and understanding and help set up a milieu that is accepting and constructive for him. He needs firm ward rules and the establishing of socially approved limit setting. Personnel must not be too permissive with him; he must learn, as soon as he comes on the ward, that he will be held fully responsible for his conduct at all times. But he should also be made to feel that the ward is a pleasant, helpful place, and that every member of the staff is concerned with helping him with his problem.

Care of the Alcoholic

The alcoholic is more readily helped to correct his pattern of behavior if he is a voluntary admission. If he has enough insight into his problem to realize that his problem has him "licked," that he is helpless to fight his compulsive drinking alone, and if he is remorseful about what his drinking problem has done to his family and others close to him, he is a good candidate for rehabilitation.

Often he is brought to the hospital involuntarily. Frequently, he is brought in in a highly toxic condition which necessitates much physical care.

If he is in the throes of delirium tremens, he must be kept in bed and prevented from injuring himself. Someone should be at his side constantly. It usually takes from five to eight days to detoxify or "dry out" a patient. During most of this time, he is both physically and psychologically a very ill man. He is usually dehydrated and he may be lacking in vitamins and minerals needed for body metabolism. He is so "jittery" that he may have to be fed intravenously. Vitamins and medications may also have to be given parenterally. He needs constant reassurance as to his worth, and that he is in a place where everything is being done for his well-being. His feelings of worthlessness and inadequacy mount in him until his nerves "scream" for alcohol. He will plead for "just one drink." In many hospitals, he is placed on disulfiram (Antabuse) on about the third day. If the patient drinks while this drug is in his body, he will suffer a most unpleasant reaction—nausea, vomiting, heart palpitations. After a few such experiences, he will avoid alcohol rather than go through such agony again.

To help him through this acute period of "drying out" it is important to offer warm acceptance, constant reassurance and encouragement, attention to all details of his physical comfort, and indications that his feelings, his fears, and his depression are understood.

It is after the first acute episode of his illness that firm limits must be set with him when he is up and around the ward. Like the psychopath, the alcoholic tends to be manipulative. He will resort to all types of subterfuge to try and get a drink.

A good sense of humor is especially valuable when caring for the alcoholic. If the patient can be helped to see the absurdities of much of his reasoning and behavior and can learn to laugh at it, much tension can be reduced.

Group therapy, in the form of Alcoholics Anonymous, has proven of special benefit to the alcoholic (See Chapter 21).

Most alcoholics are highly social people. It does not pose much of a problem to involve them in ward activities. It is especially important to assign work tasks to them that reinforce their ego pictures. One task that usually pays off is involving them in the care of a handicapped person on the ward.

All members of the staff must reinforce the alcoholic's feelings of self-worth. He must be assured that we feel he is able to conquer his problems, that he can become, once again, a person able to return to and take a responsible place in the community.

His group therapy (A.A.) should continue after he leaves the hospital. If he can become deeply involved in helping others through A.A., he stands a very good chance of remaining sober. As he gains insight into the weaknesses and frailties of his own personality structure, he can find constructive ways in which to channel his guilt feelings.

Care of the Drug Addict

The drug addict, like the alcoholic, is frequently brought into the hospital in a highly toxic state, his body wracked with his withdrawal symptoms and begging for relief.

As was discussed in Chapter 22, there are two forms of addiction, one in which there develops a physiological dependence, and one in which the dependence is psychological.

In physiological dependence, the body builds up a tolerance for the drug which makes it necessary to continuously increase the amount taken in order to get the desired effect. In psychological dependence, the body does not build up such a tolerance and the drug user may go on for months or years without having to increase the dosage.

While it is quite possible to develop an addiction to narcotic drugs when they are given daily, for relief of pain, in a hospital, this is not the cause of most addiction. Also, an addiction so acquired, provided the basic personality structure is essentially normal, is amenable to cure upon careful withdrawal and detoxification.

Most addicts take to using narcotics to escape from reality and its problems. They are suffering from a variety of underlying neuroses or from character disorders. They are poorly adjusted individuals who gain important satisfaction from the use of drugs which help them cope with or temporarily forget the upsetting aspects of their environment.

The barbiturates are, like the narcotics, physically addictive and may be even more dangerous to health during the withdrawal stage. The amphetamines, the hallucinogens, and drugs capable of producing euphoric states, or states of forgetfulness, may become psychologically necessary for those who are attempting to escape reality. Psychological addiction may be as difficult as physical addiction, but the removal of the drug is not harmful to the body.

Treatment of drug addiction is similar to treatment for alcoholism. The drug is slowly withdrawn while another non-narcotic drug is substituted for the one being withdrawn. While withdrawal and detoxification are going on, the patient must be built up physically and psychologically.

The patient must be given good physical and emotional care accompanied by warm acceptance and support in a therapeutic milieu on the ward. Group therapy is usually conducted by the nursing and medical staff.

The difficult part of recovery for the addict is his readjustment to his old environment. When he is discharged from treatment, he usually returns to friends, many of whom are still on drugs, and when he meets rejection when applying for a job in an area where he has previously been known as a "junky," he becomes depressed and frustrated and falls back into the old habit. This, and the strong tendency of society to reject him, is why 97 percent of addicts who have been detoxified at the Lexington Hospital go back to the needle and temporary euphoria.

In 1958, a business executive, Charles E. Dederich, who had overcome an alcohol problem, was motivated to open his home to a group of alcoholics and narcotic addicts for therapeutic discussions. He was a brilliant lecturer and group leader, and he stimulated his group deeply. Several of them moved into his home in Santa Monica, California, while others moved into nearby apartments. Thus *Synanon House* came into being. Its mutual self-help approach to the narcotics problem has achieved remarkable results.

Synanon patterns itself somewhat after A.A. All members act as therapists to each other and to new members. Members must have a history of drug addiction, and a desire to reject their way of life for a better one, and learn the Synanon social system.

These addicts thoroughly understand the newcomer and cannot be outmaneuvered by his manipulative behavior or his rationalizing. This organization creates for the ex-addict a new social circle to which he can belong as long as he wishes. He learns to communicate, relate, and work with others.

As his socialization progresses, he no longer finds it necessary to depend on narcotics and, with the help of his new friends, he paves the way for a gradual return to a constructive role in the community.

Synanon houses are being opened all over the country and are also being established in federal and state prisons. We are finally on the way to considering narcotic addiction as a "sickness" rather than a criminal offense.

And now let us look at the widespread damage that narcotic, hallucinogenic, and stimulant drug abuse is causing in the youngest group of drug takers, the teenage group.

Children from ten to twenty years of age have become avid users of drugs that change the concepts of reality. Some studies indicate that five out of six high school students have tried marihuana once, some a few times, and some several times a day, but many are smoking daily.

While marihuana is not physically addictive, it may be psychologically so. It is estimated that at least 40 percent of all high school students have tried LSD. This drug may be dangerous.

Many young people are taking amphetamines and sniffing glue in an effort to experience euphoria.

Many of these young people are confused about their self-identity. Many of them are unable to identify with their parents. Many have had too much of life's material goods and not enough of its spiritual values. They find it difficult to identify with the moral values held by their parents' generation. They are searching for values to which they can cling. In an explosive, uncertain world, the stability of family life and family values seem to have widely disappeared. Young people are eager and want to experiment with new ideas and concepts; they want "change" and they want it now. They are frustrated, angry, and frightened. To forbid them to experiment with mood changing drugs is like forbidding them to open a closed door that just might lead to unknown delights.

They need adequate instruction on all phases of drug taking. They need to become aware of the many dangers inherent in the taking of these drugs. They may need group therapy with a trusted leader whom they respect and upon whom they can rely to "give it to them straight."

When they are brought into a hospital ward to be detoxified, they need a very special milieu in which to live during this rather lengthy period. Since so many of them do not trust the older generation, it is helpful when most of the nursing staff is composed of young people. These nurses and technicians, while young in years, should be mature, responsible persons. They will have a natural empathy with those drug-sick patients who are within, or very close to, their own age group. The ward supervisor should be an older nurse with the qualities of understanding, patience, tolerance, compassion, warmth, and firmness. She should be able to identify and communicate with her patients, to listen intently to their problems, and to offer them the type of guidance they really want from their own parents.

Staff members working on a ward of this type need to be very compassionate, accepting, and warm. In group therapy, the young people should be encouraged to express their fears, guilt feelings, and aggressions. They need to be assisted in developing realistic ideals that will help develop balance and maturity in them. They desperately need to learn that people care about them and about their problems.

When they leave the hospital, it is helpful if they are placed in a living situation with others recovering from a drug problem. The directors of this "home" should be trained and highly skilled in handling adolescents and their problems. Here, young ex-addicts continue with group therapy and gain insight into their own weaknesses and inadequacies. They should be helped to replace these qualities with more constructive ones and to gain confidence and courage from each other.

References

De Ropp, R. S.: Drugs and the Mind. New York, Grove Press, 1960.

Erikson, E. H.: Insight and Responsibility. New York, Norton, 1964.

Kyes, J. and Hofling, C. K.: Basic Psychiatric Concepts in Nursing. ed. 3. Philadelphia, J. B. Lippincott, 1974.

Kolb, L. C.: Modern Clinical Psychiatry. ed. 8. Philadelphia, W. B. Saunders, 1973.

Care of the
Mildly Retarded

Behavioral Objectives

The student successfully attaining the goals of this chapter should be able to:

- Explain the importance of allowing the mentally retarded to develop their abilities to their fullest and describe the type of educational and emotional atmosphere that is most conducive to this aim.
- List the characteristics required of mental health personnel working with the mentally retarded.
- Describe the type of physical and emotional care needed by retarded patients with cerebral palsy and meningocele.
- Demonstrate the best way of handling a mildly retarded juvenile delinquent and explain the reasons for using this approach.

The needs of the retarded are many and varied. Perhaps the best way to discuss these would be to assess the predominant needs of each group, while realizing that the group is made up of individuals who each have special needs or a combination of needs.

The Mildly Retarded

The mildly retarded (by far the most common retardation group) are usually living in their own homes and so they make up the smallest group in our institutions. Many of them who are hospitalized should never have been institutionalized in the first place, as far as mental ability is concerned. Severe superimposed physical, emotional, or behavioral problems are the main factors underlying most of these admissions. If the mildly retarded person constitutes a danger to himself or to others, if he is too much of a physical or emotional burden on his family, if there is no family available to care for him, if his home conditions are inadequate or community resources are either absent or deficient, he is usually admitted to an institution.

The retarded child has the same basic psychological needs as the normal child; he needs to feel that he is loved and wanted as a member of the family and of groups outside the family. Surrounded with affection, handled with devoted patience, and psychologically stimulated through fondling and play, such a child should acquire the feeling of significance and security essential to the development of a stable personality.

But if he meets with mounting frustrations, humiliations, ridicule, and emotional deprivations, his anxieties will become overwhelming and will tend to be expressed in delinquent behavior.

The social training of all retarded children is very important, and it is especially so to those who are so close to normalcy. The extent to which they are acceptable as agreeable individuals by and in a community is directly proportionate to their social adjustment. This attitude of acceptance on the part of the community has a direct relation to the mental health of the growing child. If he is accepted, he will feel that he has fulfilled his main ambition of being someone in the eyes of others; if he is not accepted, he will develop a feeling of shame, failure, and frustration, of ill will and grievance against society, all of which breed discontent and unhappiness, which, in turn, lead to emotional difficulties, maladjustment, and perhaps even to delinquency and crime.

A mentally healthy child, whether of normal or of subnormal intelligence, is an asset to the community.

Every state should consider it an obligation to discover, classify, and provide suitable education for the retarded child at the mildly retarded level. Many states now have special classes for slow learners, and in some areas there are classes for the trainable as well as the educable.

By assigning the educable mildly retarded to special classes, the child is removed from a curriculum that is too difficult for him, or is progressing at too rapid a pace. In a regular class, his classmates are usually critical of him; his teacher may develop an antagonism toward him because of her apparent inability to "teach" him. He fails repeatedly. These factors all work together to reduce the child's self-confidence, his sense of security and his enjoyment of learning. He loses interest in the subject matter and falls farther and farther behind.

In a special class, the child can compete with his peers, is able to socialize better, and can develop feelings of security, self-reliance, self-satisfaction, and success.

When a mildly retarded child does begin to show deficiencies in social adaptation and develops antisocial and delinquency problems, he may be institutionalized. The institution may often do more for and with him than his family can. Staff are specially trained to help him improve his attitudes, stabilize his emotions, and develop habits of industry.

But, in general, we can say that the admission of an ambulatory, physically healthy, mildly retarded person to an institution represents a failure, either on his part, on the part of his family, or his community and its resources.

The primary aim of the staff is to help the retarded child overcome his social deficiencies and reshape his behavior as quickly as possible so as to be able to ready him for a return to the community.

Being the most intelligent group of subnormals, these people are the most easily traumatized by rejection and avoidance. As a group, they are highly sensitive to the feelings and attitudes of the people around them. They need encouragement in all their efforts at improvement, praise for work well done, emotional support when upset, and an understanding of their limitations.

Many of the residents in this group object to being hospitalized, especially if they are sent to an institution by the court for delinquency. Thus, running away is frequently a problem. They are homesick and want to return to family and home, even though the family may be rejecting and the home less than healthy. They watch for mail from home and for visits from their families. They can be very upset if the family does not write or arrive as scheduled, or if a visit home which has been anticipated does not materialize. The staff must support them emotionally, bolster their unhappy self-concepts, and rebuild their self-confidence.

When residents in this group arrive, they are examined and evaluated physically, mentally, and emotionally. The members of the professional team to which each person is assigned must study his needs, his abilities, and his deficiencies and plan a program to develop his full potential. If his behavior is unacceptable, real study must be made to determine a way, or ways, to change this behavior. At no time should he be made to feel personally rejected or unacceptable; all who work with him must help him to meet his problem constructively. He will be trained to be as productive as possible and helped to socialize to the best of his ability. When discipline must be meted out, it should be done in such a way that it is truly effective in changing behavior. The staff should carry out all promises made and adhere firmly to all restrictions imposed. They must be consistent in their expectations and demands. The members of all disciplines involved in carrying out the programming for these residents must be fully aware of the patient's needs, and must cooperate together in their efforts to fill them.

Children who have reached the age of eight are usually started in formal, structured classes taught by specially trained instructors. They receive training in the habits of living, socializing, and in good interpersonal relationships. They need patient, persistent training in their work habits, their personal grooming, and their social graces. They especially need staff working with them who exemplify the strengths and qualities needed by the children for character identification.

As they progress in their schooling and training programs, they reach a stage when they should be moved into a special unit where they can be supervised by highly skilled counselors. These counselors would live and work with them to ready them for return to the community. The counselors must actually wean these residents away from their dependency on the nursing staff.

In this special training unit, they learn to make many of their own decisions and are held responsible for their behavior. They are taken, singly and in groups, out into the community to church services, shows, civic entertainments, and on frequent shopping expeditions. They learn to order their food at restaurants and to pay for it. They must be trained in good social manners, and in socially acceptable expressions of sexuality. They must learn to handle their sex drive so as not to offend society or run into trouble with the law.

As we work with these people in our institutions today, we are becoming increasingly aware of what institutionalization has done to them in the past. Some adults have been institutionalized since early childhood; many of them remember no other home, no other way of life. They have grown up in state institutions and are the products of yesterday's "custodial care." All decisions were made for them, robbing most of them of all initiative and incentive. Because it is easier for staff personnel to do a certain thing for slow residents than to take time to teach them to do it for themselves, we have performed many, many tasks for them that they should have learned to do for themselves. We used to justify our dependency-forming actions on the fact that staffing on the wards of our retardation units was uniformly low and nurses and technicians were hard pressed to cover even the necessary physical care of their charges. Today, the staff-patient ratio has risen in most institutions. We can no longer justify our actions on this score. Now we must try to undo the damage done to these older residents. We must teach them to become more independent and encourage them to make more and more of their own decisions.

If they are to go back out into the world to work and live, they must learn to handle money, to save it, to pay bills promptly, to use a telephone, to tell time, to be punctual, to learn a trade. They must be made aware of the importance of looking clean and well groomed at all times, of practicing good personal hygiene. They must learn to conduct themselves socially. So many of these things that are progressively woven into the fabric of experience for a normal child are lacking in the experience of the institutionalized retardates and we have not realized, in the past, how our overprotectiveness has robbed them of vital experiences.

When the team thinks the resident is ready for trial placement, the patient-placement officer becomes involved in lining up a job for him in the community. Prospective employers are interviewed and receive a résumé of the resident's training, abilities, and limitations. Perhaps he will go into a sheltered workshop situation before trying an individual job in the community.

Most hospitals, when placing a resident on trial placement, will hold a bed for this resident for from six months to a year. This is to support and reinforce the resident. If he is unhappy in his work, or unable to satisfactorily perform it, he is assured that he can return to this institution at any time within this time limit.

More and more homes are being opened for retardates working in metropolitan areas. Their most difficult adjustment has been, not to the working situation, but to the living situation outside the hospital. Some residents continue to live on the hospital ward and go out daily to work.

Those who must live in cheap hotels or rooming houses find their leisure time hanging heavily on their hands. Unless they belong to a church group which will help them to socialize, they are lonely and many will drift into bars in the evenings just for companionship.

Many privately run homes for these people are being established, some partially funded by county or state funds. Here, they pay a modest sum for room and board, live with others of their own status, and have an opportunity for privacy, friendly interaction, and some structured entertainment.

Many of these mildly retarded persons can, after training in an institution, be returned to their own homes; others are placed in boarding homes, and some of the older people have been placed in nursing homes, especially if they are mildly to moderately handicapped.

Physical Abnormalities

Let us consider some of the mildly retarded who are further handicapped by physical problems or abnormalities. The retarded can, of course, have any physical debility or deformity that the child with a normal mind can have. We shall only discuss a few of these handicaps.

Cerebral Palsy

Patients afflicted with cerebral palsy can range intellectually from a normal I.Q. to profound retardation. If a child has a normal intellect, he should not be placed with retarded children but should be educated by special means so that his environment is challenging and stimulating.

A number of C.P. children are found in the mildly retarded group. Their major physical handicap is muscular spasticity. There may be severe diplegic paralysis or spastic contractures of all the limbs. They are often athetotic, epileptic, aphasic, or mute. Most of these patients need complete physical care. Some are helpless prisoners within their locked, twisted bodies and can move only their heads to some degree; some can sit upright in wheelchairs, but many of these must be braced and tied in. Most of these patients are quite aware of all that happens about them, but few are able to communicate clearly so as to make their needs easily known. Many of them are total bed care patients. If they have severely flexed arms and legs, dislocated hips, badly deformed spinal columns, or warped chest cages, as so many do, they must be handled with great care. Bathing poses a problem; legs and arms must be carefully pulled away from groin and armpit, washed and dried, then powdered thoroughly; fingers must be forced out from clenched fists and likewise washed, dried, and powdered. A small soft washcloth should be rolled up and placed in each palm with the fingers closed over it to keep opposing surfaces dry. Their teeth are often clenched and the muscles of deglutition taut. The mouth must be carefully opened and the teeth and gums brushed thoroughly twice a day with a small electric toothbrush.

Feeding those who have spasticity of the chewing and swallowing muscles can be time-consuming. They must be spoon-fed blended foods, Jello, puddings, ice creams, and liquids. Many of them will swallow a mouthful of food only to regurgitate most of it. Some of these must be fed by gavage. Spastic or atonic bowels need constant careful attention. Suction is frequently needed to clear accumulations of mucus from air passages.

These patients must be turned in their cribs hourly to relieve pressure areas. They need to be carried or wheeled out into the day room twice a day to participate to some extent with others.

The staff should talk to them softly and gently as they work with them. Many of them love music and will respond to it with a delighted smile. Some can hold soft stuffed toys, but even if they can't hold the toy, they enjoy it when a cuddly toy is used in playing with them. Many of them have large, luminous, expressive eyes, and these eyes will light with joy as you bend over them. They recognize you and usually understand most of what you say. Some enjoy being gently teased, others, able to move about better, may tease you. They enjoy being carried to the windows and having objects pointed out to them, or being held in a rocker and sung to. They respond so eagerly to your love, your touch, your presence. Their eyes will follow you as you move about the room. If you hang gay mobiles over their cribs, they will watch the moving forms and colors for long periods of time. The walls of their rooms should be decorated with colorful scenes, animals, and fairy-tale figures.

Meningocele

Another physical affliction that requires considerable physical care is the presence of an open meningocele. In the severely retarded child, this does not pose an emotional problem; in the mildly retarded it can do so. This is a condition in which there is an incomplete development of the bones of the skull or of the spinal column, or both with a resultant protrusion of the meninges, and sometimes the contents of the brain or spinal cord, beyond the skull or spine. These children must lie on their abdomens or sides. Usually they have no use of their lower limbs, and in some cases all four extremities may be paralyzed. Those who have the use of their arms are placed, during the daytime, on special carts, where they can lie in the prone position and can wheel themselves around the unit. These children can profit from formal classwork geared to their prone position, and they may learn to read, write, draw, and fingerpaint.

Every effort should be made to develop self-sufficiency in these children up to their full capacity. They are very often favorites on a ward, as most of them have nice dispositions, socialize well, and feel little, if any, pain. Many of them accept their physical handicap as a matter of fact, but others are sensitive about their affliction and need emotional support, much reassurance as to their worth, and constant evidence of love and acceptance by the staff.

Antisocial Behavior

Some mildly retarded boys and girls are sent to hospitals by the courts for antisocial or delinquent behavior. Some of these persons are psychotic; some are just angry, belligerent, resentful youngsters. If the environment of a mildly retarded child (or, for that matter, a child who is not retarded) has been of such a nature that severe maladaptation has occurred, the staff may have to deal with various degrees of delinquent or even criminal behavior.

This type of patient must be carefully assessed by the team to determine his needs on physical, mental, and emotional levels. Most of these patients are teenagers. A few may be addicted to alcohol, more are psychologically addicted today to sniffing glue or gas fumes, smoking marihuana, or taking euphoric or hallucinogenic drugs, and most of them smoke cigarettes. Few of them have learned to control their tempers; many fly into violent rages when crossed; ward fights are daily occurrences. Their language and sexual behavior may pose problems to the staff; stealing and lying are very common.

If their physical problems are minimal, they may be housed in a special unit staffed by counselors and social workers. Here, they must be taught to socialize, to develop socially approved behavior, and to identify with constructive concepts of living. They must have very firm limit setting in order to control their behavior. If they can be partially responsible (with guidance from the counselors) for setting up their own ward rules and regulations, there is a very good chance of their becoming involved in policing the activities of their more obstreperous peers and pressuring them into better behavior. Their days must be fully programmed with class attendance, physical exercise and play, and industrial training.

Never forget that, under their anger, their antisocial behavior and their rejection of adult supervision, they are deeply upset, very insecure boys and girls, with deep fears of rejection and a tremendous need for acceptance, approval, love and praise.

The mildly retarded, mentally ill person should be psychologically handled much like the mentally ill person who is not retarded, making special allowances for factors that stem from his mental limitations. His behavior must be assessed to determine his needs. In the teenage group, schizophrenia seems to be the one form of mental illness commonly encountered. In the adult retardate, we may find, besides this form, manic depression, paranoia, and both agitated and quiet depressions. Group therapy can be quite effective with these patients.

References

Aguilera D. C., et al.: Crisis Intervention—Theory and Methodology. St. Louis, C. V. Mosby, 1970.

Berne, E.: Principles of Group Treatment. New York, Oxford University Press, 1966.

Bower, E. M.: Early Identification of Emotionally Handicapped Children in School. Springfield, Charles C Thomas, 1969.

Erikson, E.: Childhood and Society. New York, Norton, 1968.

Montagu, A., ed.: Man and Aggression. New York, Oxford University Press, 1968.

Menninger, K. A.: Love Against Hate. New York, Knopf, 1945.

Milton, O., and Wahler, R. G., eds.: Behavior Disorders: Perspectives and Trends. ed. 2. Philadelphia, J. B. Lippincott, 1969.

Tredgold, R. R., and Soddy, K.: Textbook of Mental Deficiency, ed. 11. Baltimore, Williams & Wilkins, 1970.

Care of the Moderately and Severely Retarded and the Epileptic

---

Behavioral Objectives

The student successfully attaining the goals of this chapter should be able to:

- Compare the type of care required by moderately retarded and severely retarded patients as reflected by their level of ability.
- Demonstrate the kind of emotional support most mentally handicapped patients need.
- List the various ways an epileptic can be protected from injury during a seizure.
- Describe how staff personnel can provide a satisfactory emotional milieu for an epileptic patient.

The Moderately Retarded

The moderately retarded residents living in private schools and institutions have special problems and needs. As a group, they are classed as *trainable*, but some of them are *educable* to some extent. Quite a number of persons in the upper part of this group could profit from formal education. They take much longer to absorb academic experience than the mildly retarded, but some of them can learn to read and write. It might be wise to cease using the I.Q. scale as the major determinant as to whether or not a child can profit from formal schooling. More and more of these children should be placed in the classroom situation to see what their individual capabilities are, and, if their response to formal classwork looks encouraging, attempts should be made to educate them at a pace commensurate with their abilities. This is especially true of the eight- to twenty-year-old group.

The majority of the moderately retarded are trainable in the activities of daily living, in work habits, and in social graces. Some of them are quite apt at handwork; many can be trained to do housework, assist with work in the kitchens, food service areas, and laundry. Many can be trained to work on farms and to work in factories at simple construction or assembly work. They work in dietary departments, bakeries, and laundries. In an institutional setting, they may help in bathing, dressing, diapering, and feeding other patients; they can often escort other patients to and from school, doctor and dentist appointments, recreation, church services, and therapy; they are capable of running errands, of shoveling snow, and of helping with the maintenance of hospital grounds.

While it is true that most of these residents require considerable supervision of their work, it is also true that, collectively, they are able to accomplish a great deal of productive work.

Many of the patients in this group have been institutionalized when, with a little training of the patient and the family, they might have remained at home. Efforts are being made today to return many of them to their homes or to foster homes, where they can work, take pride in their achievements, and enjoy living within a family group.

Many of these patients have accompanying physical problems. Some are subject to seizures, most of which can be kept under control with anticonvulsant and sedative drugs. Others have speech difficulties and should be referred to a speech therapist for training. Many have difficulties with ambulation, muscular coordination, and body balance. The patient should be examined for neurological defects and, where feasible, sent to physical therapy for training in body balance, muscular coordination, and gait training.

In some instances, the orthopedist may order special shoes, braces, active and passive exercises, treatments, positioning, and sometimes surgery in an attempt to straighten out bone or muscle defects.

Some of the moderately retarded are hyperactive. If a patient is very hyperactive, the physician will usually prescribe tranquilizing and sedative drugs. In young children who are hyperactive and have behavioral problems, some physicians prescribe amphetamine-like drugs. While these are stimulating drugs to the adult, they often relax and calm children when given in very small dosages. The nurse must be keenly aware of the patient's reaction to drug therapy at all times and report reactions to the physician.

The patients in this group are more childlike in their thinking and behavior than are those in the mildly retarded group. Many of them play with toys or carry them around, regardless of their chronological age. They must be taught many things on the ward, such as how to toilet themselves, wash their hands and face, dress themselves, tie shoes, button buttons, handle cutlery at the table, make their beds, and hang up their clothes. They can often be taught good social manners and how to play games and socialize in groups. When they are being trained, they must patiently and repeatedly be shown how to do a simple job and then praised as they show signs of improvement. An intensive, repetitive form of training with reward for accomplishment is being widely used today. It is termed **operant conditioning.** It is especially effective in training the moderately retarded and may bring results in a small number of severely retarded.

The nurses and technicians act as surrogate mother-father figures for their patients, arbitrating their disputes, encouraging their active participation in group living, listening to their grievances, and giving them warm, affectionate support when they are upset. Patients should always feel free to come to the staff with their problems, no matter how trivial. Organized play, indoors and outdoors, daily, at regular intervals, is one of their foremost needs.

Always remember that the mental level of the patients in this group will compare with that of children between the ages of five to seven. The moderately retarded comprise the largest group in institutions. Among these are most of the genetic microcephalies, the warm, outgoing mongoloids, some of the cretins, some of the arrested hydrocephalics, many of the Little's disease group, and a great number of familial and undifferentiated varieties of mental retardation.

The Severely Retarded

The severely and profoundly retarded groups are not only greatly handicapped mentally, but they tend to have more multiple physical handicaps also. They constitute the more severely brain damaged patients. The proportion of these people in institutions is disproportionately high in relation to their incidence in the general population. The reason: it becomes increasingly difficult for the family to care for them at home as they increase in size; they become more difficult to lift and handle, and cause problems between the other family members.

The intelligence of this group is so subnormal that many of these people cannot even finger-feed themselves and must be spoon-fed. Few become toilet trained, operant conditioning has been successful in toilet training some, but in the majority of cases, the patient's mental level is just too low for the training to be complete. They must be bathed, dressed, fed, and supervised in their activities and play like very small children, and, in many cases, like infants. Some of them maturate very slowly, and they are apt to remain small and frail and look much younger than they really are. Due to superimposed physical abnormalities, they are often helpless, unable to sit up, crawl, or walk. Others maturate physically at a fairly normal pace, and learn in time to crawl and walk. Many of this group will remain immature sexually; others will develop sexually as their bodies grow and can pose problems due to their normal physical development and muscular strength.

Some of them are, due to brain injury, hyperactive. They may be aggressive toward more helpless patients and a source of physical injury to them.

Some of them are self-punishing, and take their frustration and anger out on themselves by banging their heads on walls, floor, or crib bars, or by pinching, gouging, or slapping themselves. Some are helpless prisoners in bodies that are spastic, athetoid, or palsied; some are hydrocephalic, with large heads that must be lifted, supported, and turned with great care. Many have great difficulty in swallowing and must be fed slowly and carefully; some respond well to affection and love, others seem to be indifferent to attention; some regurgitate food, or eat and smear feces, or rip off all clothing, or masturbate excessively; some are petulant and demanding; others are very quiet, gentle, and will smile or coo with delight at the sound of your voice, your touch, or just the sight of you. Many in this group have seizures, spina bifidas, meningoceles, malformation of skeletal bones, internal organs, and extremities. Many pathological conditions are seen in the brain.

Since, mentally, they range from 0 to 35 I.Q., their behavior and comprehension are comparable from the birth level to the level of a five-year-old. We tend to think of all the patients in this group as needing total care but, of course, some are much more helpless than others.

Some eat well, usually with their fingers, and some can use a spoon. Special training in eating habits can often improve their ability in this area. When this type of patient is seated at a table with others, food grabbing must be carefully watched. Usually this group needs solid foods, but these must be chopped or cut up for them; some are restricted to blended foods.

The profoundly and severely retarded patients present more physical problems and probably less emotional ones, as a whole, than do the moderate and mildly retarded patients.

If you are assigned to an all-crib-case ward, where some physical problems are concentrated, such as complete immobility, spastic arms, legs, and spines, hydrocephalus, spina bifida, cerebral palsy, and meningoceles, you must learn how to deftly handle frail bodies, how to bathe them, dress them, turn them, and how important it is to keep them dry and rotated so that bony prominences will not break down. You must watch them zealously, reporting any unusual signs or symptoms promptly. Most of them are nonverbal and cannot tell you of their distress; you must rely heavily on nonverbal communication and on keen observation.

Many of these severely brain damaged children die in infancy and early childhood, especially those with hydrocephalus and heart lesions. Many cannot fight infections.

Good bowel and bladder care is very important to these children as lack of exercise and absence of roughage in their diet tend to produce atonic bowels. Good skin care is important in the paralyzed and the spastic patient. All opposing surfaces must be kept clean and dry; decubitii must be prevented. Careful oral hygiene twice a day is essential.

These patients should have passive exercise if necessary. Patients confined to cribs should be carried to the dayroom twice a day (once right after their morning bath and again in the afternoon) and laid on covered mats on the floor where they can be played with and exercised. Those who can crawl a little should be encouraged to do so. They need exercising and a change of surroundings and a chance to be among others.

If you are assigned to an ambulatory ward of the severely retarded, you may find patients with frail, underdeveloped bodies, or symmetrical, maturely functioning bodies, or distorted and crippled bodies. Some are underactive and in need of stimulation; some are hyperactive and in need of medications and an environment that will slow down their activities.

The mentally retarded often enjoy rhythm and music. Some of the severely retarded will listen to records or T.V. music by the hour. Many of them can be taught to clap to music, march to music, and even to keep excellent time in a rhythm band.

Many of these ambulant retardates will lavish their affection on you. They will pull you to a chair and climb on your knees and beg for your hugs and caresses. It is not possible to fill all the needs of all the patients on a ward, but you must try to give of your patience, your love, your helpfulness to them all and to keep them as activated and motivated as possible and as happy and as constructively engaged as possible.

The medications and treatments that are prescribed for retarded patients, of whatever level, are not prescribed for their state of retardation, but for the superimposed physical, mental, and emotional problems they may be afflicted with. Many retardates who are healthy and well-adjusted to their environment are on no drugs or special treatments of any kind.

They must, of course, be stimulated on the intellectual, emotional, and physical levels so as to fill their days with "learning" and "doing" experiences. In this way they can be helped to develop to their full capacity and enjoy each passing day to their utmost ability.

Epilepsy

Epilepsy is commonly seen among retardates of all groups; it is especially high in the mildly retarded institutionalized patient group, not because this group has a higher incidence of the disorder, but because, in this comparatively small group, epilepsy may be one of the very few reasons for institutionalization. (See Chapter 26.)

Of the four main types of epilepsy, the grand mal type and the psychomotor type cause the most excitement and can result in the most injury to the patient.

Grand Mal Epilepsy

In the grand mal type, the patient passes through two successive stages. The first, or tonic, stage may or may not be preceded by an aura (a sensory warning) and a high, quavering cry. But whether the patient does or does not experience the aura, or cry out, he will pass into unconsciousness and rigidity and fall in this condition. As he falls, he may hurt himself by striking some object, the sharp edge of a piece of furniture, or the floor. He remains rigid for a few seconds to as long as three minutes, with all breathing cut off and his jaws rigid.

The second, or clonic stage, is usually twice to three times as long in duration as the first stage. In it, the patient convulses or jerks about on the floor, opening and closing his mouth spasmodically. The major dangers of this stage are biting and possibly "swallowing" the tongue, with subsequent prolonged anoxia. (The tongue, of course, cannot be swallowed, but falls back in the unconscious patient's throat, occluding the airway.)

Nurses, technicians, and other mental health workers should be given special training in the first aid of a patient having a grand mal seizure.

1. Help break the patient's fall if possible. Grasp him and ease him to the floor quickly so he does not strike his head.

2. Turn him on his side. This keeps his airway open. Kneel beside him and pull his body up against your thighs so he won't squirm away from you.

3. Place something between his teeth (preferably a padded tongue depressor, but in an emergency, anything, such as a piece of blanket or the sleeve of a coat, can be effectively used to keep his teeth from biting his tongue).

4. Time the second (clonic) phase of the seizure.

5. When the patient relaxes, loosen his clothing (belt, tie, and collar), put a pillow under his head, and allow him to sleep while you go and get a cart and someone to help you lift him. Take him to his room and place him on his side on top of the bed. If he has a pattern of sleeping deeply and for a prolonged time after his seizures, you might undress him completely and cover him lightly. Otherwise, leave him fully dressed except for his tie, belt, and shoes. Check on him regularly to see that he is all right.

6. If he quickly regains consciousness and insists on getting up after his seizure, help him up. If he was engaged in some ward work and wants to resume it, let him do so. This is helpful to his self-esteem, but watch him for a while, as he is often dazed and confused.

7. Chart his seizure, giving the date, the time the clonic phase started, and its duration. Indicate any perceivable injuries incurred and any first aid given.

8. Should the patient not come out of the second phase before starting to stiffen again, he may be going into status epilepticus (a series of convulsions so close together that the patient does not have time to relax between them). This condition can be dangerous and drug therapy should be instituted in accordance with hospital policy. (I.V. Valium is often helpful.) If he should not respond to this, call the physician, give him your report, and follow his instructions.

Since most epileptic patients are on drugs which prevent or decrease the severity of their seizures, one does not see too many "full-blown" seizures on the wards. You are much more apt to see aborted grand mals where the symptoms are greatly diminished or partly repressed. For instance, a wheelchair patient may jerk a few times but not slide out of his chair; saliva may flow from the corners of his mouth; his eyes may go "blank" or roll upward, and after a few seconds of this, he may return to consciousness and body control.

Psychomotor Epilepsy

As was indicated in Chapter 26, psychomotor epilepsy is the most difficult type of seizure to classify. The two distinguishing characteristics of a pure, unmixed type are automatic behavior and amnesia for the duration of the seizure.

Often, in psychomotor epilepsy, no intervention is required. The patient will continue with some automatic form of behavior from a few brief minutes to as long as 15 or more minutes.

Only when his behavioral pattern can lead to harm to himself, or to others, or to the destruction of things, is there need for intervention. If he has a pattern of rapid running—into walls or windows—he can hurt himself; sometimes severely. Knowing the pattern of his behavior while in seizure makes it possible for nurses and technicians, and sometimes even other patients on the ward, to apprehend him on his way and bring him to a stop by a concerted "tackle." If he tends to abuse others (slapping, pushing, or knocking them down) while in seizure, again his actions must be stopped. But, for many types of erratic behavior, we just stand by and let the action terminate by itself.

Petit Mal Epilepsy

The petit mal victim needs no special care. He may be in and out of seizure many times in a day and seems no worse, physically or psychologically, for his brief "blackouts."

Jacksonian Epilepsy

In Jacksonian epilepsy, where the muscular convulsions are generally unilateral, the patient is conscious, and, while he cannot stop this progression of muscular spasms, they seldom cause harm to him. Should this electrical discharge jump to the opposite hemisphere of the brain, the patient will go into grand mal, and you would give him first aid as previously outlined.

Psychological Needs

Does the epileptic have special psychological needs? He may. Certainly, the child or adult epileptic who is normal intellectually can have a number of emotional problems. Society still is fearful of his affliction and rejects his presence socially. The borderline and mildly retarded patient also suffers from the expressions of morbid fear and rejection he feels from friends, neighbors, and often from his own family. He feels doubly rejected; once on the score of his retardation, and again for his convulsive disorder. Thus it is important to provide warm emotional support for those who become upset by their affliction. Measures should be taken to build up the epileptic's ego, strengthen his self-respect, increase his sense of security, and help him feel warmly accepted on the ward.

The moderately retarded take their seizures in much better stride. Some of them are even very proud of their seizures. Some actually simulate a seizure, for it brings them prompt attention from the staff and interested concern from their companions.

The severely and profoundly retarded are usually unaware of their seizure disorder.

As for medication, the careful administration of the prescribed anticonvulsant drugs and the sedatives or the tranquilizers is the nurse's responsibility, as are careful observation of symptoms, accurate charting, and the conveying of pertinent information to the team. (See Chapter 26 for the leading anti-convulsive drugs.)

References

Carter, C. H.: Handbook of Mental Retardation Syndromes. ed. 2. Springfield, Charles C Thomas, 1970.

Gardner, L. I., ed.: Endocrine and Genetic Diseases of Childhood. Philadelphia, W. B. Saunders, 1969.

Tredgold, R. R., and Soddy, K.: Textbook of Mental Deficiency. ed. 11. Baltimore, Williams & Wilkins, 1970.

chapter

40

Community Centered Psychiatric Services

Behavioral Objectives

The student successfully attaining the goals of this chapter should be able to:

- List the 5 basic services which community mental health centers are required by law to provide.
- Describe 5 additional services which are desirable for outpatient care of mental health clients.
- Discuss the relationship between poverty and mental disorders.

The Community Mental Health Act, passed in 1964, states that a community mental health center should be accessible to the community it serves and that it should provide five basic services. These are:

1. Inpatient treatment
2. Outpatient treatment
3. Partial hospitalization (day or night programs)
4. Emergency services on a 24-hour-a-day basis.
5. Consultation and education services to community agencies, groups and individuals.

There are several other services which, while not mandatory, are desirable in order to assist in the functioning, implementation, and continuity of these five basic services. They are:

6. Diagnostic services
7. Rehabilitation
8. Pre-care and after-care
9. Training programs for professionals and nonprofessionals
10. Research and evaluation

When a center has all 10 of these services, and they are fully operational, the center is known as a comprehensive community mental health center.

The act specifies that such a center must serve as a specific area with a population between 75,000 and 200,000. In a densely populated urban area such a maximum population may be found in less than 100 square blocks;

in some remote rural areas the minimum population may be scattered over hundreds of square miles. In this event the community mental health center is not always in close proximity to area residents wanting or needing services. Ideally, though, travel time to the center should not exceed one hour.

The community mental health center, in spite of its total and comprehensive approach, is not in any sense the total Institution described by Groff in *Asylums.* It is, in fact, the antithesis of this. The patients continue to live in and deal with the real world in which they got sick. They come in with some very practical problems and some very real needs that do not lend themselves to theoretical discussion or esoteric elaboration of the point of view held by a school of thought. Practical problems like poverty, malnutrition, and rats and filth in the house require practical, immediate solutions like money, food, and the services of an exterminator, as well as the department of Licenses and Inspections. There is no place for theoretical constructs or encouraging the patient to "work it out for himself" in these situations. Terms like "hostile environment" and "quality of life" take on an entirely new meaning in a poverty situation. Words like "crisis" and "emergency" also come alive in a very special way.

The result of this interdisciplinary mix of staff, with a loud and clear input from patients and community who know what "trouble" is, is a very practical, down-to-earth approach.

The philosophy that emerges is existentialism. The therapy is reality-oriented. The emphasis is on life-in-the-world, the quality of it and the joy of it.

The patient is central in the community mental health center. The "patient" is frequently an entire family, or a married couple, or a parent and child and occasionally a separate individual.

We have emphasized the role of the center in the delivery of mental health services, that is to say, in direct patient care, and we feel that almost all workers in the community mental health system are also oriented this way. Other areas of a center's function (by federal mandate) are Research and Evaluation and Consultation and Education. There are few centers in the country today with viable, fully operating, effective departments of Research and Evaluation and Consultation and Education. Research and Evaluation is usually done by trained researchers—research psychologists, statisticians, and biometricians. It would be most helpful to get some really good studies under way that would tell us in 5 or 10 years how we are doing, how effective we really are, and where we might modify our programs to become more effective. Unfortunately, these studies are just beginning. Consultation and Education is involved in primary prevention: It is intended to increase good mental health practices in the community through schools and other institutions so that the actual incidence (number of new cases per year per unit population) of mental illness will drop. In our experience, Consultation and Education departments seldom flourish because they immediately run into two blocks that we do not have the skills to tackle as yet. One is poverty; the other is the genetic basis for mental disease. There is also a question, variously answered, as to what extent the government-funded center can get into an all-out war with other government-funded agencies like Housing and Urban Development and the Department of Welfare.

Even if such confrontations are entered in the name of patients' rights, there is a serious question about what can be accomplished at that level. A larger social plan is necessary to make a real dent in the incidence of mental disorder, and society is not yet ready to appreciate or take this step.

Of the delivery modalities within the community mental health system two have enjoyed an outstanding growth and appear to have permanently changed the face of psychiatric practice. They are crisis intervention and the partial hospital. Psychiatry in the office and psychiatry in the hospital are both diminishing rapidly. Intervention in the home, on the street, or wherever necessary, and alternatives to hospitalization are the tools of today. This "new psychiatry" is not at all confined to the mental health center. Almost all private and public mental hospitals have begun a partial hospitalization service and many are starting crisis intervention. The emphasis on these services should be most valuable to the student and the nurse regardless of the setting in which clinical experience is obtained.

The actual de-emphasis of the specifics of inpatient care may lead some students to feel they will not therefore be prepared to work on an inpatient ward. This is not true. Former specifics of inpatient care such as techniques and indications for physical restraints and postinsulin or psychosurgery are rarely required to be known today. Seclusion room care and various degrees of suicide precaution are used occasionally, vary from hospital to hospital, and can be learned in a few minutes of ward instruction. Other than these, there is little difference between the milieu and therapeutic thrust made on an inpatient ward and that made in a partial hospital setting.

The future offers wonderful challenges and opportunities for those working in the mental health field: psychiatrists, psychologists, social workers, nurses, psychiatric associates, technicians and others.

References

Hartog, J.: Transcultural aspects of community psychiatry. Ment. Hygiene, 55:35 (January) 1971.

Fast, J.: Body Language. New York, Evans and Company, 1970.

McCrosky, J., et al.: An Introduction to Interpersonal Communication. Englewood Cliffs, N.J., Prentice-Hall, 1971.

Morgan, A. J. and Moreno, J. W.: The Practice of Mental Health Nursing: A Community Approach. Philadelphia, J. B. Lippincott, 1973.

Glossary

Addiction: The compulsive use of chemical substances on which the individual has become physiologically dependent, and without which he will experience withdrawal reaction.

Affect: The mood or emotion an individual shows in response to a given situation. Affect may be described, according to its expression, as blunted, blocked, flat, inappropriate, or displaced.

Ambivalence: The coexistence of two opposing feelings toward another person, object, or idea. (For example, feelings of love and hate, pleasure and pain, or liking and disliking may exist simultaneously.)

Anxiety: Apprehension, tension, or uneasiness. Primarily of intrapsychic origin, in distinction to fear, which is the emotional response to a consciously recognized and usually external threat or danger. Anxiety and fear are accompanied by physiologic changes. Anxiety may be regarded as pathologic when present to such an extent as to interfere with effectiveness in living, achievement of desired goals or satisfactions, or reasonable emotional comfort.

Aphasia: Partial or complete loss of the power of expression or ability to understand either written or spoken language. Cause may be functional, organic or both.

Compensation: See *Defense mechanisms.*

Compulsion: An act which a person finds himself forced to do (generally against his wishes) in order to reduce anxiety. (See *Obsession.*)

Confabulation: A symptom usually seen in organic psychotic disorders (e.g., Korsokov's psychosis) in which the individual defensively attempts to "fill in" details about the past, which he cannot recall because of memory loss. Imaginary experiences are often related in a detailed and plausible fashion.

Conflict: In psychoanalytic terms, conflict describes the mental struggle which occurs when there are opposing impulses, drives, and demands of the id, ego, and super-ego.

Conversion: See *Defense mechanisms.*

Covert: Implies secrecy, or hidden reasons for conscious actions or behavior.

Crisis intervention therapy: A type of brief psychiatric treatment in which individuals (and/or families) are assisted in their efforts to cope and problem solve in crisis situations. The treatment approach is immediate, supportive, and direct.

Defense mechanisms: Unconscious intrapsychic processes that are employed to seek relief from emotional conflict and freedom from anxiety. Conscious efforts are frequently made for the same reasons, but true defense mechanisms are out of awareness (unconscious). Defense mechanisms are sometimes referred to as "mental mechanisms." The common defense mechanisms are:

1. *Compensation*—putting forth extra effort to achieve in the area in which there is a real or imagined deficiency.
2. *Conversion*—the unconscious expression of a mental conflict by means of a physical symptom.
3. *Denial*—treating obvious reality factors as though they do not exist because they are consciously intolerable.
4. *Displacement*—transferring unacceptable feelings aroused by one object or situation to a more acceptable substitute.
5. *Dissociation*—walling off certain areas of the personality from consciousness.
6. *Fantasy*—satisfying needs by day-dreaming.
7. *Fixation*—never advancing the level of emotional development beyond that in which one feels comfortable.
8. *Idealization*—conscious or unconscious overestimation of another's attributes, e.g., hero worship.
9. *Identification*—attaching to one's self certain qualities associated with others. Operates unconsciously and is significant mechanism in superego development.
10. *Introjection*—incorporating the traits of others; internalizing feelings toward others.
11. *Isolation*—separating thought and affect, allowing only the former to come to consciousness. It is a compromise mechanism.
12. *Projection*—unconsciously attributing one's own unacceptable qualities and emotions to others.
13. *Rationalization*—attempting to justify or to make consciously tolerable by plausible means, feelings, behavior, and motives that would otherwise be intolerable.
14. *Reaction formation*—expressing unacceptable wishes or behavior in a socially acceptable manner.

15. *Regression*—going back to an earlier level of emotional development and organization.
16. *Repression*—unconscious, involuntary forgetting of unacceptable or painful thoughts, impulses, feelings, or acts.
17. *Sublimation*—directing energy from unacceptable drives into socially acceptable behavior.
18. *Substitution*—unconsciously attempting to make up for a deficiency in one area by concentrating efforts in another area that is more attainable.
19. *Suppression*—the conscious, deliberate forgetting of unacceptable or painful thoughts, impulses, feelings, or acts.
20. *Symbolization*—using an object or idea as a substitute or to represent some other object or idea.
21. *Undoing*—thinking or doing one thing for the purpose of neutralizing something objectionable which was thought or done before.

Delusion: A false belief or opinion which is unreasonable and causes distortion in judgment.

Denial: See *Defense mechanisms*.

Depersonalization: Feelings of unreality or strangeness concerning either the environment or one's self or both.

Displacement: See *Defense mechanisms*.

Dissociation: See *Defense mechanisms*.

Double-bind: A type of interaction, generally associated with schizophrenic families, in which one individual demands a response to a message containing mutually contradictory signals while the other is unable to respond or comment on the inconsistent and incongruous message. Best characterized by the "damned if you do, damned if you don't" situation.

Dyad: Refers to the relationship between two people; dyadic pair can be husband and wife, parent and child, sibling and sibling. In music it describes a chord composed of two tones.

ECT: Electroconvulsive therapy. A method of treatment in which an electric current is passed through the brain causing a grand-mal seizure. Most useful in elderly depressed persons.

Ego: That part of the personality, according to Freudian theory, which mediates between the primitive, pleasure-seeking instinctual drives of the id and the self-critical, prohibitive, restraining forces of the superego. The compromises worked out, on an unconscious level, help to resolve intrapsychic conflict by keeping thoughts, interpretations, judgments, and behavior practical and efficient. The ego is directed by the reality principle, meaning it is in contact with the real world as well as the id and superego. The ego develops as the individual grows. (See *Superego, Id.*)

Empathy: The ability to "feel with" another person while retaining one's own sense of objectivity. (c.f., sympathy, "feeling for.")

Extrapyramidal reaction: Refers to the usually reversible side effect of some of the major psychotropic drugs on the extrapyramidal system of the central nervous system. Characterized by a variety of physical signs and symptoms (similar to those seen in patients with Parkinson's disease) which include: muscular rigidity, tremors, drooling, restlessness, shuffling gait, blurred vision and other neurologic disturbances.

Family therapy: Treatment of more than one member of the family simultaneously in the same session. The treatment may be supportive, directive, or interpretive.

Fantasy: See *Defense mechanisms.*

Fixation: See *Defense mechanisms.*

Functional: Refers to mental disorders (disorders of functioning) in which no physical or organic cause is known.

Gestalt psychology: The study of mental process and behavior with emphasis on a total perceptual configuration and the interrelation of component parts. Generally, refers to the "whole person" approach to assessment and treatment of psychiatric patients.

Group therapy: Application of psychotherapeutic techniques to a group of individuals who may have similar problems and are in reasonably good contact with reality, by one or more therapists. The optimal size of a group is six to ten members. As a therapy procedure, it is popular because it is a versatile, economical, and, for certain individuals, a successful modality.

Hallucination: An imagined sensory perception which occurs without an external stimulus. Can be auditory, visual, or tactile. Usually occurs in psychotic disorders, but can occur in both chronic and acute organic brain disorders.

Heterosexuality: Sexual interest and behavior toward persons of the opposite sex.

Homeostasis: A term borrowed from physiology meant to indicate the self-regulating intrapsychic processes which are optimal for comfort and survival.

Homosexuality: Sexual preference, attraction, and relationship between two people of the same sex.

Id: In Freudian theory the id is identified as the reservoir of psychic energy. It is guided by the pleasure principle, curbed by the ego, and is unconscious. (See *Ego, Superego.*)

Idealization: See *Defense mechanisms.*

Identification: See *Defense mechanisms.*

Illusion: A misinterpretation of the sensory stimuli, usually auditory or visual, of a real experience.

Insight: The ability of an individual to understand himself and the basis for his attitudes and behavior.

Intrapsychic: Refers to all that which takes place within the mind (psyche).

Introjection: See *Defense mechanisms.*

Isolation: See *Defense mechanisms.*

Latent: Adjective used to describe feelings, drives, and emotions which influence behavior but remain repressed, outside of conscious thought.

Mental mechanism: See *Defense mechanisms.*

Milieu: The immediate environment, both physical and social.

Motivation: Describes the individual's will and determination to persevere and succeed.

Neologism: A word which is invented or made up by condensing other words into a new one. Typical in schizophrenia.

Neurosis: An impairment of personality development and growth which is characterized by excessive use of energy for unproductive purposes. The chief symptom in neurotic disorders is anxiety which is either felt directly or controlled by various psychologic mechanisms to produce other subjectively distressing symptoms. Although in some of its forms and degrees it is incapacitating, it does not interfere with the individual's contact with reality; psychosis implies flight from reality, neurosis an attempt to come to terms with it.

Nosology: The scientific classification of diseases.

Obsession: A persistent, recurring thought or urge occurring more or less against the person's wishes. Often leads to compulsive acts. (See *Compulsion.*)

Organic: Refers to disorders in which a physical, chemical, or structural cause is discernable.

Overt: Open, conscious and unhidden actions, behavior, and emotions.

Paranoid: Used as an adjective to describe unwarranted suspiciousness and distrust of others.

Personality: The characteristic way in which a person behaves; the deeply ingrained pattern of behavior that each person evolves, both consciously and unconsciously, as his style of life or way of being.

Phenothiazines: The major group of psychotropic drugs used in the treatment of mental illness, chiefly the psychoses. Their chemical action is on the central nervous system.

Phobia: An irrational persistent, obsessive, intense fear of an object or situation, which results in increased anxiety and tension and which interferes with the individual's normal functioning.

Projection: See *Defense mechanisms.*

Psychoanalysis: A form of psychotherapy developed by Freud, based on his theories of personality development and disorder, generally requiring basic commitments from the patient (analysand) to the therapist (analyst) regarding time, money, and procedure. The technique of psychoanalysis involves an examination of the free associations of a patient and the interpretation of his dreams, emotions, and behavior. Its focus is mainly on the way the ego handles the id tensions. In psychoanalysis, success is measured by the degree of insight the patient is able to gain into the unconscious motivations of his behavior.

Psychodrama: A form of group psychotherapy in which patients dramatize their emotional problems. By assuming roles in order to act out their conflicts, they reveal repressed feelings which have been disturbing to them.

Psychogenic: Implies the causative factors of a symptom or illness are due to mental rather than organic factors.

Psychosis: A major mental illness characterized by any of the following symptoms—loss of contact with reality, bizarre thinking and behavior, delusions, hallucinations, regression, disorientation. Intrapsychically, it results from the unconscious becoming conscious and taking over control of the individual. In psychosis the ego is overwhelmed by the id and the superego.

Psychotherapy: The treatment of mental disorders or a psychosomatic condition by psychologic methods using a variety of approaches including psychoanalysis, group therapy, family therapy, psychodrama, hypnotism, simple counseling, suggestion.

Rationalization: See *Defense mechanisms.*

Reaction Formation: See *Defense mechanisms.*

Reality: The way things actually are.

Reality-oriented therapy: Refers to any therapeutic approach whose focus is on helping the patient to define his reality, to improve his ability to adjust and to function productively and satisfactorily within his real situation.

Regression: See *Defense mechanisms.*

Repression: See *Defense mechanisms.*

Schizophrenogenic: An adjective used to describe the object or situation which is felt to be causative in the development of schizophrenia.

Sublimation: See *Defense mechanisms.*

Substitution: See *Defense mechanisms.*

Superego: The third part of the Freudian personality theory, which guides and restrains, criticizes and punishes just as the parents did when the individual was a child. It is unconscious, and it is learned. Like the id, the superego also wants its own way. It is sometimes referred to as the conscience.

Suppression: See *Defense mechanisms.*

Symbolization: See *Defense mechanisms.*

Transactional analysis: A psychodynamic approach that attempts to understand the interplay between individuals in terms of the roles they have been assigned, have assumed, or play in their transactions with others.

Unconscious: The repository of those mental processes of which the individual is unaware. The repressed feelings, and their energy, are stored in the unconscious and directly influence the individual's behavior.

Undoing: See *Defense mechanisms.*

Word salad: A jumbled mixture of words and phrases which have no meaning, and are illogical in their sequence. Seen most often in schizophrenia. (For example, "Backter dyce tonked up snorfel blend.")

Index